Luminos is the Open Access monograph publishing program
from UC Press. Luminos provides a framework for preserving and
reinvigorating monograph publishing for the future and increases
the reach and visibility of important scholarly work. Titles published
in the UC Press Luminos model are published with the same high
standards for selection, peer review, production, and marketing as
those in our traditional program. www.luminosoa.org

On the Record

On the Record

Papers, Immigration, and Legal Advocacy

Susan Bibler Coutin

UNIVERSITY OF CALIFORNIA PRESS

University of California Press
Oakland, California

Suggested citation: Coutin, S.B. *On the Record: Papers, Immigration,
and Legal Advocacy.* Oakland: University of California Press, 2025.
DOI: https://doi.org/10.1525/luminos.237

Library of Congress Cataloging-in-Publication Data

Names: Coutin, Susan Bibler, author.
Title: On the record : papers, immigration, and legal advocacy /
    Susan Bibler Coutin.
Description: Oakland : University of California Press, 2025. |
    Includes bibliographical references and index.
Identifiers: LCCN 2024059212 | ISBN 9780520422827 (hardback) |
    ISBN 9780520405356 (paperback) | ISBN 9780520405363 (ebook)
Subjects: LCSH: Noncitizens—United States. | Illegal immigration—
    Government policy—United States. | Emigration and immigration law—
    United States. | Immigration lawyers—United States.
Classification: LCC KF4800 .C68 2025 | DDC 342.7308/2—dc23/eng/20241210

LC record available at https://lccn.loc.gov/2024059212

GPSR Authorized Representative: Easy Access System Europe,
Mustamäe tee 50, 10621 Tallinn, Estonia, gpsr.requests@easproject.com.

34 33 32 31 30 29 28 27 26 25
10 9 8 7 6 5 4 3 2 1

To the migrants, allies, advocates, and activists who seek a better future.

CONTENTS

ACKNOWLEDGMENTS

My deepest debt of gratitude is to the nonprofit staff who welcomed me into their offices, meetings, and social gatherings. I wish I could name everyone who contributed to the project and thank them personally here, but doing so would compromise the anonymity of the nonprofit. I learned a tremendous amount, and was impressed by your technical expertise, commitment to solidarity, ethical practices, camaraderie, and spirit. You touched my life in more ways than I am able to describe here, and I am better for having had the opportunity to volunteer alongside you and learn from your wisdom and care.

To the people who participated in interviews, thank you for sharing your thoughts, trust, experiences, and hopes with me. I hope that this book conveys your realities as well as your visions of a world in which legal status would no longer damage people's well-being. I also learned from you and my own relationship to documents will never be the same.

This material is based upon work supported by the National Science Foundation under Grant No. SES-1061063. Any opinions, findings, and conclusions or recommendations expressed in this material are those of the author and do not necessarily reflect the views of the National Science Foundation. I am extremely grateful to the NSF for support.

I was fortunate to work with brilliant research assistants. Véronique Fortin and Gray Abarca joined in the fieldwork, interviews, and volunteer work with care and insight. Alyse Bertenthal did background research in the project's early days, and Danny Gascon and Lucy Carrillo helped to transcribe interviews.

Some of the ideas in the book were originally presented at conferences and workshops, including at the American Anthropological Association annual meeting; American Association of Geographers annual meeting; American Bar Foundation; American Ethnological Society meeting; ClassCrits Conference; Humboldt University; Latin American Studies Association annual meeting; Law and Society Association annual meeting; Maurer School of Law at Indiana University; Max Planck Institute for Social Anthropology; "New Legal Realism" conference at UC Irvine; UC Irvine Department of Anthropology; UC Irvine Department of Criminology, Law and Society; UC Irvine Law and Ethnography lab; UC Irvine School of Law; University of Connecticut; University of Pittsburgh; and the Wenner-Gren workshop "Paper-Trails: Migrants and Documents in an Era of Legal Insecurity." I am grateful to Fred Aman, Katia Bianchini, Heath Cabot, Leo Coleman, Oscar Ruben Cornejo-Casares, Pooja Dadhania, Theresa Delgadillo, Marie-Claire Foblets, Josiah Heyman, Sarah Horton, Molly Land, Elizabeth Mertz, Alison Mountz, Georgina Ramsay, Carrie Rosenbaum, Chris Tomlins, Larissa Vetters, and many other discussants, panelists, organizers, and audience members for these invitations, and the feedback and colleagueship that accompanied them.

While none of the chapters in *On the Record* were previously published, I worked through ideas in previous publications, including in Abarca and Coutin 2018; Coutin 2013, 2020; Coutin and Fortin 2015, 2021, 2023; Coutin, Richland, and Fortin 2014; Coutin et al. 2021; and Mitchell and Coutin 2018. Thank you to my coauthors, editors, and anonymous reviewers whose feedback shaped my thinking.

Many colleagues have influenced my thinking, including Justin Richland, with whom the project was first conceptualized; my writing group members Carrie Rosenbaum, Pooja Dadhania, and Eunice Lee, who encouraged me to write this book and provided comments on chapters; Barbara Yngvesson, Jennifer Chacón, Stephen Lee, and Sameer Ashar with whom I coauthored other books while the idea for this one was brewing; the UCI Law and Ethnography lab members and my co-director Lee Cabatingan with whom I have had many conversations; and my colleagues in Criminology, Law and Society, especially Keramet Reiter. Julie Mitchell has been part of this journey, and I hope that we will write together again in the future. My graduate and undergraduate students and postdoctoral mentees were an inspiration throughout. Jennifer Chacón allowed me to audit her immigration law course when she was faculty at UC Irvine, for which I am forever grateful. I also thank my department chair, Emily Owens, for granting me the sabbatical to write this book even though I missed the application deadline.

Thank you to Fidencio Martinez Perez for permission to reproduce "Dacament #7" as cover art—this piece is so powerful and meaningful! Thank you to Austin Sarat for permission to reproduce the disputing pyramid diagram that appears in Figure 4; Bert Kritzer for background regarding the disputing pyramid concept; John Fife for assistance; and Pat Corbett for permission to include an image of the cover of *Borders & Crossings*.

I especially appreciate the editorial staff at the University of California Press. Maura Roessner, you believed in this project from the outset and it has been a dream to work with you! Sam Warren, I appreciate your enthusiasm, and the care that you took in helping me prepare the manuscript files. Thank you as well to everyone at the press who supported the book through the production process.

I could not have written this book without the support of my husband and children: Curt, Jesse, Jordy, Rapha, and Casey. You are my inspiration!

ABBREVIATIONS

BIA	Board of Immigration Appeals
CAT	Convention Against Torture
CFI	Credible Fear Interview
DACA	Deferred Action for Childhood Arrivals
DAPA	Deferred Action for Parents of Americans
DED	Deferred Enforced Departure
DHS	Department of Homeland Security
EAD	Employment Authorization Document
EWI	entry without inspection
FOIA	Freedom of Information Act
GMC	Good moral character
ICE	Immigration and Customs Enforcement
INS	Immigration and Naturalization Service
IRCA	Immigration Reform and Control Act
LPR	Lawful Permanent Resident
NACARA	Nicaraguan Adjustment and Central American Relief Act
RFE	Request for Evidence
TPS	Temporary Protected Status
USC	US citizen
USCIS	US Citizenship and Immigration Service
VAWA	Violence Against Women Act

Introduction

On a hot summer morning in August of 2012, I took the Metro into Los Angeles to the offices of a nonprofit where I was doing volunteer work and observations as part of a study on how legal service providers and their clients documented immigration cases. As I exited the Metro station, I heard the sounds of a vendor calling, "Tamales, tamales, tamales!" I declined a coupon that someone was handing out, and walked past a cluster of men sitting at a bus stop, crossing the street to walk along the edge of an urban park. The lake that is the park's most prominent feature was beautiful in the sunlight, and there seemed to be more people around than usual: unhoused people, joggers, folks taking a break from their workday, vendors. A vibrant community.

When I arrived at the nonprofit at about 9:40 a.m., the reception area was already bustling with people. Only two months earlier, President Obama had announced the Deferred Action for Childhood Arrivals (DACA) program, and, when the application period opened in August, the nonprofit had been deluged with would-be applicants: individuals who had entered the United States before turning sixteen, were under the age of thirty-one, had lived in the United States continuously since 2007, and either were studying or had completed their educations (USCIS 2024a). In this context of heightened demand for legal services, I prioritized my role as a volunteer over my role as a researcher.

That morning, one of the attorneys had asked me to meet with her client to prepare a U-visa declaration. U-visas are available to crime victims who suffered substantial harm and who collaborated in investigating the crime. My task was to ask the organization's client to tell me about these events in Spanish, and I would type their declaration in English. As I passed by the attorney's office to pick up the

1

case file, she told me that she had a pile of documents that needed to be translated into English. "So today, I'm going to be your personal assistant?" I asked, and she laughed. And that is more or less how the day went!

I found an empty office—luckily not one located along a hallway that was sweltering because the air conditioning in that part of the building had broken. I logged into a computer to open a blank Word file. Before calling in "Juan," the man for whom I was preparing a declaration, I reviewed his file.[1] U-visa files generally contain the completed U-visa forms, a signed certification of cooperation with law enforcement (a document that can require many hours of attorney work to obtain), and the police report.[2] I had been taught to review the police report to make sure to explain any discrepancies with the declaration. When I read this police report for Juan's case, I was struck by a phrase written down by one of the officers (and I paraphrase): "the suspect fled, and citizens flagged down a police car to indicate which way he was going." What caught my eye was the term "citizens." To officers, the public can be described as "citizens," not in reference to their immigration status or nationality, but rather to a presumed relationship between police and civilians. In the version of this relationship that is the basis for a U-visa case, "citizens" collaborate with the police, helpfully assisting them in enforcement activity. For these reasons, some police forces were not supportive of policies that required them to check for legal citizenship (Provine et al. 2012).

After reviewing the file, I called in Juan from the reception area and prepared the declaration, which I will not summarize due to confidentiality. I had been advised that in this particular case, the attorney needed to be able to make a "cumulative trauma" argument because the crime to which he was subjected was not deemed "severe." I was told to spend some time in the declaration detailing Juan's past suffering so that it would be clear why the crime, given Juan's history, was traumatic. Nonetheless, when Juan told me of his experiences, I was surprised that the crime was not considered severe.

I followed my usual procedure in taking down Juan's declaration. At the beginning of our appointment, I outlined what we would cover: when he came to the United States, any past suffering, the crime, the impact of the crime (I had been told to ask what he was thinking while it was occurring), and Juan's plans for the future. As Juan spoke, I experienced some tension between wanting to write down his words verbatim (as I would try to do as an ethnographer, albeit in English) and focusing on the elements needed for his legal case. For instance, Juan spent some time sharing his philosophy that one should not depend on the government for anything. I summarized those views very briefly, writing something like, "In the future, I hope to earn enough money to be able to support myself and to never have to depend on the government." As an ethnographer, I would have tried to record this philosophy, as it seemed to me that he was defending himself, as a person who had immigrated, against the charge that immigrants use public resources.

But those comments did not fit within the scope of what I had been taught to include in a U-visa declaration.

When we were finished, I had to find the attorney who had asked me to prepare this declaration so that she could review it. I spent some time looking for her. She was not in her office, even though one of her clients was sitting there. I finally found her making photocopies. She said she would be available shortly, so I went back to chat with Juan again. He had given me several additional documents for his file—letters attesting that he was employed, his birth certificate, his daughter's birth certificate, and a letter from a relative about the trauma he suffered. I collected these and, as time passed, I decided to photocopy them, so that I could accomplish something while waiting. The employment verification letters struck me as a particularly peculiar element of these sorts of cases—undocumented people are not permitted to work, but somehow, employment verification letters strengthen their cases.

Finally, after about twenty minutes, I left to look for the attorney again. She was in another office (not hers) meeting with several clerks who were preparing DACA applications. Such continual interruptions were common for attorneys at the nonprofit: they sometimes did their own photocopying, they had to supervise DACA clerks and volunteers preparing declarations, and they also met with clients. I stood outside of the second office, waiting for her. When she came out, she joked, "Are you stalking me?" "Yes," I answered. She said that she did not have time to review the application right then, so I should print out the declaration and she would review it at a later date.

I also asked the attorney about the documents that Juan had brought. She said to copy them, keep the original copies of the letters, and give the original copy of the birth certificates back to Juan. She also asked me to translate the documents that were in Spanish. As I completed my volunteer tasks, I found myself wondering how closely the adjudicator would review these and other documents. How could someone like Juan produce a compelling documentary record, given the obstacles associated with being "undocumented"?

DOCUMENTING DOCUMENTATION

My experience preparing Juan's U-visa application that morning introduces a number of themes that recurred over the four years I spent doing fieldwork and volunteer work one day per week in the legal services department at this nonprofit: the unmet demand for high-quality, affordable legal services in immigrant communities; the tension between encountering oneself in official documents and producing one's own narrative; the fact that people who lacked legal status could also be regarded as insiders, even as "citizens" who could flag down a police car; the limitations of legal avenues for immigration relief, such as challenges proving psychological trauma;[3] the catch-22 of needing to document activities, such as presence or employment, that technically are prohibited to undocumented people; the role of criminal histories and public benefits in definitions of deservingness; my own role as an engaged researcher; and the power and limitations of documents that can confer status but also can fall short in representing life events. Such documentation challenges were characterized by a central paradox: US immigration law simultaneously forbids the presence of those who immigrated without authorization and requires those who are potentially eligible for immigration status to document their presence and activities. This paradox subjects the "undocumented" to intensified documentation requirements, resulting in bizarre situations. An unhoused person might struggle to provide an address on an immigration form; someone whose marriage or birth certificate contained errors might be unable to regularize their status; a spouse who was eligible for a green card through marriage might have to leave the country to get it and then be barred from reentering; some DACA applicants might have boxes of documents as evidence of their time in the United States while other applicants might have a gap in their records; and numerous individuals are responsible for retrieving documents—such as birth certificates—from their countries of origin even though they may not be authorized to reenter the United States if they leave (Mitchell and Coutin 2019). In sum, in immigration proceedings, the documents of daily life took on extraordinary significance both for immigrant community members and the service providers who advocated on their behalf.

On the Record examines the role of documents and documentation within immigration cases, focusing on the barriers that these create, the opportunities that they sometimes provide, and the craft through which service providers and people who have immigrated interpret and deploy records as part of legal advocacy. By "documentation," I mean the process through which service providers and people who have immigrated gather and produce records as evidence in support of legal claims. In so doing, service providers and immigrant residents frequently redeploy records that were originally created for other purposes, thus producing new and altered understandings of social realities. Documentation practices take place within a broader climate of stiffened immigration enforcement coupled with US claims to be a humanitarian nation. This climate produces competing tendencies toward heavily scrutinizing immigration cases and exercising discretion for humanitarian reasons. Moreover, even though US intervention is a key reason for immigration to the United States, immigration law treats immigration as an individual decision for which those who immigrate are held to blame. This sense of suspicion infuses the documentation process (Krajewska 2017), creating a heavy and continually increasing burden for legalization applicants who must appeal to the humanitarian impulses of a system that is largely repressive.

The experiences of immigrant residents are part of a broader phenomenon in which onerous administrative burdens limit access to resources, thus exacerbating inequality (Edwards et al. 2023; Herd and Moynihan 2018). Documentation challenges are pervasive in highly bureaucratized societies, and many vulnerable communities, such as racialized minorities, people receiving public benefits, and people who are unhoused, may lack records that are requested of them or find themselves characterized in official documents in ways that they reject (Robinson et al. 2023). Scholars have argued that administrative burdens take three forms: (1) *learning costs*: the effort expended to understand how administrative processes work, who is eligible, or even that an opportunity exists; (2) *compliance costs*: the time, money, and energy expended filling out forms, obtaining documents, and attending hearings and appointments; and (3) *psychological costs*, such as stress, anxiety, uncertainty, and stigma (Moynihan, Herd, and Harvey 2015; Herd and Moynihan 2018). Administrative burdens have multiple sources, "including the role of policy design, bureaucratic dysfunction, federalism, and the private provision of social welfare benefits" (Herd et al. 2023, 12). Scholars have argued that administrative burdens are imposed deliberately, and therefore are "policymaking by other means" (Herd et al. 2023, 12). For example, if politicians wish to reduce the number of people who receive welfare, they can make the requirements more onerous. Such seemingly technical changes may be a hidden way to accomplish politically unpalatable policy objectives (Herd et al. 2023; Moynihan, Herd, and Harvey 2015). Administrative burdens disproportionately affect marginalized communities (Fox, Feng, and Reynolds 2023), either by preventing them from accessing services, or by intrusively compelling them to participate in programs, as when child welfare courts require parents to go to counseling or to take drug tests (Edwards et al. 2023).

Analyzing the documentation practices of immigrant residents makes three contributions to the literature on administrative burden. First, my analysis explores how, by defining immigrant residents as a suspect population undeserving of the rights afforded to citizens, the law is an additional source of administrative burden. Second, in contrast to programs that are designed to meet a societal need, such as public assistance for those experiencing poverty, legalization opportunities for illegalized residents are a policy *exception* begrudgingly made available to people who are viewed as *outsiders* potentially subject to deportation. The administrative burdens imposed by immigration law and policy are therefore particularly high. Third, I observed that a number of nonprofit clients assumed an *anticipatory administrative burden*, in that they started saving documentation before they had an actual case. Assuming this anticipatory burden was a form of agency. As Horton points out, "documents are concrete distillations of state power. . . . Yet, because documents are the result of practices of inscription, they are simultaneously a potent site of resistance" (2020, 4). Assuming an anticipatory administrative burden enabled these clients to prepare for any future opportunities, but also reflected their liminal status as residents whose presence in the United States was insecure.

It is perhaps surprising that the immigrant residents I met through the nonprofit were willing to submit applications for immigration relief despite such administrative burdens. Indeed, scholars have noted that social groups that are subject to heightened policing and surveillance develop strategies to avoid institutions that generate records of their presence. Forrest Stuart (2016) found that unhoused residents living on skid row in Los Angeles avoided contact with the police, while Sara Brayne, who studied police use of big data, reported that "individuals who have been stopped by police, arrested, convicted, or incarcerated are more likely to avoid surveilling institutions such as medical, financial, educational, and labor market institutions that keep formal records (i.e., put them 'in the system')" (2021, 114). Such system avoidance exacerbates social inequality by preventing marginalized groups from accessing services, however, it may not be feasible for at-risk groups to avoid recordkeeping institutions entirely. Asad Asad (2023, 12) found that Latinx immigrant community members in Dallas, Texas, practiced "selective engagement"—that is, they made practical decisions about "which types of institutional surveillance are to be pursued and which are to be avoided"—and agencies that provided immigration assistance were among those that were pursued. Furthermore, surveys of Latinx residents before and after the 2016 presidential elections revealed that anger over Donald Trump's anti-immigrant rhetoric led to increased civic engagement, rather than to political withdrawal (Jones-Correa and McCann 2020). Because I carried out my project in a legal services department, I primarily encountered people who were interested in applying for status (if eligible), rather than those who sought to avoid immigration officials altogether. Most of the nonprofit clients I met had been in the United States for decades, so I was not able to study how new arrivals understood documentation. Moreover, during the time when I did the research, comprehensive immigration reform was being discussed and forms of executive relief were announced, creating a sense of hope. That said, nonprofit clients described earlier moments when they had not pursued an immigration case, as well as their doubts about their current case, thus providing insight into their concerns about applying for status. As I discuss in more detail later in this book, service providers at the nonprofit worked hard to build trust with their clients. For example, they spoke to Spanish-speaking clients in Spanish, expressed empathy, and provided high-quality services. In addition, due to the many unscrupulous notaries and attorneys who defraud immigrant residents by persuading them to pay high sums to prepare and submit applications for remedies for which they are not eligible, unwarranted system engagement often causes more problems for some immigrant residents than does system avoidance. A central goal of nonprofit staff was to provide their clients with the knowledge that would enable them to make informed decisions about whether to pursue an immigration remedy or to simply wait, in hope for a future opportunity.

By studying the documentary process that legal advocates and immigrant residents develop in the face of these challenges, *On the Record* transcends what sociolegal scholars have often characterized as a "gap" between law-on-the-books and law-in-action. The forces that make documents both necessary and scarce imbue them with power such that documents ("the books") are themselves active. One can see such "documents-in-action" in the file that I carried with me to prepare Juan's U-visa declaration; the attorney's plan to review and perhaps meet with Juan to edit his account; the birth certificates produced in Juan's country of origin and photocopied for his immigration case; the letters in support of Juan's case; and the U-visa itself that Juan and his attorney hoped to secure. While these documents are not precisely "law," they *are* "legal" and do comprise a corpus of material, even a network, that is both "fixed" and in motion.

Methodologically, conducting ethnographic fieldwork regarding documentation suggests that there are relationships between anthropological and legal knowledge. Thus, the day that I prepared Juan's U-visa declaration, I also wrote field notes about my experience. These differed in content, as the declaration adhered to legal norms in both style and content (for instance, each paragraph was numbered and the document concluded with a translator's certification), whereas my field notes followed anthropological conventions, such as using pseudonyms, and omitted the details of Juan's case, which were confidential. Indeed, while writing the declaration, I was aware of these similarities and differences: interviews were a core component of both fieldwork and case preparation, but the sorts of information recorded and the interviewee's ability to direct the conversation differed in each. As an ethnographer, I typically followed a rough interview guide but also sought to enable interviewees to talk about what they considered significant. As a volunteer, I also followed a rough template, as I had been trained, but focused on elements that attorneys considered legally significant. My own ethnographic documentation, such as interview transcripts and field notes, was not part of a legal record but nonetheless trafficked in related assumptions that documents were a form of evidence, could convey narratives, and had authors. Carrying out fieldwork regarding documentation therefore creates opportunities to reflect on such resonances.

My interest in documentation practices grew out of my previous research regarding political and legal advocacy on immigration issues. By doing fieldwork and volunteer work with religious activists who supported Central American asylum seekers during the 1980s, and with nonprofits that provided legal services to Central American residents in the 1990s, I learned how asylum claims were documented, the effects of lacking identity documents, and the creative strategies that service providers and immigrant residents developed in a legal context that was stacked against them (Coutin 1993, 2000). During the first decade of the 2000s, I carried out fieldwork in El Salvador and in the United States, focusing on the significance of the Salvadoran population in the United States for the country of El Salvador, the experiences of youth who were born in El Salvador and raised in the United States, the limitations of nation-based categories of membership for people who lived transnational lives, and the ways that deportation dislocated individuals, removing them from families and communities (Coutin 2007, 2016). These projects taught me that high level policy decisions play out in people's lives in empowering and devastating ways, that advocacy takes mundane as well as dramatic forms, and that when taken cumulatively, individual actions can impact policy. Central American scholars have emphasized the importance of historical memory as a means of recuperating submerged pasts and envisioning more just futures. As Karina O. Alvarado, Alicia Ivonne Estrada, and Ester E. Hernández write, "Central Americans and U.S. Central Americans maintain hope, resistance, creativity, agency, voice, and memory as part of our identities and cultures that are often overlooked" (2017, 4). These interests in recognition, historical memory, and law led me to focus on documentation as a form of legal advocacy.

Though it builds on my previous work, *On the Record* also differs in that it examines the minutia of filling out forms and documenting cases in a broad range of immigration-related procedures involving Spanish-speaking residents from multiple nations, not only from Central America. Between 2011 and 2015, I carried out fieldwork one day per week in the legal services department of the nonprofit, with the exception of times when my teaching schedule, administrative responsibilities, or conference travel kept me away. I had a long-term relationship with the nonprofit, where I had also volunteered in the 1980s and 1990s, helping to document asylum cases. Legal staff welcomed me as someone who was sympathetic to their mission and who also was willing to volunteer. I was permitted to shadow service providers as long as their clients granted permission, and I was told that I could write field notes reflecting on my volunteer experiences as long as I did not include identifying information. I sat in on consultations, watched as attorneys and paralegals completed forms, and attended meetings, trainings, and public presentations on immigrant rights. As a volunteer, I was trained to take declarations, fill out immigration forms, and translate documents from Spanish to English (and occasionally, vice versa), topics that will be addressed in subsequent chapters. I also made photocopies, assembled application packets, helped out in the reception area, and generally supported the organization's work. I was able to employ two graduate student assistants, Véronique Fortin and Gray Abarca, who joined me in fieldwork and volunteer work, and who wrote field notes for the project. Véronique and I also conducted two focus group interviews with naturalization class participants, and Gray and I did interviews with twenty-four nonprofit clients. Véronique is now a law professor at Université de Sherbrooke, and Gray is a Research Scientist at an agency dedicated to promoting healthy behaviors. A former paralegal, who I do not name here in order to preserve the organization's anonymity, also became involved in the research and joined me on a research trip to El Salvador to interview officials there about issuing documents for Salvadorans in the United States. These collaborations enriched the project and led to a number of academic publications (Abarca and Coutin 2018; Coutin and Fortin 2015, 2021, 2023; Coutin, Richland, and Fortin 2014).

This book is based primarily on participant observation, which largely took place at the nonprofit itself. On a "typical" day, I observed three to four appointments for approximately four hours, volunteered (e.g., translating documents, meeting with a nonprofit client to prepare a declaration or complete forms) for approximately two hours, and attended a staff meeting for approximately two hours. Yet, this pattern varied considerably. There were periods, such as that described at the outset of this chapter, when the nonprofit's workload was exceptionally heavy, leading me to focus on volunteering. But there were also periods when I was able to observe as many as six appointments in a single day, or when an entire day was devoted to a document preparation training or workshop. Some fieldwork and volunteer work took place outside of the nonprofit, such as when I accompanied service providers as they gave public talks, or helped out at naturalization fairs. I made one two-week research trip to El Salvador, to learn how officials there supported the documentation needs of Salvadorans living abroad.

Participant observation was supplemented by interviews, which provided crucial information about nonprofit clients' backgrounds, immigration histories, legal strategies, and future goals. Altogether, forty-one people were interviewed for the project, including thirty-four nonprofit clients, and seven officials and experts during the research trip to El Salvador. Seventy percent of the interview participants identified as women, and 30 percent identified as men. This gender-skewing resulted from the focus groups tapping into two friendship groups of women in the naturalization class and from the fact that six of the officials and experts interviewed in El Salvador were women; remaining nonprofit client participants were divided evenly between female- and male-identifying. Interview participants' ages ranged from twenty-four to eighty-one and averaged forty-eight years. Nonprofit clients came predominantly from Central America (twenty-three participants) and Mexico (ten) with one nonprofit client (who was petitioning for a family member) coming from the United States. Nonprofit clients' legal status at the time of the interview varied. Thirteen were Lawful Permanent Residents, eleven were undocumented, four were US citizens (petitioning for relatives), and eight had received another status (U-visa, Temporary Protected Status [TPS], or withholding of deportation). The nonprofit clients who were interviewed generally worked in the service industry or manufacturing, or were unemployed, self-employed, homemakers, or retired.

CHARACTERISTICS OF INTERVIEW PARTICIPANTS

Number of participants	34 nonprofit clients
	7 officials and experts in El Salvador
Participant's gender	29 female-identifying
	12 male-identifying
Nonprofit clients' country of origin	17 El Salvador
	10 Mexico
	4 Guatemala
	1 Honduras
	1 Nicaragua
	1 United States
Nonprofit clients' legal status at time of interview	13 Lawful Permanent Resident
	11 undocumented
	4 US citizen
	3 TPS
	2 withholding of deportation
	1 U-Visa

The 2011–2015 period in which this research was conducted was a critical time in immigration policymaking, one in which documentation processes that continue today were established. President Obama had been elected in 2008 on a platform that promised comprehensive immigration reform (Aguirre 2009). In order to obtain bipartisan support for legalization, Obama first sought to secure the US-Mexico border (Hernández 2010), earning Obama the moniker of "Deporter in Chief" (Golash-Boza 2018), yet bipartisan support proved elusive. Unable to pass legislation, Obama sought to act administratively. In 2011, Immigration and Customs Enforcement (ICE) Director John Morton issued memos that directed ICE officers to prioritize "criminal aliens" for deportation and to exercise discretion in favor of law-abiding long-term residents on humanitarian grounds (Wadhia 2011, 2015). This guidance was not always followed by officers in the field. Furthermore, immigrant rights advocates demanded more: work authorization and permission to remain in the United States with a pathway to citizenship. In 2012, with an eye toward systematizing discretionary relief, the Obama administration launched the DACA program and, in 2014, sought to expand such administrative relief to undocumented parents of US citizens and Lawful Permanent Residents and to additional child arrivals. However, in 2015, a court enjoined this expansion. Legal battles over deferred action have continued to this day as the Biden administration once again grapples with the possible demise of DACA. Moreover, though the Biden administration has claimed to be supportive of immigrants, continued controversies over border policies have led Biden to "stiffen enforcement for those who try to come without a legal right to stay" (White House 2023b).

By carrying out fieldwork at a Southern California nonprofit during this critical period, I was able to witness how stiffened enforcement and humanitarian discretion shaped the legal strategies of service providers and immigrant residents. The nonprofit was an appropriate site for this project because it is a leading immigrant rights organization, both locally and nationally. Lead plaintiff in a number of class action suits that won key rights for immigrants, the Los Angeles office also provided extensive immigration services to Southern California Spanish-speakers. Services were offered on what Chiara Galli (2023, 115–116) refers to as a "low-bono" basis—that is, fees were lower than those charged by private attorneys, and service providers were "motivated by humanitarian and social justice concerns rather than profit." At the time of my research, the nonprofit's legal services included TPS, naturalization, DACA, U-visas, Violence Against Women Act cases, asylum, family visas, Special Immigrant Juvenile visas, general consultations on immigration law, and more. This broad range of services coupled with the nonprofit's commitment to advocacy made it an ideal setting to study documentation practices.

ON THE RECORD

The central intervention of this book is to take documentation seriously, both as process and product. To do so, I treat the records that legal service providers and immigrant residents collect and generate as an "archive" assembled strategically around legal and administrative criteria while also asserting immigrant community members' own understandings of their lives. I use the term "archive" to highlight the intentionality of collecting documents that are part of a broader set of materials, kept by individuals or held by institutions (e.g., banks, schools, courts, police) as part of their own information systems. Immigrant residents develop expertise in documentation by living in the United States without full legal citizenship. As long-term residents who, in many cases, are undocumented or have only temporary authorization, immigrant residents understand the power and limitations of documentation. For instance, they may be able to work, but not legally, or they may be able to get drivers licenses but not social security numbers.[4] This fundamental tension between being a long-term resident and being unauthorized created a double bind: nonprofit clients often had to document activities, such as employment or their years of presence in the United States, despite working in the informal sector or trying to remain undetected. Furthermore, immigrant residents had to develop legal strategies without full knowledge of the records that the state had compiled about them (Kalhan 2014)—and submitting Freedom of Information Act (FOIA) requests did not always remedy this problem. Records therefore played a dual role, creating obstacles (such as a criminal conviction) but also sometimes creating openings (as when a kin relationship conferred eligibility for lawful residency). Service providers' experiences navigating such obstacles and openings also gave them expertise in documentation as a craft, in knowing how to fill out forms, make arguments, manage risks, anticipate US Citizenship and Immigration Service (USCIS) requests for evidence, and assemble paperwork. Service providers mediated between their clients and administrative audiences, advocating for the former while also anticipating responses from the latter. In so doing, they brought forward their clients' voices while also shaping these into administratively recognizable forms.

Analyzing the archival practices of service providers and immigrant residents highlights how subaltern groups "document back" to the state. The notion of "documenting back" draws on Maori and Indigenous Studies scholar Linda Tuhiwai Smith's concept of "researching back." In *Decolonizing Methodologies*, Smith writes, "Part of the project of this book is 'researching back,' in the same tradition of 'writing back' or 'talking back,' that characterizes much of the post-colonial or anti-colonial literature. It has involved a 'knowing-ness of the colonizer' and a recovery of ourselves, an analysis of colonialism, and a struggle for self-determination" (Smith 2012, 8). In the same vein, undocumented or temporarily authorized residents develop a "knowing-ness of the immigration state" through its demands for identity documents. Within governmentality literature, such "knowing-ness" is generally viewed as an internalization of the gaze of the state, one that leads subjects to discipline themselves. As Rose, O'Malley, and Valverde point out, according to governmentality scholars, "technologies of the self were formed alongside the technologies of domination such as discipline. The subjects so created would produce the ends of government by fulfilling themselves rather than being merely obedient" (2006, 89). In the case of illegalized community members, such technologies of the self might lead them to discipline themselves as they attempt to live in ways that would define them as "deserving" (García 2014; Menjívar and Lakhani 2016). Yet, I argue that in addition to being disciplined, immigrant residents are able to use their "knowing-ness" in the ways highlighted by Smith, to recover themselves, analyze power relations, and seek self-determination. In short, they develop their own expertise regarding documents and documentation, an expertise that attempts to deploy records in ways that "speak back to the state in its own language" through claims for regularization (Abarca and Coutin 2018, 8). Disciplinary facets of governmentality therefore also give rise to tactics of resistance that implicitly or explicitly challenge state practices and understandings (Coutin 1995).

Examining how illegalized residents and their advocates "document back" to the state also sheds light on papereality as a relational dimension of citizenship. Dery defines papereality as a feature of bureaucratic organizations, in which there is "a world of symbols, or written representations, that take precedence over the things and events represented" (1998, 678). Examining the archival practices of advocates and immigrant residents suggests that rather than being limited to bureaucracies, papereality has become a feature of social life, such that marginalized people can claim power by gathering their own documentation. In so doing, they attempt to bring "the things and events represented" into conformity with the documentary account that they produce, instead of allowing official records to determine their existence. Of course, proving any claim in US courts requires assembling paperwork, but in the case of illegalized residents, the need for and ability to produce documentation takes on added significance. Immigrant residents' efforts to document their own lives respond to the twin tendencies toward enforcement and humanitarianism. That is, noncitizens must provide documentation to counter suspicion (e.g., I *was* really here; I *was* contributing to society), and to appeal to officials' compassion (e.g., Deporting me *would* hurt my children). Papereality is relational in that the legal cases of people who have immigrated are constructed in relation to other accounts, whether these take the form of laws, popular discourse, or records generated by officials. As a relational practice, the production of papereality is spatialized, as documents circulate and reference other documents. Yet papereality also exists *outside of* space, as people can be physically present but legally nonexistent, positioned "elsewhere" or "outside" of national polities. And moreover, papers are increasingly giving way to digital records, which may not physically exist, even as officials sometimes insist on "wet" rather than digital signatures. Both citizenship and alienage emerge between papereality and the "other" domain to which documentation can only refer but not actually reach.

Attending to archival practices as a relationship between papereality and events that lie outside of documentation provides a fresh take on what has often been characterized as a "gap" between "law-on-the-books" and "law-in-action" (Gould and Barclay 2012). Traditionally, "gap studies," as they came to be called, viewed written law ("law-on-the-books") as *inactive*, in contrast to "real law" as practiced ("in action") by the bureaucrats, judges, and community members who carried it out (Calavita 2016; Morrill and Edelman 2021; Suchman and Mertz 2010). In contrast, studying how immigrants and advocates deploy documentation in an effort to claim status suggests that law "on-the-books" is far from static. Over the five-year-period of the research for this book, legal terms such as "admitted and inspected" and "misdemeanors" were redefined, while new programs such as DACA and provisional waivers were implemented. This book provides insights into how organizations and immigrant residents may respond if new programs— such as expanding current numeric caps on visas or updating "registry," which allows those who have been in the United States continuously since January 1, 1972 to apply for residency—are adopted in the future. Where gap studies often suggested legal reforms to realign legal practices with written law, my own analysis suggests that although the boundary between law and that which lies outside of law can shift (and promoting such changes is precisely the point of regularization efforts), this boundary cannot be eliminated (Coutin, Maurer, and Yngvesson 2002). "Law" and "illegality" are therefore dimensions of social reality (Coutin and

Yngvesson 2023), much as "length," "breadth," and "height" can be understood as dimensions of space. Temporally, the domain that lies outside of recordkeeping both precedes and results from documentation. Thus, a birth takes place *before* a birth certificate is issued, even as the birth certificate produces a birth as a legally cognizable event. Such moving between papereality and "the things and events represented" is the essence of archival advocacy. As Susan J. Pearson observes, "If our documents are meant to say who we are, then we ought to have a say in our documents" (2021, 292).

In studying archival advocacy, I treat advocates' and immigrant community members' accounts of documentation as sources of insight, informed by their knowledge of the roles of papers within (il)legalization. Just as work by undocumented and immigrant scholars challenges popular narratives of deservingness (Abrego and Negrón-Gonzales 2020), so too do community members insist on their value, regardless of immigration status. Their accounts are "inherently political," in the sense that anthropologist Aimee Cox discusses in relation to her interlocutors:

> When Janice and the other residents [in a shelter] considered the meaning of events, their commentary was regularly informed by what it feels like to live in bodies that are given multiple unstable identifications . . . constantly reminded of where they did and did not belong, how they should and should not be seen, and the consequences for stepping outside of the boundaries meant to define and contain them as poor Black girls. How they experience their lives is thus "inherently political," even while their politics are inaccessible in the narratives that situate them in various, often competing discourses. (2015, 5).

Similarly, immigrant residents have experienced being asked for papers that they do not have, or presenting documentation that is deemed insufficient. Service providers likewise represent clients who are treated by authorities as suspect, and who therefore face heightened documentation requirements. Such experiences give both service providers and immigrant residents a sort of "documentation expertise"—that is, a specialized knowledge of forms, records, and transactions. Their articulation of this expertise, much like their documentation practices, engages the broader systems within which they are situated, and thus takes on political meanings, even when not explicitly political. Thus, when an attorney told me to detail Juan's suffering in order to support a cumulative trauma argument, this attorney was insisting that Juan's experiences mattered and were deserving of legal recognition. Detailing such suffering was a way to contest narrow legal definitions of harm. Similarly, Juan's comments about self-sufficiency in some ways echo dominant tropes that condemn welfare use (Gustafson 2009), but also reflect insights borne of possibly being considered a public charge. Later chapters also engage illegalized residents' insights. For example, chapter 2 discusses Sonya's view that the residue of everyday life could potentially confer status, notes ways that illegalized residents assess their own deservingness, presents Gloria's insight that she became undocumented *before* she left her country because she did not have enough documentation to secure a visa, shares Arnulfo's perspective that complying with immigration authorities' requests did not guarantee outcomes, and analyzes an interlocutor's comment that she was living in a "cage of gold." These and other insights have shaped the book's central arguments about how the securitization-humanitarianism nexus that is at the heart of US immigration law makes documents vitally important to illegalized residents, generating strategies through which they pursue status, but also uncertainty about what the state will do.

In sum, exploring the archival practices of advocates and immigrant residents sheds light on how those whose lives are to some degree, "off the record," nonetheless counter illegalization by "documenting back" to the state. Their documentation efforts are part of a broader phenomenon, in which undocumented people, including undocumented students and researchers, "talk back to all of the scholarship"—and, I might add, political speeches and legal narratives—"that has been produced *about* their experiences" (Abrego and Negrón-Gonzales 2020, 2). Such students and researchers have argued that immigrant residents are knowledge producers rather than mere research subjects (Alonso Bejarano et al. 2019), and have produced accounts of immigration that begin with US intervention abroad rather than with people entering US territory (Martinez et al. 2020). As Marco Saavedra queries in the poem, "Que?" (in Martinez et al. 2020, 78):

> What if the illegal is you?
> Your institutions, your economy
> your system of reality

This question flips the frame through which immigration in understood, noting ways that by denying others' humanity, US institutions become illegitimate and therefore illegal.

(IL)LEGALIZATION AND UNDOCUMENTATION

By 2011, when I embarked on this study, approximately 11 million residents of the United States had been subject to *illegalization*—that is, they were defined as outsiders whose presence was prohibited (Warren 2018). This number has remained similar: using 2019 data, the Migration Policy Institute (n.d.) estimated the unauthorized population at 11,047,000. Significantly, for most of these residents, illegalization was not the result of a judicial determination but rather was produced through daily life, as officials, employers, universities, healthcare providers, police, landlords, bank personnel, and others requested documents that they did not have (Dreby 2015).[5] Furthermore, illegalization was often incomplete in that living in the United States produces connections that defy illegalization. Such connections include ties with employers, friends, neighbors, relatives, religious institutions, local businesses, schools, clubs, and organizations. Despite these connections, documents play a central role in illegalization. Work authorization is required for formal employment, identity documents can be required to travel both domestically and internationally, people can be pulled over at sobriety or immigration checkpoints, a traffic stop can involve a request for a driver's license, and people's abilities to access healthcare, attend college, qualify for financial aid, drive, enter a club where one has to be over twenty-one, and much more are influenced by having or lacking particular documents. Illegalization is therefore also a form of *undocumentation*—that is, of being made to lack papers, a condition that is created by the government and that therefore can be changed (see also Boehm 2020; Abrego and Negrón-Gonzales 2020). Yet, while illegalized residents may lack Employment Authorization Documents (EADs), US passports, US birth certificates, or social security numbers, they are often hyper-documented in other ways, as they may collect receipts, pay stubs, and other documentation that would prove their presence in the United States, if an opportunity to regularize their status arose (Chang 2011; Abarca and Coutin 2018; Ordóñez 2016). Thus, illegalization, legalization, and the gradations between involve documentation strategies, whether on the part of illegalized residents, other community members, or the state.

The population of illegalized residents in the United States was not always so large. Historically, while immigration law was deeply exclusionary,[6] it also was built on the principle that people who immigrated were "Americans in Waiting" who would eventually naturalize (Motomura 2006). While there were periods of mass expulsion, as when Japanese Americans were interned during World War II or when those of Mexican descent (including US citizens) were deported during the 1950s, it was during the 1980s that the mass production of long-term illegalized residents began in earnest. Three factors were key to this development. First, US intervention, political violence, and economic oppression displaced growing numbers of people from their countries of origin (Hamilton and Chinchilla 1991; Sassen 1989). Second, with the rise of neoliberalism, the US labor force, which had always relied on immigrant labor, underwent further transnationalization, both through assembly plants relocating beyond US borders and through recruiting laborers, often undocumented ones, from beyond US borders. This flexible workforce was both expendable and exploitable, due to the risk of deportation (De Genova 2002). Third, within the United States, avenues for regularization were increasingly restricted even as border enforcement stiffened, trapping unauthorized populations within the country (Bean, Vernez, and Keely 1989). The mass production of undocumented workers was simultaneously a process of racialization and criminalization, as, in 1965, numeric restrictions imposed on those from the Western Hemisphere (Vázquez 2015), rendering mass migration from Mexico illegal (Ngai 2004), and the criminal justice system increasingly targeted migrants as racialized "others" (García Hernández 2013).

The US policies that illegalize long-term immigrant residents are in some ways typical of highly developed countries that are immigration destinations, and in other ways are atypical. Like the United States, other destination countries have adopted restrictive measures that treat immigration as a security issue. Such measures include establishing checkpoints to examine identity documents, making eligibility for services contingent on legal status, detaining and deporting those without authorization, and linking crime control and immigration enforcement (Barbero 2020; Borrelli and Walters 2024; Bosworth 2012; Bowling and Westenra 2020; Khosravi 2009; Moore 2020; Panebianco 2022; Van der Woude, Barker, and Van der Leun 2017; Van der Woude and van der Leun 2017; Zotti 2021). In multiple destination countries, people who lack authorization or who have pending immigration claims must live for years with uncertain futures (Artero and Fontanari 2021; Hasselberg 2016), while those who are apprehended at border entry points may be removed without a meaningful opportunity to assert their rights (Barbero 2020). Despite such similarities, the United States differs from peer countries due to what legal scholars refer to as "immigration exceptionalism"—that is, a judicial doctrine known as "plenary power" that gives Congress and the executive branch full discretion over immigration policy as a matter of national sovereignty, thus limiting the judicial review of government action vis a vis immigrant residents (Rubenstein and Gulasekaram 2017).[7] The plenary power doctrine has allowed immigration law to evade "substantive constitutional restraints" (Legomsky 1984, 255), and immigration policies that could otherwise be considered racially discriminatory continue unchecked (Rosenbaum 2018; Chang 2018; Saito 2003; Lee 2023), potentially contributing to the death of border crossers and immigrant residents who are treated as expendable (Lee 2023). Indeed, the US judiciary's unwillingness to limit Congress' and the president's ability to deport long-term residents who have weak connections to their countries of origin "makes the United States an outlier as compared to both its neighbors and to former colonial powers" (Chacón 2023, 15–16).

In the face of daily practices that illegalized their presence, the immigrant residents I encountered at the nonprofit experienced both hope and anxiety regarding documentation. Hope derived from the fact that laws and policies change over time, with new programs (such as DACA) sometimes being created. As well, people's personal circumstances sometimes changed in legally beneficial ways. Marrying a US citizen or Lawful Permanent Resident could potentially confer eligibility for a spousal petition, though having lived in the United States without status could create a barrier to qualifying (Gomberg-Muñoz 2016). Furthermore, many illegalized residents had friends and relatives who had obtained residency, which made status appear to be within reach, and many felt that they were at least as deserving. The pressure to obtain status was intense. Illegalized residents needed legal status to advance in their jobs, study, remain with their US citizen children, petition for family members living outside of the country, and visit relatives from whom they had been separated. But applying for status was also seen as somewhat risky. What if submitting paperwork backfired, leading to deportation? Would a brief encounter with the police many years ago come back to haunt them? What records did immigration authorities have about them? Would outstanding debts be held against them? What if they were unemployed or if a family member had received public assistance? Would that look bad? Decisions about whether to pursue regularization had high stakes—but so did *not* applying.

In this high-stakes context, nonprofits such as the one where I did fieldwork played an important role as "brokers" who mediated between illegalized residents and the state (De Graauw 2016; Tuckett 2018). In Southern California, as in many regions of the United States, there are insufficient free or low-cost, high-quality immigration-related legal services to meet demand, and, generally, there are no public defenders for immigration cases (though, increasingly, some cities are providing free legal services to those in removal proceedings) (Annobil 2009). The immigration legal services market is therefore populated by public notaries claiming to have immigration expertise, predatory attorneys who go to court without first meeting their clients, preachers who prepare immigration paperwork for congregants, and more (Longazel 2018; Pedroza 2018; Shannon 2009). Illegalized residents who hope to regularize their status are vulnerable to such practitioners, who may claim to have "connections" that can expedite clients' cases or secure status that is otherwise unavailable. All too often, employing such services leads to being placed in removal proceedings. Unlike such unlicensed or substandard practitioners, reputable nonprofits educated clients about immigration law, provided contracts spelling out their fees and services (as required by California licensing and ethics rules), and delivered accurate assessments of clients' prospects of regularization, even when the news was disappointing. The nonprofit where I volunteered combined services with advocacy by participating in immigrant rights coalitions, holding rallies and marches, working with local and state authorities, and leading or participating in class actions. It also conducted public outreach by speaking to the media about immigration issues and holding regular community-based "know your rights" presentations on immigration. This nonprofit's relationship with the USCIS was not always adversarial; for instance, nonprofits participated in USCIS information sessions and conference calls regarding policy changes, and successfully competed for federal grants to support naturalization services. Nonprofits often had strong ties to local and state government as well, securing funding from government agencies and developing connections that enhance their advocacy work.

As an organization that moved within policy circles while also being rooted in immigrant communities, the nonprofit had to translate between policy and advocacy, community members' and officials' worldviews, documentation requirements and the records that community members could access. Legal staff therefore developed specialized expertise in document preparation. They kept abreast of changing requirements, knew the specific documents that USCIS had requested in the past, and understood how these had to be formatted and assembled. I noticed that legal staff had memorized the forms that they worked with regularly. They knew the numbers of questions that proved tricky, the page numbers of the forms, and the section headings. Most legal staff were also bilingual in English and Spanish and had therefore learned both technical and "everyday" Spanish terminology for US legal concepts. For instance, a "fee waiver" was referred to as "perdón de pago" (literally, a payment pardon). Their work with clients gave them familiarity with popular conceptualizations of US immigration law. Legal staff's familiarity with immigration procedures allowed them to decipher the processes that had generated notices, forms, or documents that their clients had received.[8] They could advise their clients where to obtain the documentation that they needed for their cases, and how long particular procedures or requests would take. This expertise, and the fact that Southern California is home to a sizeable and diverse immigrant population, made this nonprofit an ideal fieldwork partner and site.

PARALEGAL ETHNOGRAPHY

The approach that I used during fieldwork can be described as a *paralegal ethnography*, in that it combines "para-ethnography" and "legal ethnography," and was carried out from a subject position akin to that of a paralegal. Holmes and Marcus (2006) coined the term "paraethnography" to describe the ways that social actors engage in quasi-ethnographic inquiries—for example, by carrying out observations and informal interviews to understand emergent trends. Holmes and Marcus explain:

> within these milieus of contemporary fieldwork operate reflexive subjects whose intellectual practices assume real or figurative interlocutors. We can find a preexisting ethnographic consciousness or curiosity, which we term para-ethnography, nested in alternative art space in Tokyo or São Paolo, at an environmental nongovernmental organization (NGO) in Costa Rica, the central bank of Chile and the headquarters of the major pharmaceutical firm in Zurich or Mumbai. (2008, 82–83; see also Islam 2015; Reichman 2011).

The legal services department of a nonprofit is one such site, as service providers adjust their practices to meet clients' needs; indeed, providers' documentary expertise is gleaned not only through formal legal training, but also through para-ethnographic engagement in that they hone their legal craft as they interact with clients, officials, and each other. By carrying out fieldwork alongside these practitioners, my own ethnographic inquiry likewise participated in informal forms of knowledge production. At the same time, by situating myself in a legal context, shadowing service providers, observing case preparation, and talking with providers and their clients, I was performing classic techniques used in legal ethnography

4.	**Race** *(Select one or more)*				
	☐ White	☐ Asian	☐ Black or African American	☐ American Indian or Alaska Native	☐ Native Hawaiian or Other Pacific Islander

FIGURE 1. Race question on the 2013 version of the N-400 "Application for Naturalization" form.

(Starr and Goodale 2002). My own role during fieldwork was similar to that of a paralegal—that is, someone who, under the supervision of an attorney, provides legal assistance, interviews clients, takes notes, completes forms, prepares declarations and affidavits, documents cases, and provides administrative support. I carried out such tasks as a researcher and volunteer. One important aspect of paralegal ethnography is that it involved stance-taking (Faria et al. 2020; Simpson 2020) in that, as a quasi-member of a legal team, I helped to advocate for clients.

Being a "paralegal ethnographer" helped me to see documents themselves almost as ethnographic subjects. Through my fieldwork, I became aware of documents' efficacy and limitations. I learned, for example, how "Employment Authorization Documents" (EADs) or work permits could be used as a form of identification. I came to see supplementary documentation, such as bank statements, medical records, transcripts, and awards for community service, as immigration documents. I saw how service providers and their clients interacted with documents and forms, and, when I worked as a volunteer, I played a role in gathering evidence. I learned how to fill out immigration forms and became aware of the tricky questions, such as the fact that the question about race on the 2013 version of the N-400 form did not allow applicants to select "Hispanic" or "Latino," forcing them to choose between categories with which they did not identify (see Figure 1). My engagement with documents was embodied and emotional as well as analytical. I sometimes developed a headache when struggling with a complicated translation, I felt exhausted when I skipped lunch to attend to multiple nonprofit clients, I was anxious for the nonprofit's clients, and I experienced exhilaration when I learned that applications had been approved. In sum, fieldwork gave me the opportunity to engage with documents as these were deployed as part of legal claims.

Of course "ethnography" refers to both the written product of fieldwork as well as to the method employed. As a paralegal ethnography, each chapter of *On the Record* takes up a different facet of documentation practices. Chapter 1, "Securitization, Humanitarianism, and Plenary Power," details how broader historical and political forces structure encounters between noncitizens who are seeking status and the federal officials who will decide their fates. The twin forces of securitization and humanitarianism shape the files that immigrant residents compile when applying for immigration remedies. Chapter 1 details how, in addition to being a judicial doctrine, plenary power is manifest in immigrant residents' daily lives, defining them as outsiders who are subject to the president's and Congress' political will. It undergirds the forms that immigrant residents fill out, the social exclusions they experience, and the administrative guidance provided by government authorities. Plenary power renders the state omnipresent yet absent, as immigrant residents are scrutinized as security risks but cannot always tell what the government has in its files. The power to exercise discretion also creates vulnerabilities for the state in that immigrant residents can attempt to sway decision-making in their favor. The state thus is made to appear through immigrant community members' actions, much as the outline of a figure also reveals the ground that surrounds it.

Chapter 2, "Routine Exceptionality," analyzes how those who have immigrated navigate plenary power. The state's exercise of discretion sets up a dynamic in which applicants for immigration remedies must demonstrate that they are exceptional—for instance, that unlike others who immigrated without authorization, they need asylum, are victims of crime, or have essentially become "American" in all but name. Drawing heavily on conversations and interviews with immigrant residents, this chapter explores how noncitizens inhabit the subject positions created by immigration law. On the one hand, they adopt the law's logic, documenting the conditions that make them worthy of a favorable exercise of discretion. On the other, immigrant residents' legal strategies, such as saving documents in an effort to compel the state to recognize their claims, repurpose documents in ways that undermine the categorical demarcations on which law depends.

Chapter 3, "Legal Craft," focuses on the strategies through which advocates mediate between immigrants and the state. Legal craft is practiced in a context of uncertainty, in which state policies may shift, adjudicators are relatively inaccessible, and the difficulties that immigrant residents face in accessing "their" records give rise to an imbalance of knowledge. Examining such documentation challenges sheds light on the opportunities and double binds that immigrant residents and service providers experience as they attempt to turn recordkeeping systems to community members' advantage. Deciphering these opportunities and double binds involves a sort of technocratic expertise in mundane but nonetheless crucial facets of immigration law—how to fill out a form; how long it takes for applications to be processed; the amount and type of evidence that officials require. Examining the legal craft practiced by advocates and immigrants highlights records' quasi-magical ability to transform persons.

Chapter 4, "*Otro mundo es posible* (Another World Is Possible)," analyzes the alternative visions of belonging that advocates and immigrant residents put forward. According to immigrant residents, justice entailed transforming the conditions that led them to immigrate, making documents more readily available, reuniting families, creating regularization opportunities, erasing distinctions based on immigration status, and treating those who immigrate to the United States with respect and dignity. Service providers prefigured such a world through their own advocacy work as they expressed empathy with clients, translated between state categories and their clients' understandings, provided a high level of service, and sought to empower their clients. In so doing, they strived to make immigration rights "real" (De Graauw 2016). The vision of justice articulated by immigrant residents and prefigured through service providers' actions suggest ways that government officials could practice an ethic of care rather than securitization.

Finally, the Conclusion, "Documenting Back," considers how the alternative accounts explicated in chapter 4 speak to the forms of power and legal processes analyzed in earlier chapters. The chapter begins by synthesizing the arguments of the earlier chapters and then reflects on paralegal ethnography as a form of "documenting back" through witnessing. The chapter concludes by detailing ways that the analysis presented in *On the Record* helps to explain current impasses in immigration reform efforts, even as it also presents ways to move forward.

Securitization, Humanitarianism,
and Plenary Power

In March 2015, my research assistant Gray Abarca observed a "charla"—a community presentation about immigration policy—in the nonprofit's event hall. The most striking thing about this event was the sparse attendance: only fifteen to twenty-five people came to the event. In contrast, a few months earlier, in November 2014, shortly after President Obama announced Deferred Action for Parents of Americans (DAPA) and an expansion of DACA eligibility known as "DACA+," I had attended a charla where the room was packed with over two hundred would-be applicants, straining to see a power point in the front of the room. Yet, in February 2015, the day before DACA+ was to be implemented, a federal Court in Texas enjoined both DAPA and DACA+, after Texas and twenty-five other states sued the Federal government, arguing that the president had exceeded his authority in establishing these programs. This lawsuit became a template for subsequent lawsuits challenging executive actions taken by the Biden administration, and the DAPA and DACA+ injunction left immigrant residents who had hoped to apply in a state of uncertainty. By March 2015, even as organizations such as the nonprofit where I was doing fieldwork and volunteer work continued to fight the injunction, many who could have potentially benefited from DAPA and DACA+ had become discouraged. As Gray wrote in his field notes, "Undocumented folk are accustomed to not hoping too much and expecting to stay in limbo (interestingly enough, it seems that potential DAPA folk are in some limbo within a limbo)."

Understanding why "undocumented folk are accustomed to not hoping too much," as Gray put it, requires examining how historical and political forces structure encounters between noncitizens who are seeking status and the federal officials who will decide their fates. A key aspect of these encounters is the skewed balance of power that made it possible for immigrant residents to be told overnight that these programs were enjoined and might not be implemented at all. Most fundamentally, this power differential is grounded in the notion of immigrants as *aliens* who are foreign to the United States regardless of the amount of time they have resided within US borders (Bosniak 2006). As noncitizens, migrants' constitutional rights are limited: they have only the rights afforded to "persons," not those for which citizenship is a prerequisite (Varsanyi 2008; Chacón 2010b). In contrast to the precarious position occupied by immigrant residents, the United States, as a matter of sovereignty, claims the authority to regulate its relationship with foreign governments, set foreign policy, control its borders, and govern "aliens" within its territory (Coutin, Richland, and Fortin 2014; Torpey 2000). Through the "plenary power doctrine," courts have given the political branches of government "full" or "plenary" power to regulate such matters without judicial interference. The sense that immigrant residents threaten US security runs deep in US history, from the 1798 Alien and Sedition Act through the notion of "perpetual foreignness" that undergirded Japanese internment, to the fear that Latinos are taking over the United States (Chavez 2013; Honig 1998). As García Cruz writes, "The United States has created a 'state of emergency' against immigrants, which has entailed limited legal protection while giving the nation-state complete power to enact discriminatory policies in the name of national security" (2020, 115).

Since the 1980s, the securitization of immigration law has intensified, even as officials have claimed that the harshness of the US immigration system is mitigated by the use of discretion on humanitarian grounds. For example, the Policy Manual of the US Citizenship and Immigration Services states, "The favorable exercise of discretion and the approval of a discretionary adjustment of status application is *a matter of administrative grace*, which means that the application is worthy of favorable consideration" (USCIS 2024c; emphasis added). Yet, though securitization and humanitarianism might appear to be opposing forces, in that the former is punitive while the latter promises relief, a closer examination reveals that they exist in relation to each other, forming two sides of one coin (Ticktin 2005, 350). When securitization is accompanied by the exercise of discretion on humanitarian grounds, punitiveness is mitigated in ways that soften its harsh edges, but that leave securitization itself intact. Humanitarianism can thus help to legitimize securitization (Abarca and Coutin 2018). As former Department of Homeland Security (DHS) secretary Janet Napolitano wrote in the June 15, 2012 memo authorizing DACA: "Our Nation's immigration laws must be enforced in a strong and sensible manner. They are not designed to be blindly enforced without consideration given to the individual circumstances of each case" (2012, 2). Humanitarian goals can sometimes be cited as justifications for border enforcement. For example, US "Prevention through Deterrence" policies forced border crossers into inhospitable and deadly terrain resulting in skyrocketing deaths. Proponents argued that such deadly policies promoted public safety (De Leon 2015). Likewise, the Biden administration has justified increased use of expedited removal along the US-Mexico border as a strategy to "expand and expedite legal pathways for orderly migration" (White House 2023a). Humanitarianism can itself be a form of securitization. Forrest Stuart (2016) has documented the "therapeutic policing" through which unhoused people are removed from the streets in the name of recovery and rehabilitation. Humanitarian programs can perpetrate legal violence by forcing people into the mold of victims in order to qualify (Abrego and Lakhani 2015; Herd and Moynihan 2018; Menjívar and Abrego 2012), and can also discipline immigrant residents as they attempt to demonstrate deservingness for humanitarian relief (Fassin 2011; Ticktin 2005). Indeed, recent humanitarian forms of relief, such as DACA, are actually enforcement mechanisms: what is being deferred is deportation.

The coupling of securitization and humanitarianism is widespread internationally. The anthropologist Miriam Ticktin has documented how European Union control over immigration and French control over citizenship created anxiety and ambiguity in France regarding who "belonged" there. French police had the discretion to pursue enforcement, deciding who to question, who to detain, for how long, and in what conditions, even as humanitarian exceptions to removal were granted for immigrants facing medical emergencies or who had extreme accounts of persecution. Ticktin writes that "law, in certain critical realms, operates according to the logic of exception, rather than as a regime of normative justice based on general rules and rights. . . . The significance of this point is not primarily legal, but political: it demonstrates a move away from the logic of democratic politics to a different logic of political belonging where law does not function to put limitations on the state" (2005, 348). Such suspension of law in the name of securitization, a suspension that empowers the state to grant exceptions according to political will, has occurred in other countries as well. Artero and Fontanari (2021, 643) have detailed how after concerns about immigration rose in Italy in 2015, asylum law operated through a "process of obfuscation" that made asylum seekers' status and futures unclear, thus acting as a means of deterrence and illegalization. Panebianco (2022) points out that in the Mediterranean, border enforcement has been externalized by encouraging Libya to interdict migrant vessels before they arrive, thus allowing EU countries to avoid violating humanitarian norms. Australia has also practiced border externalization by locating both enforcement and humanitarian assistance in the Middle East and Southeast Asia in order to prevent migration (Watkins 2017).

In the United States, the linkage of securitization and humanitarianism is evident not only in high-level legal decisions and Congressional debates but also in more mundane moments such as at the charla that Gray attended, when disillusionment seemingly led to poor attendance. Immigration is an arena of social life that is both *hyperlegalized* (Calavita and Jenness 2013) in that undocumented residents are continually made aware of the implications of legal status, and *extralegal*, in that immigration policy is seen as political and therefore less subject to judicial review. The implications of the plenary power doctrine can be felt in immigrant residents' everyday lives as they confront police who are allowed to racially profile them (Chacón 2010a), employers and other gatekeepers who ask them for identity documents, and programs that are enjoined before being implemented (Chacón, Coutin, and Lee 2024). US immigration policy serves the interests of powerful groups in the United States. Immigrant workers have been recruited to meet labor needs, only to be deported when competition with US workers becomes too intense or when those needs subside (Ngai 2004; Calavita 2020; De Genova 2002). Shifts in responsibility for the administration of US immigration policy from the Department of Labor, to the Department of Justice, to the Department of Homeland Security reflect changing conceptualizations of immigrants as workers, law enforcement targets, and security risks (Calavita 1992, USCIS 2012). Indeed, practices such as targeting so-called "criminal aliens," the increased use of detention and deportation, the blending of immigration enforcement and local policing, and the expansion of convictions that carry immigration consequences have further marginalized immigrant community members (García Hernández 2013; Stumpf 2006). Not surprisingly, criminal convictions were a key focus of the charla that Gray attended (see Figure 2).

To avoid being treated as security threats who should be deported, undocumented residents appealed to the state's "humanitarian" side, attempting to persuade immigration officials to exercise discretion in their favor. In so doing, residents took advantage of the ways that humanitarianism makes the state vulnerable: the state has to sometimes live up to the promise of administrative grace in order to appear legitimate. In this sense, there is an interdependency between the administrative state and undocumented communities that are the target of its governance practices. As Gray Abarca and I wrote (2018, 8), "Ironically, since alienage derives from the member-nonmember divide, the sovereign state needs noncitizens to constitute the possibility of absolute rule, even as the presence of undocumented workers demonstrates the limits of this possibility. Likewise, noncitizens would not exist as such were it not for the very power that can exclude them." Relatedly, in his study of the history of passports, John Torpey (2000, 6) draws attention to the interdependency between migration and sovereignty by noting that "regulation of movement contributes to constituting the very 'state-ness 'of states." Through this interdependency, the presence of undocumented residents allows the state to appear benevolent in granting status to those deemed deserving, and resolute in controlling its borders

FIGURE 2. Slide displayed at Charla on Executive Relief, November 22, 2014, "Verify everything about your criminal records before applying." Photo by author.

against external threats. Yet, at the very moment that the state appears, it is also challenged, through immigrant residents' demand for it to be something other than a state: a community in which distinctions between citizens and noncitizens would cease to be salient. It is through these dynamics of appearance, challenge, and coexistence that the judicial doctrine of plenary power takes shape.

To explore securitization, humanitarianism, and plenary power in US immigration policy, this chapter analyzes the legal history through which the plenary power doctrine developed, the immigration programs through which undocumented residents can appeal for a favorable exercise of state discretion, the ways that state power is manifested in forms and documents that guide applications for legal status, and the vulnerabilities and openings that these processes create.

Such vulnerabilities include the precedents that allow at least some administrative programs to endure, even in the face of opposition.

FOUNDING MOMENTS: INTERTWINING
SECURITIZATION AND HUMANITARIANISM

In 1888, Chinese immigrant Chae Chan Ping attempted to enter the United States at the port of San Francisco, where he presented a reentry permit that the US government had issued to him in June of 1887, when he visited China after having lived and worked in the United States for twelve years. Unfortunately for him, the United States rescinded his and other Chinese immigrants' reentry permits in the interim. Ping was only permitted to disembark after a *habeas corpus* petition was filed on his behalf. Chae Chan Ping's case challenging the denial of reentry reached the US Supreme Court, which, in a unanimous decision, allowed the denial to stand. Justice Stephen Johnson Field explained the decision as a matter of sovereignty: "The power of exclusion of foreigners being an incident of sovereignty belonging to the government of the United States as a part of those sovereign powers delegated by the Constitution, the right to its exercise at any time when, in the judgment of the government, the interests of the country require it, cannot be granted away or restrained on behalf of any one" (*Chae Chan Ping v. United States*, 609). The plenary power doctrine was born out of this exercise of discretion.

The Chinese Exclusion Act case, as Chae Chan Ping's effort to remain in the United States came to be known, introduces themes that undergird immigration policymaking today (Augustine-Adams 2005; Chang 2018; Kagan 2015; Rosenbaum 2018; Saito 2003). The Court's decision defined Chinese residents as outsiders on the basis of both *race* and *foreignness*. In discussing Chinese immigration, Justice Field noted "differences of race. . . . They remained strangers in the land, residing apart by themselves and adhering to the customs and usages of their own country" (*Chae Chan Ping v. United States*, 595). US immigration law continues to have racially disparate impacts, and racial profiling is considered legally permissible in immigration enforcement (Chacón 2019, Rosenbaum 2018). To the *Chae Chan Ping* Supreme Court, the relationship between foreign nationals and the United States was a matter of politics and foreign policy, not law, and therefore fell outside of the Court's jurisdiction. Drawing an analogy between immigration policy and treaty obligations, Justice Field wrote, "The question whether our government is justified in disregarding its engagements with another nation is not one for the determination of the courts" (*Chae Chan Ping v. United States*, 602). The Court felt authorized to rule on its own *lack* of jurisdiction (Coutin, Richland, and Fortin 2014). To justify its claim that decisions about entry of noncitizens were part of foreign policy, the Supreme Court defined the Chinese as a potential security threat and immigration as akin to war: "To preserve its independence, and give security against foreign aggression and encroachment, is the highest duty of every nation, and to attain these ends nearly all other considerations are to be subordinated. It matters not in what form such aggression and encroachment come, whether from the foreign nation acting in its national character, or from vast hordes of its people crowding in upon us" (*Chae Chan Ping v. United States*, 606). The securitization of immigration policy is thus a key feature of the plenary power doctrine. Yet, as articulated in the Chinese Exclusion Act case, this doctrine also allows for positive uses of discretion. Justice Fields writes that the US government could revoke reentry permits "at any time, at its pleasure." (*Chae Chan Ping v. United States*, 609). Presumably, if reentry permits could be revoked at the "pleasure" of the government, so too could they be extended. Securitization and the possibility of exercising discretion (favorably or negatively) were intertwined in the very moment that the plenary power doctrine was announced.

This intertwining of securitization with limited humanitarian discretion has characterized immigration policy, in different forms and with different emphases, throughout US history. When US employers recruited Chinese workers to build the US railroads, Filipino and Mexican workers to pick crops, and Mexican and other agricultural and industrial workers during World War II (Calavita 1992; Moore 1949; Ngai 2004) officials sought to weed out those suspected of labor organizing or political agitation (Calavita 1992, 2020). Such recruitments privileged US interests over humanitarian considerations (Gonzalez 1999). When the need for their labor subsided, these workers were frequently forced out, as occurred in Operation Wetback during the 1950s, treating immigration as a source of expendable workers (De Genova 2002). Immigrant residents have been subjected to what Krajewska (2017, 1) refers to as "identity policing," namely "efforts of nation-states—primarily governments, police, and other authorities—to collect and record identifying information about individuals who permanently or temporarily reside in their territory."[1] US immigration policy has prioritized visas for immediate family members of US citizens and Lawful Permanent Residents a humanitarian measure that promotes family unity, even though much of immigration policy seems designed to keep family members apart (Enchautegui and Menjívar 2015; Lee 2019).[2] Moreover, civil rights principles were incorporated into the 1965 Immigration Act, which replaced racially biased nation-based quotas with a more open preference system (Ngai 2004; Keyes 2014). In 1996, immigration reforms furthered criminalization through collaboration between federal and local law enforcement; targeting those with criminal convictions; expanding immigration consequences for crimes; restricting regularization opportunities; and increasing detention (Morawetz 2000). The 2000s have seen an intensification of security concerns manifested notably with the former Immigration and Naturalization Service (INS), which was housed in the Department of Justice, being reorganized as the US Citizenship and Immigration Services (USCIS), Customs and Border Protection (CBP), and Immigration and Customs Enforcement (ICE) and housed in the Department of Homeland Security. Humanitarian programs, including asylum, family-based visas, U-visas,

Temporary Protected Status (TPS), and deferred action, continue to exist but face legal and political challenges.

Together, securitization and humanitarianism structure relationships between immigrant residents and the state. Immigrant community members are suspected of being security threats but also can potentially sway authorities to exercise discretion in their favor. To do so, they must convince the state that they are deserving, according to categories and standards that they did not create and with which they may disagree, while knowing that authorities may also have collected records about them. These panopticon-like dynamics can lead to an internalization of state categories of deservingness (Menjívar and Lakhani 2016; García 2014), even as immigrant residents and their allies seek to expand regularization opportunities (Coutin et al. 2021). Temporary programs that can be withdrawn at the government's will position immigrant community members as supplicants who must appeal to authorities' "administrative grace" (Chacón 2015). Colleagues and I have written about this elsewhere:

> The discretionary state (associated with expansive executive authority) has the power to decide the fate of its noncitizen subjects by awarding, denying, and determining the benefits of . . . forms of liminal legality. The discretionary state is omnipresent, brought into being through the exercise of discretion (which affirms its sovereignty), fragmented (in that there may be internal dissension), unstable (in that is programs can be suspended or ignored), and *law-like* but differentiated from formal *law*. (Coutin et al. 2017, 953).

Of course, immigrant residents may refuse to occupy the position of "supplicant" that is associated with discretionary power, instead putting forward rights claims, insisting that they are here to stay, and assuming the authority to define their own identities (Coutin et al. 2017, 955). For example, rejecting narratives that blame immigrant parents for bringing children to the United States, youth have adopted the slogan, "unapologetic and unafraid" (Seif 2011).

While plenary power has primarily been understood as a judicial doctrine (Augustine-Adams 2005), there are also connections between (a) the way that this doctrine defines immigrant residents as outsiders and immigration policy as a matter of political will, and (b) immigrant residents' experiences of being regarded as security risks even as they seek to remain in the United States on humanitarian grounds. The securitization of immigration law is grounded in the notion that outsiders threaten the country (Chavez 2013) and undergirds exclusionary policies ranging from expanding the definition of an aggravated felony under the Clinton administration (Morawetz 2000) to the Muslim ban implemented by the Trump administration (Chang 2018). Likewise, the notion that immigration policy is a matter of political will means that discretion is a matter not only of deciding how to interpret law but also of filling in gaps between law and the extralegal (i.e., will). As Justin Richland, Véronique Fortin, and I observed, "Substituting political will for legal judgment explicitly acknowledges that, though authorized through legal deference, plenary power is a naked form of power, apparently inherent in sovereignty" (Coutin, Richland, and Fortin, 2014, 108). As a "naked form of power," plenary power is affirmed and contested not only in court rulings, but also in the forces that shape immigrant residents' lives and legal strategies.

SEEING LIKE A DISCRETIONARY STATE

One way to think about the *charla* that Gray attended in March 2015 is that public presentations on immigration law are designed to educate immigrant community members about how the US government sees their lives. US immigration policies focus on the aspects of individuals' immigration histories that undergird both securitization and humanitarianism. Regarding securitization, officials want to know how people entered the United States, whether they have committed crimes, if they were previously deported, and whether they pose a security risk. For example, during the *charla*, the speaker explained the following, in Spanish:

> Some crimes will disqualify you for deferred action; other crimes will not disqualify you, but they [authorities] have discretion to deny your application. Okay? Even though you fulfill the requirements, if you have been found guilty of very serious crimes, it may be that the Immigration agency sends your case for deportation. So if you have criminal convictions, it is very important for you to obtain your court record and consult with an attorney before submitting your application. You do not want to put yourself in danger of deportation.

Regarding humanitarianism, officials are interested in discretionary factors, such as ties to relatives in the United States, medical hardships, risk of persecution if deported, and any achievements that make immigrant residents particularly meritorious. During the March 2015 *charla*, the speaker emphasized the characteristics that would have qualified an individual for DAPA, had the program gone forward:

> First you have to be father or mother of a citizen or permanent resident; the important thing is that the relation had to exist on November 20 of 2014. So any child born afterwards does not qualify. You also have to have lived continually in the United States since the first of January of 2010. You have to have been physically present in the United States on November 20 of 2014. And you can't have had legal status on that date and you can't have certain criminal convictions.

Comparing these two quotes, one can see that regarding criminal convictions, the boundaries of acceptable records are not clear; authorities have discretion to deny cases; and individuals may not know the details of their own histories. In contrast, humanitarian factors, such as having children who are US citizens or Lawful Permanent Residents and having lengthy periods of residence in the United States, are limited by eligibility dates and the suspicion of criminality.[3] Other seemingly relevant information, such as rehabilitation following a conviction or having a child after the eligibility date, would not have been "seen" by the state evaluating a DAPA application.

The notion that states "see" reality in particular ways was developed by the anthropologist James Scott in his 1998 book, *Seeing Like a State*. Scott writes that state actions require "mak[ing] a society legible" (1998, 2) through "state simplifications . . . [that] did not successfully represent the actual activity of the society they depicted, nor were they intended to; they represented only that slice of it that interested the official observer" (1998, 3). For example, a state that is interested in resource extraction might look at a forest and only see timber, not the ecosystem that enables forests to flourish. In the case of immigration, officials may see only the aspects of immigrant residents' lives that are relevant to their own decision-making. Furthermore, the securitization of immigration policy produces an asymmetry between *security*, which is emphasized, and *humanitarian considerations*, which are secondary. The state sees like a white, settler colonial power that controls territory and can decide who is allowed to be present.[4] The state's gaze is infused with suspicion, with the assumption that those who are seeking status may pose security risks or be committing fraud. As members of a suspect group, immigrant residents are seen as undeserving, such that any award of status or deferral of removal appears benevolent or generous on the part of the state, an act of "administrative grace." As Sati observes, "Undocumented immigrants were made to grovel for a humanity that ought to be presupposed" (2020, 27). This asymmetry between the state and undocumented residents creates a high administrative burden for immigrant community members: they need to document the aspects of their lives that officials will see as meritorious for particular legalization avenues while avoiding triggering suspicion of wrong-doing (Horton 2020). This evidentiary burden is intensified by the fact that immigrant residents who are applying for status may not know what records the state has about them, which is why the *charla* speaker advised anyone who might have a criminal history to obtain their court records. The onerous nature of evidentiary burdens appears to deliberately place obstacles in the path of those who seek to regularize their status (Herd et al. 2023).

Several key evidentiary practices that reveal how the state "sees" cut across the programs through which immigrant residents can potentially regularize their status. These key evidentiary practices include calculating temporal presence, narrating merit and hardship, proving relationships, building exceptions into law, and assessing criminality. First, calculations of temporal presence are important because the state "sees" and evaluates the legal significance of presence in specific ways in different pathways to regularization.[5] For example, asylum applications generally must be submitted within one year of entering the United States; DACA requires demonstrating continuous presence in the United States since June 15, 2007; Lawful Permanent Residents (LPRs) must reside in the United States for five years before they are eligible to naturalize (three years if married to US citizens); eligibility for cancellation of removal requires ten years of continuous presence; and adults who are unlawfully present in the United States for six months or one year face a three- or ten-year bar on lawful reentry. Thus, in some cases, documented presence is required and in others—such as when trying to avoid a bar on lawful reentry—it is damning. To document their presence in the United States, immigrant residents had to provide records that had their names, a date, and an address. Such records included bank statements, employment records, rent receipts, school records, check stubs, receipts, letters, sign-in sheets, and records of doctor appointments. Lengthy temporal gaps between documents could be seen by the state as evidence that the applicant might have left the country, so service providers tried to keep gaps to a minimum. Naturalization applicants often provided copies of their passports so that entries and exits could be calculated: if an official failed to stamp a person's passport when they reentered the country, then the applicant was suspected of being away longer than claimed.[6] Brief, casual, and innocent trips outside of the country were not considered interruptions of continuous presence, as long as they cumulatively totaled less than six months. These ways of "seeing" temporal presence assumed that if something happened, it could be documented, even though illegalized residents used cash for transactions, worked in the informal economy, and set up accounts (such as rental agreements) in other people's names.

Second, another way of "seeing" was to consider hardship and merit, usually through narratives accompanied by supporting documentation. For example, asylum applicants detailed experiences that made them fearful of persecution; U-visa applicants narrated the suffering caused by crimes; and applicants for provisional waivers (to "waive" the three- or ten-year bar for certain family visa petitions) explained why it would be an extreme hardship for their US citizen or Lawful Permanent Resident spouse or parent if they had to remain outside of the country. The state wanted narratives to match criteria but not so well that narratives appeared to be invented. Narratives therefore needed to be individualized, even if the practice being narrated was patterned and widespread. To see hardship or merit, the state required levels of suffering or achievement that went beyond the ordinary. As a volunteer who wrote out U-visa declarations, I was advised to ask applicants to explain how they felt after surviving tragedies, which felt insensitive. Narrative accounts were supplemented by medical records, letters from therapists, documentation of country conditions, police reports, supporting letters from relatives and coworkers, or other evidence of the events described. Even in the absence of written declarations, application files in some ways put forward an implicit narrative by assembling a record of hardship, presence, and achievement. To be seen as meritorious, these accounts and records had to focus on the elements of people's lives and histories—employment, family ties, educational achievements—that the state considered relevant whether or not these were key factors for applicants.[7]

As Sati observes, "Undocumented immigrant groups are all but forced to operate under the establishments' framings" (2020, 35).

Third, seeing like a discretionary state entailed locating individuals within a set of kin relations, while also *not* seeing relationships that were not considered legally significant. Through the family visa petition system, US citizens can petition for residency for their spouses, parents, children, and siblings, while Lawful Permanent Residents can petition for spouses and unmarried children. Children's age (under or over 21) and marital status are relevant to how long such a petition will take—it can take decades in those categories (such as siblings) that are lower priorities. Other relationships, such as aunt-nephew or grandparent-grandchild, are not eligible for the petition process even though, in actuality, a child might be raised by an aunt or grandparent. Kinship is also important when determining who is included in an immigration benefit (for example, asylees can include their spouses and children as derivative asylees), who would experience hardship in an instance of removal (e.g., in cancellation of removal cases, only hardship to a US citizen or Lawful Permanent Resident spouse, parent, or child is considered), or whether a provisional waiver of unlawful presence can be granted (if a US citizen or LPR spouse or parent would suffer due to family separation). To be "seen," kin relationships require documentation, such as birth certificates, blood tests, marriage certificates, or adoption records. Official records are required due to the fact that, as Pearson (2021, 6) notes, "the state [has] gained a monopoly on epistemological authority." In the case of relationships that are suspect—marriages, parentage of children born out-of-wedlock—additional documentation can be required, including letters attesting to the validity of a marriage, photos of relatives spending time together, cards or letters establishing that a relationship existed, proof that a parent has provided a child with financial support, evidence of living together. To the discretionary state, discrepancies within these records could be taken as signs of fraud.

Fourth, seeing like a discretionary state meant incorporating exceptions into law by distinguishing the deserving from the undeserving. People who are in the United States without authorization generally are subject to removal unless they can demonstrate that they are eligible for relief. Qualifying for status required demonstrating that one is exceptional in some way, whether due to having a well-founded fear of persecution, a qualifying relationship to a US citizen or LPR family member, a job that could generate a work-related visa (something that I did not study, as such visas were not handled by the nonprofit), a history as a crime or trafficking victim (U- or T-visas), or some other form of eligibility. Some opportunities were limited to those from certain countries, such as awards of TPS due to humanitarian issues in a particular country (and clearly, it is problematic to think of dire circumstances as an "opportunity"). Of course, DACA itself is an exception, a form of prosecutorial discretion designed to give "consideration . . . to the individual circumstances" of those who immigrated as children and "lacked the intent to violate the law," as former DHS Secretary Janet Napolitano (2012, 1–2) put it. Procedural exceptions are also possible. For instance, naturalization applicants can seek fee waivers based on their income, beneficiaries of family visa petitions can seek provisional waivers for a bar on reentry, and U-visa applicants can ask officials to excuse minor violations, such as petty theft, especially if they can tie these to the crime they experienced (e.g., an abuse victim who is experiencing economic deprivation might shoplift to obtain food). While the varied avenues through which one can seek status might suggest that regularization is within reach, the reality is that the vast majority of undocumented residents are ineligible for any remedy. Gaining status is exceptional.

Fifth and finally, seeing like a discretionary state meant presuming that anyone seeking legal status in the United States might pose a security risk or be submitting a fraudulent application. "Good moral character" (GMC) was a required element of eligibility for numerous forms of relief, and was assessed both through criminal records checks (an absence of arrests or convictions) and positive demonstrations of deservingness (good works, such as certificates for volunteering at a school or religious institution). Certain criminal convictions (such as drug- or gun-related convictions) made individuals statutorily ineligible for status, as did convictions for aggravated felonies, which, for immigration purposes, were defined broadly (Morawetz 2000). Moreover, arrests could also be taken into account, despite the precept that people are innocent until proven guilty. In a 2012 video charla that the nonprofit created, a speaker advised potential DACA applicants of the following:

> Examples of factors that DHS is going to use to determine if you're a threat to public safety are arrests for certain things, even if they don't result in criminal charges. Say, you get arrested for maybe soliciting or vandalism or something, but the charges always get dismissed for one reason or another, or—you know—drug arrests, but then they ended up getting dismissed—um—a lot of arrests, even if they don't result in criminal charges, that could be taken into account. Also, tattoos that are visible in the photos that you submit to USCIS, so you want to be really careful if you have visible neck or face tattoos that might be a problem when you send your photos to USCIS.

A hint of criminality—such as a tattoo, which people get for many reasons that are unrelated to criminal activity—could be seen as threatening. For forms of legalization where the state had discretion to weigh criminality alongside other factors, the severity and timing of the offense were taken into account. In the case of naturalization, GMC has to be demonstrated for a five-year period, though earlier offenses can be taken into account. As the USCIS Policy Manual explains: "In general, the applicant must show GMC during the five-year period immediately preceding his or her application for naturalization and up to the time of the Oath of Allegiance. Conduct prior to the five-year period may also impact whether the applicant meets the requirement" (USCIS 2024g). Applicants were also penalized for factors, such as mode of entry, related to their immigration histories. Thus, those who "entered without inspection" (EWI) rather than with a visa were ineligible to adjust their status within the United States, and therefore were subject to the three- and ten-year bars on reentry. Anyone who falsely claimed to be a US citizen while entering the country was permanently barred, while those who left the country after having been ordered deported in absentia may have unknowingly executed a deportation order. Finally, suspicion pervades the state's gaze, such that discrepancies in individuals' records (e.g., differences in dates or the spelling of names) could be interpreted as signs that documents were forged, even if errors were introduced by people other than the applicant.

These ways of seeing prioritize suspicion of wrongdoing (criminal convictions, fraud) over markers of deservingness, which are limited by eligibility dates, the need for evidence, and individuals' immigration histories (e.g., entry without inspection). The administrative burden of applying for status is placed on immigrant residents rather than on the state. For example, when officials lost applications, nonprofit staff sometimes advised clients to resubmit the application and pay the fee a second time, since it would be difficult to locate and reactivate the original submission. Likewise, if immigration authorities were delayed in renewing a work permit, it was the applicant who suffered potential loss of employment and income.

The security/humanitarianism asymmetry pervaded not only evidentiary practices but also the process of applying for legal status. These asymmetrical ways of seeing materialized within the application forms and administrative guidance documents created by state agencies.

MANIFESTATIONS OF PLENARY POWER

Immigration-related forms can be understood as a manifestation of the ways that plenary power structures an encounter between immigrant residents and the state. The N-400 form through which Lawful Permanent Residents apply for naturalization is perhaps the most quintessential expression of the ways that securitization and humanitarianism are embedded in state exercises of discretion. Through naturalization, individuals transcend the boundary between noncitizens and citizens, formally becoming part of the US polity, so this form serves as a portal while also playing a gatekeeping function. Those who complete the N-400 form have already overcome many hurdles: they have immigrated to the United States, obtained permanent residency, fulfilled the requisite periods of residency, and prepared for language and civics exams (or sought waivers for these tests). The US government encourages Lawful Permanent Residents to naturalize and, in fact, promotes naturalization through outreach and grants to community organizations (USCIS 2023).

Yet the N-400 form could potentially be daunting to would-be applicants. The first eleven parts (pages 1–11) of the 2019 version of this twenty-page form

Part 12. Additional Information About You (Person Applying for Naturalization)

Answer **Item Numbers 1. - 21.** If you answer "Yes" to any of these questions, include a typed or printed explanation on additional sheets of paper.

1. Have you **EVER** claimed to be a U.S. citizen (in writing or any other way)? ☐ Yes ☐ No

2. Have you **EVER** registered to vote in any Federal, state, or local election in the United States? ☐ Yes ☐ No

3. Have you **EVER** voted in any Federal, state, or local election in the United States? ☐ Yes ☐ No

4. **A.** Do you now have, or did you **EVER** have, a hereditary title or an order of nobility in any foreign country? ☐ Yes ☐ No

   B. If you answered "Yes," are you willing to give up any inherited titles or orders of nobility that you have in a foreign country at your naturalization ceremony? ☐ Yes ☐ No

5. Have you **EVER** been declared legally incompetent or been confined to a mental institution? ☐ Yes ☐ No

Form N-400 Edition 09/17/19   Page 11 of 20

FIGURE 3. Beginning of Part 12 of the September 17, 2019 edition of Form N-400, "Application for Naturalization."

focus on demographic information and facts relevant to the applicant's eligibility, such as whether they have been Lawful Permanent Residents for five years, previous names used, social security number, contact information, current and previous addresses, names of and information about parents and children, race, ethnicity, hair and eye color, previous employment and schooling, time outside of the United States, and marital history. Though difficult to complete (not everyone keeps good records of their previous addresses and employment), such information generally serves the purpose of determining identity and eligibility. Questions allow applicants to indicate that they are eligible for an accommodation due to a disability, that they qualify to waive language requirements, or that they wish to change their names when they are naturalized. In "Part 12, Additional Information about You" (pages 11 through 16), a series of highly stigmatizing questions are asked about criminal history, security risks, false citizenship claims, moral failings, and immigration history (see figure 3). Some of the questions seem anachronistic: "Do you now have, or did you **EVER** have, a hereditary title or an order of nobility in any foreign country?" (question 4A). Most, though, imply that the person who is seeking naturalization may have engaged in reprehensible conduct. Examples include, "Have you **EVER** claimed to be a U.S. citizen (in writing or any other way)?" (question 1); "Have you **EVER** advocated (either directly or indirectly) the overthrow of any government by force or violence?" (question 11); "Have you **EVER** committed, assisted in committing, or attempted to commit, a crime or offense for which you were **NOT** arrested?" (question 22); and "Have you **EVER** been a habitual drunkard?" (question 30A). The concluding parts of the N-400 form (parts 13–18) consist of signatures, attestations, information about the form preparer and interpreter (if any), renunciation of foreign titles, and the oath of allegiance. The lengthy list of questions in part twelve demonstrates how security concerns dominate discretionary decision making, as compared to, say, humanitarian consideration of the need for accommodations due to disabilities, a topic given only brief treatment in the application form.

Instead of viewing forms such as the N-400 applications as neutral or technical means of obtaining information, scholars who study bureaucracy and documents have examined forms as a means of producing "'papereality,' defined as a world of symbols, or written representations, that take precedence over the things and events represented" (Dery 1998, 678). As Matthew Hull argues, "Documents are not simply instruments of bureaucratic organizations, but rather are constitutive of bureaucratic rules, ideologies, knowledge, practices, subjectivities, objects, outcomes, and even the organizations themselves" (2012, 253). Thus, the questions on a form, the order of the questions, the ways questions are worded, and the possible answers permitted (e.g., yes or no, open-ended, checking a box) are a way of imagining the world, and both reflect and shape the ways that states see and that migrants and their allies can be seen (Vismann 2008). What is *not* asked about— the silences within forms—can be as significant as what appears (Constable 2005). Furthermore, forms have both a material reality and an aesthetic quality. It matters how much space is left to answer a question, whether only "wet" signatures are acceptable, if forms are to be completed digitally, and the degree to which a completed form stands in for the person whose reality is represented in the form. Is the completed form messy? Has white-out been used? Are there spelling errors? Or is the completed form crisp and professional? At the same time, a form stands in for government in that applicants may imagine themselves speaking to officials through the form. The encounter between applicants and the state that occurs through forms is disciplinary in nature. As Urla (2019, 264) observes:

> Governance unfolds in the inglorious realm of middling administration, examinations, classifications, protocols, and policies often seen as technical or routine. It is effected not in a single institution, but through an array of disparate forms of expertise, institutional practices, architectural forms, and laws that traverse a number of sites in and outside the state and its institutions, that may work in sporadic or totalizing projects, and that collectively, if not always seamlessly or coherently, coalesce into what Foucault called the apparatus or *dispositif* of governance.

Though disciplinary, the encounter that occurs through forms also enable applicants to potentially sway state officials. Approvals help to legitimize denials by showing that the state does not "blindly" enforce the law, as Janet Napolitano put it.

A close read of two forms—the N-400 Application for Naturalization (just introduced) and the I-821D Consideration of Deferred Action for Childhood Arrivals (DACA) forms—and the accompanying instructions reveals how the plenary power doctrine shapes the relationship between the US state and its noncitizen subjects. These two forms are appropriate for comparison because they represent two extremes in the regularization process. Those who are applying for naturalization already have lawful permanent residency, so what is at stake in the application process is whether they satisfy the requirements to become US citizens, the last step in immigrating to the United States. In contrast, DACA is not a status, but rather a form of presence, and it derives from a policy memo rather than a statute. Successful DACA requestors are considered to be lawfully present, but without legal status. DACA confers no pathway to citizenship and is a form of prosecutorial discretion. In fact, the I-821D form and instructions refer to those who submit this form as "requestors" rather than "applicants," thus positioning them as supplicants who are asking for humanitarian "consideration" on the part of the state. Both of these forms—one at the boundary between citizens and non-citizens and the other at the boundary between undocumented immigrants who warrant "consideration" and those who presumably do not—convey authorities' power to exercise their will as a matter of "sovereignty belonging to the government of the United States" (*Chae Chan Ping v. United States*, 1889, 609).

The N-400 and I-821D forms enable applicants and requestors to appeal to officials, even as these forms also emphasize administrative categories and procedures in ways that limit how appeals can be structured. On the one hand, the forms and instructions convey openness on the part of officials. For example, both forms explain the eligibility requirements and the sorts of evidence that should accompany the form; the N-400 instructions advise applicants that they can access a guidebook to naturalization, and the I-821D instructions conclude with a helpful checklist for requestors. Relatedly, the forms and instructions convey a willingness to modify some procedures to accommodate individual circumstances. Naturalization applicants are instructed that they may be able to take a modified oath, that they can be exempted from testing requirements based on their age and number of years in the United States, and that "USCIS is committed to providing reasonable accommodations for qualified individuals with disabilities and/or impairments" (USCIS 2019b, 6). Domestic violence victims who are seeking naturalization are advised that they can report a "safe address" where they can receive mail, instead of where they are actually staying. Forms include some open-ended questions and invite (or require) applicants and requestors to submit additional pages to explain their answers. DACA applicants, for example, can fill in a blank in their own words to indicate how they meet DACA's education requirement, though specific wording (e.g. "graduated from high school") is suggested (USCIS 2021a, 4). Likewise, after providing examples of appropriate forms of evidence, the DACA instructions invite requestors to submit "any other document that you believe is relevant" (USCIS 2021b, 6).

On the other hand, this openness is accompanied by clear reminders that USCIS, not applicants/requestors, has the power to decide whether to grant requests. Applicants and requesters are repeatedly informed that they must complete forms using black ink, answer every question by writing "not applicable" rather than leaving a blank space, and check the correct number of boxes, lest their application/request be denied or delayed. The I-821D form stresses the discretionary nature of relief, indicating that "USCIS will evaluate the totality of the circumstances in reaching a decision on deferred action," and that "even if you satisfy the threshold criteria for consideration of DACA, USCIS may deny your request if it determines, in its unreviewable discretion, that an exercise of prosecutorial discretion is not warranted in your case" (USCIS 2021b, 11). This "totality of the circumstances" phrasing and the reference to "unreviewable discretion" imply a kind of omniscience in which the balance of power lies with USCIS, not with applicants. Though the N-400 form and instructions do not mention discretion, these materials do repeatedly remind applicants that their applications may be denied. The negative terms "revocation," "reject," "deny," and "denied" appear in the N-400 instructions twenty-six times, in contrast to seven instances of the more positive terms "approve," "approval," and "grant." There is clearly an asymmetry between a limited degree of openness within this form and an overarching concern with control.

This asymmetry between openness and control intensifies the administrative burdens faced by naturalization applicants and DACA requestors, as they must prove their realities to a skeptical state while facing the catch-22 of having to document activities that were, of necessity, somewhat informal. Of course, naturalization applicants have lawful permanent residency and therefore are living in the United States with legal status, fully able to participate in the formal labor market. However, they too may experience gaps between their self-understandings and the papereality that they present to officials through the N-400. Thus, DACA requestors and naturalization applicants have to provide their "current legal name" defined as "the name on your birth certificate unless it changed after birth by a legal action such as a marriage or court order" (USCIS 2019a, 4), and this is the name that will appear on DACA recipients' work authorization, potentially creating conflicts with school or other records, if they have also used other names (Sanchez 2018). Both forms treat gender as a binary, even though applicants may be transgender, and both forms also have restrictive definitions of ethnicity and race. For "ethnicity," applicants and requestors must choose between "Hispanic or Latino" and "Not Hispanic or Latino," even though applicants might have parents of multiple backgrounds. For race, they may select "all applicable boxes" from the following list: "White," "Asian," "Black or African American," "American Indian or Alaska Native," and "Native Hawaiian or Other Pacific Islander" (USCIS 2019a, 5). In my experience, people from Central America frequently felt that none of these categories applied to them. The DACA request form must be accompanied by an abundance of additional evidence to prove applicants' identity, age, presence in the United States on June 15, 2007, continuous presence since that date, education, and criminal history (if any).

Yet, while the evidentiary burden falls on applicants and requestors, decisions about how to handle documentation fall to USCIS, which can require originals but which advises applicants that if they submit originals that are not required, "**your original documents may be immediately destroyed upon receipt**" (USCIS 2019b, 3). Furthermore, USCIS advises DACA requestors that any originals that they submit may not be returned. USCIS reserves the right to request additional evidence, obtain additional information through vague "agency verification methods," and share information with other agencies for routine uses (USCIS 2019b, 17). Even though applicants and requestors are required to prove their claims, USCIS may consult its own records—something that is particularly tricky when someone could be listed in gang databases without their knowledge (Muñiz 2022). Application forms and supporting documentation *affirm* the realities to which they refer and also *create* these realities, both by putting forward a particular representation (e.g., people may have to approximate the dates that they lived at particular addresses) and by trying to obtain citizenship or lawful presence, something that, to some degree, immigrant residents may already have in a de facto sense.

The asymmetry between USCIS's seemingly unfettered capacity to exercise discretion as compared to the applicants' more limited ability to present information is further exacerbated by a pervasive concern with security and fraud. As previously noted, the N-400 form requires applicants to answer fifty questions about their criminal histories, moral failings, and risk to national security. These questions are broad in scope. For example, the N-400 instructions advise applicants, "If you have ever been arrested or detained anywhere in the world, by any law enforcement officer, for any reason, and **no charges were filed,**" then applicants must submit an original arrest report and an official document certifying that no charges were filed (USCIS 2019b, 13). While there are fewer security-related questions on the I-821D form, the DACA request process created a new and vague term, a "significant misdemeanor" conviction, which can render requestors ineligible for DACA. Yet, without knowing what counts as a significant misdemeanor, it is difficult to know whether to apply. Within immigration processes, criminal records have permanency, even if they are expunged for other purposes. Thus, naturalization applicants are told, "You must disclose this information even if someone, including a judge, law enforcement officer, or attorney, told you that it no longer constitutes a record or told you that you do not have to disclose this information" (USCIS 2019a, 14). Further, instructions indicate that USCIS can go beyond the reported information to check applicants' criminal histories with law enforcement agencies, such as the FBI. Alongside these security concerns, the much more minor infraction of not following instructions by using the wrong color of ink or leaving a question blank can lead to denials.[8]

Forms such as the N-400 and the I-821D exemplify key features of plenary power. They enable the state to appear benevolent, yet, it is state agents who have "full" or "plenary" power to exercise discretion, and in the case of DACA, their decisions are unreviewable. Officials' ability to exert control is evident in these forms through repeated admonitions that failing to follow instructions may result in denials, expansive concern with criminal history, extensive documentation requirements, and limitations on how requestors and applicants can narrate deservingness. The ways that the state manifests itself within forms, guidance documents, and administrative practices create opportunities and challenges for immigrant residents.

VULNERABILITIES AND OPENINGS

Immigrant residents' and advocates' legal strategies are shaped by the vulnerabilities and openings that plenary power creates. As noted earlier, in the Chinese Exclusion Act case, the US Supreme Court defined the ability to exclude foreigners and govern access to US territory as a matter of sovereignty. The state's exercise of plenary power is therefore intrinsic to its existence, creating something of a fraught interdependency between the state and migrant subjects. Immigrant residents experience what Justin Richland, Véronique Fortin, and I have elsewhere termed, routine exceptionality: "Their presence demands law—the petition, the recognition claim—even as this demand simultaneously seeks an exception to law in that officials have the discretion to decide" (Coutin, Richland, and Fortín 2014, 99). To appear sovereign, the state treats resident noncitizens as outsiders, shaping their everyday lives through policies that racialize them as "foreign" and presume that they threaten national security. Recall Justice Fields' concern about "aggression" and "hordes . . . crowding in upon us" (*Chae Chan Ping v. United States*, 1889, 606). Because immigrant residents are presumed to be undeserving outsiders, any grant of status appears generous. For instance, granting a respondent in a removal proceeding "voluntary departure"—the ability to depart the country "voluntarily" at their own expense rather than being formally removed, is considered a form of immigration relief (Novy 2019). Thus, humanitarianism legitimizes securitization by allowing authorities to exercise the will conferred by plenary power "gracefully." For example, a 2013 ICE directive on recognizing parental interests while enforcing immigration law stated, "U.S. Customs and Immigration Enforcement (ICE) is committed to intelligent, effective, safe and humane enforcement of the nation's immigration laws" (ICE 2013, 1). Similarly, a Biden administration executive action in support of DACA stated, "DACA reflects a judgment that these immigrants should not be a priority for removal based on humanitarian concerns and other considerations, and that work authorization will enable them to support themselves and their families, and to contribute to our economy, while they remain" (White House 2021).

As noted earlier, the relationship that plenary power establishes between the state and immigrant residents is asymmetrical in that security concerns are prioritized over humanitarianism, opportunities for regularization are limited while consideration of risks is expansive, and officials have the power to decide whereas immigrant residents are positioned as applicants or requestors. These asymmetries create vulnerabilities for immigrants, such as the possibility that programs can suddenly be retracted, as occurred with DAPA, DACA+, and the reentry permits that were revoked through the Chinese Exclusion Act, and as potentially may occur as litigation over DACA continues. Laws and policies can also be changed retroactively (Morawetz 2000). As a 2015 Congressional Research Service report on removals explained, "An action that does not make an alien removable at the time it occurs may make the alien deportable at a later date if Congress changes the law" (Siskin 2015, 6). The precarity of relief, the retroactivity of policy, and the uncertainty of promised or proposed reforms place residents who are seeking status in limbo. Some immigration policies take effect almost automatically, without granting immigrant residents a day in court to challenge removal. For instance, "reinstatement of removal" occurs when someone who was previously removed reenters the United States without authorization and is apprehended. The earlier removal order can simply be reinstated by DHS without any judicial action. Reinstatement can only be challenged in extreme cases, such as when someone faces a probability of persecution under the Convention Against Torture (CAT). Generally speaking, opportunities for relief are limited to narrow grounds or restrictive eligibility dates, whereas if someone has "ever been arrested or detained anywhere in the world, by any law enforcement officer, for any reason" (USCIS 2019b, 13), then this arrest or detention can be considered by US immigration authorities. Proposals for immigration reform evince a lack of political imagination in that they typically include lengthy periods of provisional status, increased enforcement, and further restrictions on regularization (Chacón, Coutin, and Lee 2024).

A good illustration of these asymmetrical relationships is provided by the USCIS Policy Manual's discussion of "Extreme Hardship" (USCIS 2024d). This section of the manual provides guidance for adjudicators who are considering whether extreme hardship considerations warrant granting a waiver to a bar of inadmissibility. To even be considered, the extreme hardship must be experienced by a "qualifying relative"—that is, a US citizen or Lawful Permanent Resident spouse, parent, or child of the applicant (depending on the form of relief requested), not by applicants themselves. Authorities, the policy manual advises, have considerable leeway: they may construe hardship "narrowly should they deem it wise to do so" but a "restrictive view of extreme hardship is not mandated" (USCIS 2024d). The policy manual acknowledges that a denial of a relative's admission would generally produce hardship, thus demonstrating a broad awareness that US immigration policies are cruel.[9] But, "to be considered 'extreme,' the hardship must exceed that which is usual or expected" (USCIS 2024d). Interestingly, "normal" amounts of hardship can be added together to reach the "extreme" level: "If there is no single qualifying relative whose hardship alone is severe enough to be found 'extreme,' the extreme hardship standard would be met if the combination of hardships to 2 or more qualifying relatives in the aggregate rises to the level of extreme hardship" (USCIS 2024e). The manual's guidance on hardship also enumerates "common" hardships that are not considered extreme, such as family separation and economic harm (USCIS 2024f). This discussion of hardship demonstrates the limitations imposed on humanitarian considerations, the ways that immigrant residents are positioned as outsiders, and the power imbalance between state authorities and immigrant subjects.

Despite these asymmetries, the state's need to appear administratively "graceful" creates openings through which applicants can attempt to improve their circumstances and sometimes alter policies. For example, when immigrant residents seek a favorable exercise of discretion, they cite existing categories of deservingness but also may share their own understandings. For example, as I will discuss further in the following chapter, a letter of support from a coworker of a legalization applicant might say, "She washed and ironed my clothes for me, without charging me anything, therefore I know that she has good character." These understandings become part of the record of individual cases and can potentially suggest new interpretations of legal categories. Relatedly, immigrant residents may attempt to minimize citizen-noncitizen distinctions by appealing to authorities as fellow human beings. A U-visa applicant made such an appeal in a handwritten declaration, telling officials, "Everything that I have told you all is true, nothing is a lie, and I lived through it in my own flesh. I hope that you have been able to read what I have written and that you have been able to understand me." While the state's gaze is limited, what is not "seen" by the state can nonetheless have power, fueling calls for change. The long-term presence of community members who are potentially subject to deportation creates sympathy on the part of some municipalities, which may refuse to collaborate with federal law enforcement (Lai and Lasch 2017; Gomberg-Muñoz and Wences 2021). Though they are unstable, deferred action and TPS establish precedents that are sometimes honored by the courts, preventing rescission. For instance, despite restrictionist efforts to eliminate DACA, US courts have allowed recipients to keep and renew deferred action, though no new applications are being reviewed. Lastly, the state is not monolithic: there are partisan conflicts, competing agency priorities, and disagreements within and between branches of government. Such fragmentation can create openings for immigrant residents to seek change. In so doing, immigrant residents and their allies may refuse to occupy the position of supplicant, instead insisting that they have rights. The ways that these dynamics play out in immigrant residents' everyday lives is the subject of the next chapter.

2

Routine Exceptionality

In September 2014, I sat in a Long Beach sandwich shop to talk with Sonya, who had immigrated to the United States from El Salvador in 1994. I had met Sonya a few weeks earlier, in the nonprofit's waiting area, where she and a friend had gone for a consultation, and she had agreed to be interviewed for my research. We arranged to meet one morning after she got off work. While I sipped orange juice and she had coffee and a croissant, Sonya shared the many ways that she had suffered. Her own mother left her in El Salvador when she was only six or seven, and she in turn had to leave her children behind, something that she described as "painful" but also a "necessity," both for economic reasons, and because of the Salvadoran civil war: when she had to flee bombings, she witnessed dismembered bodies, and her livestock were killed by stray bullets. After arriving in the United States, she lived with her mother, but was mistreated. She said that she had lived like an animal, doing all of the housework and sleeping on the floor. She eventually married, but her husband was also abusive.

Over the years, Sonya made multiple attempts to regularize her immigration status. She had been apprehended crossing the US-Mexico border in 1994, and she submitted an asylum claim at that time. After being released on bond, she had a court case in Texas and had to travel there from Los Angeles by bus alone, without speaking English. Her case was transferred to Los Angeles and then she had a hearing that she didn't know about, after which she found out she had been ordered deported in absentia. Nonetheless, she was able to qualify for Temporary Protected Status (TPS) in 2001, and that is what she had had ever since. Sonya described what TPS had meant to her: "It has helped me work, [helped me] with everything. Now, well, it is my protection now." Her husband applied for a green

45

card for her and her older daughter, and although her daughter's residency papers came through, hers did not. She did not understand why. Sonya had submitted her marriage certificate and photos of her wedding, but she suspected that immigration authorities considered her marriage fraudulent. She was left wondering and waiting, but had not pursued the family visa petition further because she and her husband divorced.

Sonya's long-term goal was to acquire permanent legal status for the sake of her six-year-old daughter, who was born in the United States. She related, "I beg God for everything to turn out well for me, because it is many years of waiting and waiting." She had been told that she might be able to qualify for a visa as a domestic violence victim, so, through the nonprofit, she had submitted a FOIA request for her immigration file. She also hoped that her older daughter, who had gained residency through her husband and who was planning to naturalize, could petition for her. But she worried about her daughter having to gather the evidence—taxes, proof of employment—needed to support a family visa petition, especially because her daughter was not working. If applying through her older daughter was not possible, Sonya reflected, she could wait for her six-year-old daughter to turn 21 and petition for her.

In the meantime, Sonya was saving documentation of her own, such as letters from El Salvador, tax records, and check stubs, in hopes of someday applying for permanent residency. She reflected, "For me, it would be such happiness. Yes, because with residency, I would be able to walk around more freely . . . And with the possibility that in a short time, I could become a citizen, because that is my ambition, to become a citizen."

Sonya's experience of living in the United States for decades with precarious status and an uncertain future is an example of *routine exceptionality*—that is, the need to submit a *legal* claim to appeal to authorities' *political* will. An immigration claim is legal (a matter of law) and extralegal (political, an exception to law) at the same time (Coutin, Richland, and Fortin 2014). Furthermore, in contrast to programs that are designed to meet a societal need, such as reducing poverty, legalization opportunities are designed for exceptional circumstances, in which long-time residents who are considered outsiders are able to meet highly restrictive eligibility criteria. Therefore the high administrative burden in immigration cases seems designed to discourage applicants. Yet, would-be residents and citizens stake immigration claims not only by filing paperwork and having court hearings; in addition, they often save documents as though they have a pending case and are under scrutiny. Thus, Sonya assumes an anticipatory administrative burden by treating the residue of everyday life—check stubs, letters—as potential evidence in a future immigration case and views her daughter's employment history through the lens of imagined officials who might be evaluating a family visa petition. In so doing, Sonya exerts agency in the face of uncertainty, preparing to establish the legality of her presence in the United States. While the paperwork that Sonya collects may seem mundane, it is important to remember that extraordinary circumstances, namely, the violence of the Salvadoran civil war and the harsh realities of poverty, led Sonya to migrate, catapulting her into the state of "illegality" from which she has struggled to emerge. And while in this state, she experienced further violence, including labor exploitation and dehumanizing domestic abuse. Her interactions with immigration officials were overshadowed by uncertainty—she did not learn of her California immigration court appointment in time to attend, she later learned that she had been ordered deported, and she never knew what came of the spousal petition that her husband submitted. Uncertainty exacerbated her experience of time as indefinite, as "many years of waiting and waiting" (see also Hasselberg 2016). To exit this state of uncertainty, she was dependent on officials who might grant a family petition, might recognize her as a domestic violence victim who was deserving of residency under the Violence Against Women Act (VAWA), and hopefully would extend TPS eligibility so that she could continue to renew her temporary status in the meantime. These possibilities created a sense of hope: maybe she *would* qualify, maybe her ambition of becoming a US citizen *would* be realized. Yet, the door that she hoped to walk through was not unlike the door described in Kafka's parable, "Before the law." In Kafka's account, the door of law is open but guarded by a gatekeeper, while a man who hopes to enter sits before it for years, wasting away. As he nears death, the gatekeeper tells him, "Here no one else can gain entry, since this entrance was assigned only to you. I'm going now to close it." The appearance of openness coupled with barriers that, all too often, are insurmountable resonates with illegalized residents' experiences of routine exceptionality.

While having a precarious status and being subject to authorities' political will exposes immigrant residents to emotional and material deprivation, immigrant residents have a degree of agency: they *can* potentially sway the sovereign, and, in fact, the state needs them in order to draw the citizen–noncitizen distinctions on which its sovereignty depends. Living in the United States as illegalized and/ or temporarily authorized residents gives noncitizens an expertise in documentation (Abarca and Coutin 2018). By amassing evidence of their deservingness, those who seek to regularize their status hope to persuade the state that they are deserving. Furthermore, in putting forward such claims, whether through formal applications for status or by performing "deservingness" on a daily basis (García 2014; Menjívar and Lakhani 2016), unauthorized residents can attempt to shift the categories through which deservingness is measured. In so doing, they not only see themselves through what they imagine to be the gaze of the state, in addition, they attempt to alter the lens that is used, so that the state sees them as they would like to be seen. Appealing to that which is beyond law as well as to rights enshrined in law enables immigrant residents to attempt to redefine the securitization–humanitarianism nexus, such that their own humanity and need for security become apparent. In Sonya's account, for example, immigration law both threatens her ability to remain with her family and is what she must appeal to in an effort to secure status.

To examine how immigrant residents who live in the United States experience routine exceptionality, this chapter analyzes interviews with nonprofit clients, as well as conversations that occurred while I shadowed service providers. The process of illegalization that gives immigrant residents expertise in documentation begins as residents leave their country of origin, continues through the uncertainty that characterizes illegalized residents' lives in the United States, and informs the strategies through which they strive to gain status. My analysis is grounded in the notion that being subjects of immigration law gives immigrant community members expertise, including the ability to craft strategies to improve their conditions. One such strategy is to "document back" by saving documents in anticipation of a regularization opportunity (discussed in this chapter), and then preparing application forms and supporting documentation (which will be discussed in chapter 3). Documenting back requires overcoming distrust of the institutions that police immigrant residents' presence.

ILLEGALIZATION AND INTERDEPENDENCY

Immigrant residents' documentation expertise is informed by their experiences of illegalization. While the securitization of US immigration law suggests that the United States strives to prevent unauthorized entry and to remove those who lack status, there is also a multifaceted interdependency between the United States and its noncitizen subjects. The US economy profits from immigrant workers' labor (De Genova 2002; Calavita 2020; Ngai 2004); the arrival of migrants at US ports of entry supports a narrative of national superiority; the presence of unauthorized entrants in the country's interior justifies the existence of a highly profitable detention-and-deportation complex (Welch 2002); and grants of refugee status enable the country to appear benevolent. Most fundamentally, there is a structural relationship between the United States and noncitizens in that regulating the presence of "foreigners" enables the United States to act as a sovereign nation. Gray Abarca and I have argued as much:

> The relationships through which the state enacts plenary power can be understood through relational frameworks according to which entities, objects, and beings are formed through and exist in relation to—and not independently of—other entities, objects, and beings (Barad 2007; Haraway 2003). In effect, relationships themselves "do" things, because they are a web of shifting configurations from which social beings and entities emerge (Desmond 2014). The state–noncitizen relation is such an entanglement. In this understanding, the sovereign state is not a substantive configuration existing independently of its relationship to noncitizens; rather, it comes into being at least partially through this relationship. . . . Sovereignty is thus a relationship—not a property or possession. (2018, 8)

Illegalization is one manifestation of the state–noncitizen relationship in that the practices that illegalize undocumented residents simultaneously produce the United States as a sovereign nation, just as granting status also enables the state to assume the position of a sovereign power.[1] As Hansen and Stepputat (2005, 31) note, sovereign power "needs bodies and 'bare life' to manifest itself." Furthermore, US complicity in the factors that propel movement—human rights violations, civil war, repressive policing practices, resource extraction—connects immigration law to other policy arenas. As Nora Hamilton and Norma Chinchilla (1991, 106) concluded in an article about Central American migration, "Overall, U.S. foreign policy appears to have been more effective in generating refugees than U.S. immigration and refugee policies have been in preventing their entry."

The notion that immigrant residents and the state are interdependent challenges popular accounts of immigration as a matter of individual choice that can either follow or violate rules. In reality, of course, the "rules" shift over time (for example, President Biden changed the long-standing rule that asylum seekers can request asylum at a port of entry; see Jordan 2023) and can be impossible to follow (income requirements prevent some people from petitioning for their family members). Furthermore, large-scale immigration takes place through a process of displacement, in which human rights violations, violence, dispossession, or the disappearance of job opportunities force people to move (Sassen 2014), even as particular industries—such as US agriculture—actively recruit immigrant workers (Gonzalez 2015; Calavita 2020). Indeed, some scholars have argued that historically, the United States unofficially tolerated unauthorized immigration, both to meet labor needs and as a "safety valve" to limit social dissidence abroad (Bach 1978; Jenkins 1977; Harwood 1984). Kitty Calavita (1998) pointed out that in capitalist societies, there is a conflict of interest between employers who want to hire undocumented workers at low wages, and labor unions that, historically, supported restrictive immigration policies in order to protect their members. She argues that regularization programs that appear to grant immigration opportunities but that, in practice, are riddled with barriers are a form of "symbolic law" through which capitalist states manage this contradiction. One case in point is that recent proposals for comprehensive immigration reform, such as the 2013 Border Security, Economic Opportunity, and Immigration Modernization Act, which never became law, have included measures that kept people in a provisional status for years. While US labor unions have changed their stance in recognition of the fact that immigrant workers—including the undocumented—make up a sizable portion of their membership (Kreychman and Volik 2005–2006), illegalization is still potentially a way of producing value. As Nicholas de Genova (2002) has noted, within capitalist labor markets, immigration is a flexible and expendable source of workers who, due to their deportability, may be hyper-exploitable. As the forbidden other, unauthorized residents are an object of desire.

The relationship between the United States and its noncitizen subjects begins outside the United States. Major immigrant-sending countries (including Mexico and Central American nations) have a history of US intervention and resource extraction, both of which uproot people from their places of birth. US complicity in a politics of displacement is not acknowledged in immigration policies (Dadhania 2023), which limit immigration and travel opportunities to narrow categories, such as qualifying for a family petition, or obtaining a tourist or work-related visa. Only Lawful Permanent Residents and US citizens can petition for their family members to immigrate to the United States legally and only certain categories of relatives qualify. Moreover, there are long waiting lists for most such petitions. As a result, family-based immigration is rarely a solution for urgent circumstances, such as escaping gang violence. Likewise, nearly all nonimmigrant visas (such as a tourist visa) require having an economic profile or the type of job that convinces US consular officials that an individual does not intend to immigrate. During a focus group interview, Gloria, who immigrated to the United States in 1991 when she was in her mid-twenties, explained how her poverty had prevented her from obtaining a visa:

> One comes in this way [without authorization] because one is poor, one does not have the money to be able to get a visa, a passport. If one had, let's say, at least properties and a good job, and one were to go to obtain a visa, but with what is one going to present oneself to . . . the American consulate [to show] that one had properties or one were going to say, "I have a good job, I have these properties." So it is very, very difficult. Even more so when one is young, because they say, "Oh, you are not just going there on vacation."

In that she was unable to provide the US consulate with the documentation of intention to return home (e.g., employment and property ownership), Gloria was undocumented *before* she left El Salvador. Even while living in her country of origin, Gloria had developed the ability to view her life through what she imagined would be the eyes of the US state and to determine that she would be found wanting.

Those such as Gloria who are forced to immigrate but for whom legal travel documents are out of reach enter a clandestine realm in which their identities, and indeed their very humanity, is erased. Significantly, the routes that migrants travel—on top of rather than within trains, on backroads instead of highways, across deserts instead of hospitable terrain, and in storage compartments rather than seats—are simultaneously prohibited yet hyper-legalized, defined by the law yet placed outside of it. Moreover, while these routes transcend borders, they are also defined in relation to the United States, since US enforcement strategies compel migrants to travel in such extralegal fashions (Álvarez Velasco 2009). Gloria's account of her journey to the United States describes the violence of these prohibited routes:

> I was on the road for 22 days. . . . One suffers cold, hunger, people who dislike one, well, because one is not from their country. And sleeping outside—they only allowed us to sleep in the yards of their houses—outside, withstanding the cold, like animals. . . . Starting from Guatemala to here, starting from Mexico to here, is where the movie [the adventure] begins for one. The mistreatment on the part of the very same *coyotes* from Mexico. And crossing the river, one feels that one will be carried away because many cross on rafts, but many cross on foot. And when I was smaller, the water carried me away, and the others had to help me because there were twenty-three of us. And then, to get on the train there, the train they call *la bestia* [the beast] . . . To get on that train, another movie. . . . And then the only thing that one can eat is canned beans and bread. . . . And [when the train approached a stop], it doesn't matter if you fell on a branch, if you fell on a rock, you had to throw yourself off because you didn't want them to capture you. And with the same [fear], to get up and run away. . . . They took us [women] away into the hills like they wanted to rape us. . . . And when we came to an overflowing river, where the water moved with force . . . the current carried me away . . . and when we got to the desert, I was fainting, and the man said—and other men wanted to help me—he said, "Leave her, one may be left behind," he said; "one may die but not three," said the coyote.

Gloria survived this journey, eventually obtaining permanent residency through a family visa petition, and, at the time of our interview, taking citizenship classes in order to naturalize. However, note the deprivation that she experienced while traveling, the dehumanizing experience of sleeping outside like an animal, the gendered violence of possibly being raped. She was at risk of being captured by authorities, being carried away by the current, or being left behind to die. She was abandoned to this traumatizing and "lawless" space outside of normal travel routes due to ineligibility for a visa under US law.

As people enter the clandestine realm of illicit travel, their identities are erased, in contrast to the careful documentation of identity that occurs at authorized border crossings and ports of entry. Focus group participants explained that when they had immigrated to the United States from Central America during the late 1980s and the 1990s, the smugglers who guided them throughout the journey destroyed their passports and other identity documents so that they could not be identified if they were apprehended. Their goal was to avoid being deported back to Central America, a great distance from which to travel on a subsequent attempt. Juana Maria, who was in her 70s at the time of our interview and who fled El Salvador during the civil war when her business was repeatedly assaulted, related the following:

> I put my name in big letters on a small paper and I put it here well hidden, well hidden in the small pocket of a pair of pants. In my mind, as they said that they were killing people, that one could become lost. Because we came *mojados* [undocumented], as they say. I came *mojada* . . . So I said, "if something happens to me, by my name they will find me." And I said, "here I carry my name." And it said, "El Salvador." So that they would return me to my country. However it might be.

Unlike the airport, where one presents a passport to a TSA, customs, or immigration agent in order to travel internationally, Juana Maria's journey as "mojada" required her to hide her identity in her clothing, in the hope that if she died en route, she would not become an unidentified body. Rather, she sought to identify herself to those who might find her, and who would read her name and country of origin, enabling her family to repatriate her remains (De Leon 2015). By hiding her own handmade (instead of government-issued) identification document—a small piece of paper—in her clothing, Juana Maria insisted on her value. Juana Maria's story is indicative of the extreme fear, risk, and violence to which migrants were subjected as they were remade—or in some instances, destroyed—through migration.

Of course, not all interviewees traveled clandestinely. Some were able to obtain tourist or work-related visas, and some qualified for residency through a family petition, entering the United States with a green card. While such individuals avoided the indignities described by Gloria and Juana Maria, even authorized travel could be mired in complications and uncertainty. Arnulfo was a US citizen who had immigrated to the United States from El Salvador during the 1980s, obtained residency through the Nicaraguan Adjustment and Central American Relief Act (NACARA) in 2003, and naturalized in 2012. He had been separated from his wife and children for most of this time, but he had filed petitions for them, and they had slowly been rejoining him in the United States. When we met in 2014 for an interview, Arnulfo and his wife (who had immigrated in 2011) expressed great frustration about the obstacles that their oldest son, in a medical profession, had encountered:

> He already got another person to give him a letter of support; he already did the whole process as required. Now the decision is with the embassy. Here, there is nothing [more to do]; there the decision is theirs; either they approve or don't approve. But I keep waiting. It has been four years since he got the first letter of support. They went; they required him to get a medical examination. And then the time period arrived, and this man could not give me the other documents that were missing, so it was cancelled. Now, we have to pay again for another medical exam, which my son already did again. My son after this exam, they have put it in for six months [meaning it is valid for six months]. When the doctor says that's it, that there is no problem, he has to repeat the exam again, which costs around $500 to $600. Expenses, excuses. Because every time that I go to do paperwork, I have to lose a day [of work.] There [in El Salvador], they [his son and daughter-in-law] also lose a day, their time, and money, because without money, there is nothing . . . There is great confusion about my son's case; the embassy has not sent me any notifications about it. And what my son tells me is that he has to go to appointments at a psychiatric clinic, seemingly for people who use drugs or are crazy, I don't know. But the embassy has not sent me a note, telling me, "We are going to submit your son to these exams which are necessary for this or that reason." They don't, I have never received a letter from them.

There is no explanation. They do not say anything about why they are doing this. Well, the word for me is frustration. Frustrated because, even though they [his son and daughter-in-law] are doing everything that is asked of them, there is no certainty of saying that they [immigration officials] are going to approve it this month, this year. No, because each time, they ask for more things.

I have quoted this passage at length to show how, from Arnulfo's point of view, the legal immigration process is opaque and Kafkaesque, with shifting and inexplicable requirements that are imposed with complete disregard for the expense, effort, and emotional investment that fulfilling them requires (Horton 2020; Gerson 2023–2024). Even though Arnulfo's son seemingly was eligible to enter the country as a relative of a US citizen, and even though they had obtained the required letter of support to show that he would not be a financial burden, Arnulfo's son faced additional medical requirements. The first exam seems to have expired before it could be submitted to the embassy, so Arnulfo's son had to repeat this exam. Then the embassy required Arnulfo's son to complete a series of psychiatric evaluations, without indicating why. Arnulfo's comment that despite doing everything asked of them, there was no certainty that the embassy would issue his son a green card is the epitome of routine exceptionality.

The interdependent but fraught relationship established as immigrants embark on their journeys continues after they enter the United States.

A CAGE OF GOLD

One November morning in 2011, as I was shadowing a service provider at the non-profit, a Honduran woman who I will call "Morelia" came in to renew her TPS and work authorization. When the service provider stepped out to make a photocopy, I asked her if she had ever been to Morelia, in Mexico, the city that was her name-sake. She replied that she had not, and that in fact, she was unable to go anywhere. "We are in a cage of gold," she commented. I asked her how long she had TPS and we quickly calculated that it had been something like twelve years. "This year," she said, "I thought that they were going to say, 'All of the Hondurans and Nicaraguans [with TPS], residency!' but no. Maybe they are waiting for something that will work for all instead of just for particular groups."

Morelia's comment about being in a cage of gold and her unrealized hope that there would eventually be a way for TPS recipients to regularize their status conveys what it is like to experience routine exceptionality. Unauthorized residents' experience of being placed in an alternative reality—a cage, to use Morelia's term—continues after entry as people face restrictions on their movement and other indignities. In the "cage" of precarious legality, they are visible to the state (for instance, Morelia regularly shared personal information when she renewed her TPS status) even though they cannot discern the state's future actions (such as whether there would be new legalization opportunities). Yet, the cage is "of gold" in that those who are in the United States can often access work opportunities. Theirs is an embodied and emotional existence as they experience uncertainty and material deprivation.[2] In describing these challenges, they critique the system within which they are located. Morelia's comment about being in a cage of gold, for example, counters the notion that by immigrating to the United States, one can achieve the American Dream. Instead, she points out, she is trapped in a place that—so far—had denied her the opportunity to obtain residency.

The challenges experienced by illegalized residents and those with precarious legal status are well documented in the academic literature. Such residents are at risk of detention and deportation (Kanstroom 2007; Golash-Boza 2015), and may be over-policed due to their race and ethnicity (Chacón 2012; Vega 2018). Illegalized residents lack work authorization documents, and so may work in the informal economy or at low-paying jobs where they face exploitative labor practices (Horton 2016; De Genova 2002). Financial and documentation challenges place them at risk of housing insecurity (Chinchilla, Yue, and Ponce 2022). Such stress contributes to chronic and life-threatening health issues that can be exacerbated by lack of medical insurance (Lee 2019). Multiple facets of daily life can be impacted by lack of documentation. For instance, going on a date poses challenges as individuals could be asked for an ID to enter a club (Enriquez 2020). Higher education is difficult to access due to the out-of-state tuition fees charged in many states as well as ineligibility for federal financial aid (Flores, Escudero, and Burciaga 2019; Gonzalez 2016). Noncitizens cannot vote in the United States, and may not be able to vote in their countries of origin either, due to distance (Bauböck 2005; Ruth, Matusitz, and Simi 2017). Family separation is an ongoing challenge, as undocumented and temporarily authorized people may, like Morelia, be unable to travel internationally or petition for their family members to immigrate legally (Gomberg-Muñoz 2016). Indeed, illegalization is an "everyday" experience (Dreby 2015) that has been characterized as a form of "legal violence" (Menjívar and Abrego 2012).

Here, I highlight how illegalization produces routine exceptionality—that is, the need to appeal to law while also seeking a legal exception. For illegalized residents, both documentation and the lack of documentation are protective and othering. Documentation provides temporary authorization, allowing recipients to work legally, remain in the country for the time being, and possibly access higher education and other resources. Yet temporary documentation marks one as different. Arnulfo, whose efforts to petition for his son in El Salvador were described in the last section, recounted what it was like to have temporary status through an application for political asylum that remained pending for over ten years until he qualified for residency through NACARA:

I got the [work] permit. Immigration gave it to me. I spent ten years renewing it. The advantage of the work permit was that I could work. Well, that Immigration couldn't deport me, because I was under the law. And the disadvantages were that I could not leave the country. I could not petition for my family. I could not bring my family. I could not visit them, because that was not permitted according to the law.

Arnulfo appeals to the law repeatedly in this passage: he was under the law; he followed the law; he worked legally. But the bases for his status—a claim for asylum, which is a discretionary form of relief that can be granted by US officials, and then residency under NACARA for humanitarian reasons—were exceptional. In the legal liminality of temporary authorization (Menjívar 2006), Arnulfo was denied basic rights that others enjoy.

Likewise, Diana, who had immigrated from Mexico to the United States without authorization in 1994 at the age of seventeen, felt marked by being undocumented (see also Abarca and Coutin 2018). During a 2015 interview with my assistant, Gray Abarca, Diana explained:

When I would see the police, I would be like, "Oh!" Always afraid. Now I am not so afraid, but it's like a cloud of—like something very heavy. Like they are coming for me, as though I were such an important person. Or as though there is a sign on my body, "Here she is! Here I am!" So it is very limiting. . . . To identify oneself as, "Yes, I am an immigrant," I feel that that can be a moment of power. But there is also much shame.

Diana had consulted with multiple attorneys, only to be told that there was no way for her to regularize her status. She was haunted by the fact that she had temporarily used a false ID, thus creating multiple versions of her identity. In her previous quote, she describes the overwhelming ambivalence of her circumstances. She feels as though she stands out, as though there is a sign on her body alerting authorities to her presence, even as she also believes herself to be unimportant. Likewise, she finds it empowering to claim an identity as an immigrant, but is ashamed of this status. Perhaps the heavy cloud that envelops her, potentially hiding but also drawing attention to her, is akin to the documentation that allowed Arnulfo to remain in the United States but without the right to be with his family. Both Diana's cloud and Arnulfo's documentation were representations of partial inclusion: Diana and Arnulfo were present, but with limited rights, visible but not fully recognized.

Diabolically, documentation (or lack of documentation) traps people, making it difficult to navigate borders and inspection points while also creating the hope of eventually regularizing their status. The need to follow the law in order to regularize his status trapped Arnulfo in the United States, preventing him from seeing his family until he was able to gain residency. Similarly, Diana was trapped by her undocumented status in that she could not reenter the United States legally if she left the country, but by remaining in the United States, she hoped to eventually qualify for status. In fact, we met her at a *charla* on the 2014 executive relief program announced by President Obama.

Another undocumented person who hoped to eventually regularize his status was Manuel, who we also met at a charla at the nonprofit. Manuel had immigrated to the United States from Mexico in 1989, originally intending to return, but after starting a family in this country, he hoped to stay. He too felt trapped: "Here it is nothing more than working, sleeping, and working, sleeping, and working. And without papers it is a prison. I say, I have thought about returning, but for my children's sake I do not do it, because I know that they might not be able to adapt there." The multidimensionality of the United States as a place where one could provide for one's children and potentially regularize but also where one suffered was not unlike the (extra)legality of routine exceptionality. In fact, it was so routine for police to confiscate undocumented residents' cars that Manuel only owned old and inexpensive vehicles, whose state of disrepair unfortunately created grounds for a police stop: "We Latinos have the tendency, those of us who do not have papers, of having old cars, because we know that they take them away from us [due to driving without a license], that if the police stop us, they are going to take them away from us, so they are cars that are not worth much." Manuel's description of driving an old car because it could be confiscated echoes Diana's account of feeling as though there were a sign on her body, announcing her status.

As they are trapped in the United States, immigrant residents are separated from family in their countries of origin. Juana Maria and Elena, who participated in a focus group in 2012, eloquently described how their intense longing for children that they had left behind led them to imagine encounters, as though their children had become a spectral presence:

Juana Maria: I left El Salvador as an undocumented person; that is the hardest thing. When I boarded the bus in Guatemala, and because it was night, sleep overcame me, and I lay down in the seat. I looked at the photos of my children. I looked at them. When I closed my eyes, I saw my children.

Elena (recognizing this experience): One hears that they are speaking to one.

Juana Maria: One hears that they are speaking to one.

Elena: Yes.

Juana Maria: And once I got work in a factory here. Sewing. Suddenly I was working, when there was an entryway there, and there I saw my son enter, who I left behind at the age of twelve. I say to him, "[gasp!] My son!" And it was in real life! Mother! Me working! In real life. "My son! How did you come?" When suddenly, he vanished. What videos I saw. It was a vision. One sees one's children. They draw themselves. One, look, the full 24 hours, you don't rest, thinking of your children.

> *Elena:* I believe you, because something similar happened to me. I also, since I came to this country, worked only in sewing. Sewing and sewing. That was in '87. I worked here on 23rd and Main. And I worked and cried, worked and cried. But I heard my daughter crying.
>
> *Juana Maria:* It's that one hears them!
>
> *Elena:* It's that she spoke to me. "Mami." And my co-worker who was in front of me said, "Elena, don't cry. Don't worry." "It's that I can't [stop]. I can't."
>
> *Juana Maria:* It is very difficult.

This exchange conveys the anguish that Juana Maria and Elena experienced as newly arrived residents, longing for children to the point that they had waking dreams of their children appearing before them, speaking to them. It was as though Juana Maria and Elena were in a multidimensional reality, occupying both the sewing factories where they worked and the space where their children lived at the same time. Their children were tantalizingly close yet unbearably distant at the same time. Such painful separations are a common and foreseeable consequence of US immigration policies that impose lengthy waiting periods for relatives to immigrate legally, prevent undocumented and temporarily authorized persons from petitioning for family members at all, and make border crossings increasingly deadly (L. E. Sanchez 2023). Guillermina, for whom I prepared a U-visa application, was stoic while describing how she had been victimized through a crime. But when I asked her to describe her dreams for the future, she began to cry. Guillermina said that she dreamed of being able to travel so that she could visit her mother's grave, put a flower on it, and ask her mother's pardon for not being there when she died. US immigration law can be cruel.

As Guillermina's, Elena's, and Juana Maria's narratives indicate, living in a cage of gold is an embodied and emotional experience. The documents that trap people in the United States and that can potentially become part of immigration files are also objects of emotional investment—what Herd and Moynihan refer to as the "psychological costs" of administrative burdens (Herd and Moynihan 2018). For example, Magdalena approached the nonprofit for assistance in petitioning for her siblings, only to discover that there were errors in their birth certificates. "De la emoción, no se fija" (due to emotions, one doesn't notice), Magdalena remarked, pointing out the strong emotions parents might experience when registering their children's births. Numerous interviewees stressed the fear that they would be apprehended by immigration officials. Diana reflected, "It is as though the immigration system is everywhere . . . And the terror—I feel that it is terror that we have." Terror, fear, and anxiety manifest themselves physically in pain, *nervios* (nerves), and the inability to breathe. Emelia, who was waiting to learn whether she could obtain a pardon for a previous criminal conviction, felt that stress and uncertainty were contributing to pain in her feet, making it difficult for her to walk. Efraín, another nonprofit client, shared how painful it was to seek advice regarding immigration situations, even at trusted organizations. Efraín said, "I am going to explain something to you. It is like someone who has a wound; they know that they have a wound but that they don't want the doctor to look at it because they think that it is going to hurt. It is the same for the immigrant. They know that they need this, but they are afraid of getting into this because they don't know well. They have doubts, do you understand me? That's why they are afraid; they don't want to touch this theme." My assistant Gray Abarca's field notes regarding a TPS renewal that he observed convey the ways that immigration law acts as emotional bait: "[The TPS renewal applicant] commented that he hopes to do his residency one day, though he knows that it is not likely. He made hand gestures to explain the way immigration policy works, showing to the effect that opportunities will be right around the corner, but they are always false hope; that as the chances to gain legal status grow closer, they seem to get farther away, especially when people get hopeful at the prospect." This description of opportunities that simultaneously grow closer and more unreachable is reminiscent of Kafka's parable, described earlier.

For undocumented and temporarily authorized immigrants, these emotions and their embodied effects are linked to the panopticon-like condition of being subjected to the state's gaze while being unable to ascertain what the state sees. My field notes and interview transcripts are replete with examples of immigrant residents wondering what records the state has about them, what became of paperwork that they submitted, and whether future regularization programs will be open to them. I have already presented Arnulfo's complaint that there was no certainty that the US embassy would issue his son a green card; Sonya's experience waiting and wondering what happened to the petition that her husband submitted on her behalf; Morelia's hope that someday TPS recipients would be able to secure permanent residency; and Diana's fear that at any time, the police could come for her. Similarly, it was not uncommon for those who approached the nonprofit to ask about files that the state might have about them. For example, an attendee at a *charla* on immigration law in 2015 asked the presenting attorney, "If a person was apprehended by Immigration while entering [the country] around the year 2000, does that still remain on their record today?" It was not clear to this attendee whether such immigration records endured, in this case, over a fifteen-year period. Magdalena, who was presented above and who was attempting to petition for her siblings, was not sure whether immigration officials would notice the minor errors that appeared in their records. According to my notes, Magdalena speculated "that there is only a 25 percent chance that Immigration will notice the error of her father having two different ages on her birth certificate and her sister's birth certificate. The problem is, what if twelve years go by and then they discover the error? Will it cause further delays?" For these and other residents, it was as though the state were reviewing its records of their lives, whether or not they had filed for status. Indeed, a key feature of being in the golden cage of undocumented or temporary status is hoping that law will eventually align with the de facto realities of people's existences.

COUNTERING ILLEGALIZATION

On February 18, 2015, the day that DACA+ was supposed to go into effect, my graduate student research assistant Gray Abarca went to the nonprofit for a day of volunteer work and fieldwork. (I was teaching and could not be there.) A Texas judge had unexpectedly enjoined DAPA and DACA+ the previous day, making it impossible to submit applications and leaving the future of these programs unclear. Nonetheless, Gray reported, the lobby was full. In his field notes about this experience, Gray wrote the following:

> There was a line extending from the receptions desk to the bottom of the entrance stairs. I saw the new staff attorney who is leading the DACA/DAPA process going down the line to ask people what they were here for. I wasn't exactly sure what she was doing, I think it was a rapid screening of people who had come specifically for DACA/DAPA. Those who were there for that reason were given an intake form for a consultation. . . . I had one person come in who was obviously distressed because he was worried that the one opportunity he had (DAPA) to gain legal status was taken. How awful to be given hope and then thrown back into limbo; more awful to be told by the staff that we basically have no idea what is going to happen (I mean, there is an appeal by Obama's administration, and they are expected to be successful because it was after all an executive order; but we didn't want to tell them that to avoid giving even more false hope).

The line of people outside of the nonprofit that morning is evidence of undocumented residents' desire to counter illegalization, as well as the fragility and inaccessibility of the legal mechanisms available to them.

Though many hoped to eventually gain residency, some considered status so far beyond reach that success would require divine intervention. For example, Juana Maria, who had hidden her name and country of origin in her clothing so that her body could be identified if she died en route to the United States, had promised God that if she were able to return to El Salvador with papers, then she would immediately go to the cathedral in San Salvador to light a candle:

> I asked God before leaving [El Salvador], and I said to God that if I—I am Catholic, right?—and I said that if I returned to my country someday—I was going to return—but that he would give me the opportunity to have documents, blessed be God, and I promised my god that if I were to return, the very first thing that I would do is to visit the cathedral. And that is what I did. I left the airport and from there to the temple. And from the temple to my house.

Juana Maria's account of visiting the cathedral before she even went to her own house after many years living outside of El Salvador suggests that she credited God with giving her residency, which she obtained through NACARA. Similarly, other interviewees who were hoping for positive outcomes in their cases stressed that matters were in God's hands. Sonya, who had TPS and who hoped to reopen an earlier asylum case, commented, "And, God willing, may God help me to move forward, that they will reopen the case." Such appeals to the divine are not only indications of religiosity but also signs of the high stakes for those who hoped to overcome illegalization. In this area of law, in which new immigration opportunities could be created or canceled, and officials could exercise discretion favorably or deny a petition, success seemed to require divine help.

One way that some residents sought to counter illegalization was by obtaining false documents—though this strategy could backfire by miring them more deeply in illegality. Numerous interviewees described purchasing identity documents so that they could obtain jobs. For instance, Manuel, who I interviewed in 2014, related that he used them "only for work. And when I began to work in a parking company, they did ask me for them. I had to get false papers." In fact, such practices were so common that they seemed to be unofficially tolerated. At one immigration *charla* that I attended, an audience member asked if they would be adversely affected by using a false social security number, and the speaker replied, "If you only use the social to work, sometimes to get a [drivers] license, normally that does not affect you."[3] To interviewees who had entered the country during the 1980s or early 1990s when it was common for Central Americans to obtain work authorization by applying for asylum or TPS, official work authorization also appeared to be something that the government gave out almost arbitrarily. Juana Maria, who entered the United States in 1989, recalled that a friend told her husband, "Look, they are giving out work permits." She had no money, but the friend loaned her husband $200 and she was able to apply, most likely for asylum, which, during the 1980s, enabled her to secure work authorization.[4] For Juana Maria, obtaining legal papers appeared to be a financial transaction (though not everyone was able to seek work authorization in this way). Interviewees who arrived later or from other countries, where asylum was less viable and TPS was not an option, were sometimes haunted by the decision to get false papers. Diana had purchased a false ID on Alvarado Street in Los Angeles, but after her employer noticed two individuals with the same social security number and then someone came by her house looking for her, she left her job and fled. Diana lived in fear that this record of a double identity, her true name and her false one, would come to light if she applied for status.

Yet, even residents who did not have pending applications hoped to produce a record that would eventually enable them to qualify for status. In so doing, they viewed their life through what they imagined would be the perspective of officials. For example, Gloria recalled the advice she was given by her lawyer:

"Look," she told me . . . And I always say this to those who want to fix [their papers]. "Do you want to get papers? You have to be a good citizen. Work a lot. And behave well. Not have a single felony. . . . Don't steal, don't do reckless things because that is bad here." And I always go around saying that to young people . . . I tell them, "You have to behave well in this country because those who behave badly are sent away. They do not want them here."

Of course, in reality, many people who "behave well" according to the standards that Gloria describes do not automatically become eligible for status, nor is "behaving well" by itself a defense against deportation. Furthermore, "contorting themselves into what they perceive as the caseworker's [or in this case, the immigration official's] image of the deserving client" is part of the administrative burden that applicants face (Herd and Moynihan 2018, 26). However, Gloria is correct that good moral character (GMC) is often one of the requirements for gaining status, and that work and criminal histories can be considered. For many, behaving like "a good citizen," as Gloria recommends, may be both a form of "passing" (García 2014; Elias 2017) and a strategy to acquire status.[5] Aligning the facts of one's life to align with opportunities for regularization can support status claims. For example, marrying a US citizen potentially confers eligibility for a spousal visa (Gomberg-Muñoz 2016), while taking classes or volunteering can generate evidence of presence and character. At the same time, viewing one's life through the eyes of the state could lead to fear of being deemed undeserving. Dora, who, before the program was enjoined, had hoped to qualify for DAPA, worried that the fact that she had obtained public assistance for her US citizen children would make her ineligible; Marta feared that having received three months of food stamps would disqualify her; and Manuel expressed concern about the impact of not having listed his wife on his income tax returns every year. In fact, the strategy of countering illegalization by obtaining false papers and the strategy of producing a record of deservingness were potentially at odds, since obtaining false papers could be considered fraud. Diana was anguished about having used someone else's ID during her first years in the country. An attorney had told her that she only needed to demonstrate good moral character for seven years, but she feared that she could never escape the legal implications of this act.[6]

For some, the best way to counter illegalization was to practice what Asad (2023) terms "selective engagement," going about one's life in the United States but avoiding risky situations. Diana had put her utility bills in the name of other people so that she could not be identified, while Daniela and her husband opened bank accounts in the name of their school-aged daughter, because she had identification documents that they lacked. Such workarounds posed challenges if immigrant residents had to document their presence in the United States. Avoiding checkpoints was another way to hide presence. Of course, restricting one's movement was one of the ways that illegalization was manifested in people's lives.

Immigrant residents I met at the nonprofit sometimes had multiple long-term strategies through which they eventually hoped to qualify for status (though, of course, there were also many who had no option). Living with these possibilities—which frequently could be described as "long shots," at best—required viewing one's own life and relationships as potential avenues for regularization. For example, Sonya, whose experiences were described at this chapter's outset, had TPS which provided temporary protection but no path to permanent residency. She had been the beneficiary of a spousal petition whose outcome was unknown; her young daughter could potentially petition for her after turning 21; and, because she had experienced domestic violence, she could potentially self-petition under the Violence Against Women Act's provisions. Yet, she lived with uncertainty—which, if any, of these possibilities had the greatest likelihood of success? How long would each take? And, if she applied, was there a risk of being deported? Similarly, Efrain, who had immigrated from El Salvador on a tourist visa, had two possible immigration cases. His US citizen sister had filed a family visa petition for him, which he saw as 95 percent certain to result in residency, but he had been advised that it would take twelve years for the petition to become current. His second option, which he saw as only 30 percent likely to succeed, was a U-visa case. He had been a victim of a crime, however, the police had not agreed to certify that he had collaborated in the investigation, a common obstacle for potential U-visa applicants (Dingeman et al. 2017; Lakhani 2013). Although he could not apply for a U-visa without this certification, he was saving the police report and the documentation of his injuries in the hope that there would be a change in personnel and that he could obtain the necessary police signatures. The fact that Sonya, Efrain, and others lived with a sense of possibility, and sometimes sought to maximize their eligibility for status, were signs of persistence and hope.

Of course, approaching organizations such as the nonprofit for legal advice and applying for legal status if eligible were also ways of countering illegalization, at least on an individual level. Collectively, such applications, and the personal archives that people assembled in the hope of being able to apply someday, were a way for illegalized community members to "document back" to the state in a language that they hoped it would understand.

DOCUMENTING BACK

During a 2015 interview, Laura, who immigrated to the United States in 1994 fleeing the Guatemalan civil war and who hoped to qualify for DAPA, told my research assistant Gray Abarca how she saved documents for potential future immigration cases. Gray summarized the interview as follows:

> Laura has been meticulously storing pretty much *any* form of documents that indicates her presence (as well as her children's) in the United States, including taxes, gas bills, receipts of remittances, letters she sent to and received from Guatemala, rent invoices, even store receipts (like from Macy's). She keeps them all in a box, and she is aware of the plethora of documents that she can use towards her case, which

is probably why she feels the level of optimism she feels. In fact she stores so many documents that her daughters have teased her for it, but she has passed on this tradition of archiving to them, something she is clearly very proud of.

Laura's commitment to saving documents stemmed from previously being asked for documents that she did not have. She explained, "I had an experience when I went to court and they denied me asylum, they asked me for this paper and that paper. . . . And I realized that they, to regularize, were going to need paper and documents as evidence. And that is what made me save paperwork." Her efforts to save documents paid off in 2012, when DACA was launched and her two daughters had everything they needed to successfully apply. These experiences taught Laura of the power of papers—what Dery (1998) terms "papereality." Laura told us, "Remember that here, papers speak." She reiterated that words are insufficient if they are not accompanied by documentary proof.

Illegalized residents' understandings of the power of papers give residents the opportunity to "document back" to the state by amassing records that put forward a narrative of deservingness. As I noted earlier, the notion of "documenting back" builds on the work of Maori Studies scholar Linda Tuhiwai Smith, who discusses the importance of "researching back" to those in power, as a form of resistance. Recall that Smith advocates "'researching back,' in the same tradition of 'writing back' or 'talking back,' that characterizes much of the post-colonial or anti-colonial literature. It has involved a 'knowing-ness of the colonizer' and a recovery of ourselves, an analysis of colonialism, and a struggle for self-determination" (2012, 8). "Documenting back" is similar in that it too demonstrates illegalized residents' "knowingness" of the state in that the records that residents assemble adopt the law's logic, documenting the humanitarian conditions that make residents worthy of a favorable exercise of discretion. As Horton notes, "Regularization . . . requires that 'undocumented' migrants develop an intimate relationship to bureaucratic records" (2020, 11). At the same time, such records are part of "a struggle for self-determination," as saving papers not only attests to the merit of illegalized residents' own requests for status but also contests the state categories through which deservingness is assessed. The documents that immigrants collect and assemble—bank statements, receipts, check stubs, school records, rental contracts, letters, affidavits—enable illegalized residents to insert their own understandings of merit into the documentary record. They do so through statements in letters of support, the quantity of documentation that they assemble, and the multiple meanings that are part of repurposed documents. For instance, school or financial records may be submitted to prove presence on a certain date but these documents also depict applicants as community members who go to school, deposit checks, and participate in daily life. By making illegalized residents socially visible and by putting forward their own interpretations, documentation shapeshifts the categorical demarcations on which law depend.

In documenting back, illegalized residents assumed an anticipatory administrative burden in order to be prepared for future legal opportunities, assembling evidence of deservingness based on their understandings of state practices and criteria.[7] Assuming this burden was a way of exerting agency in response to the securitization/humanitarianism nexus in which they were situated. On the one hand, the threat of deportation made them aware of the insecurity of their futures in the United States, while on the other, the possibility of future regularization opportunities and their own sense of merit led them to hope that they would eventually prevail. This anticipatory burden in some ways resembles anticipatory grief, such as when immigrant residents mourn the possibility that a family member will be deported, or that a relative in their country of origin will pass away before they return (Falzarano et al. 2022; Martínez Rosas 2020; Nesteruk 2018; Sanchez, Philbin and Ayón 2021). Yet, rather than anticipating a tragedy (as occurs with anticipatory grief), immigrant residents who assume an anticipatory administrative burden are hoping for a happy event—namely, successfully applying for legal status. Their efforts to save documents now may actually alleviate their future evidentiary burden if such a moment materializes, but may also be for naught. Therefore, although saving documents is a form of agency and an act of hope, it is also a burden. Residents who are not illegalized do not have to keep documentation in order to prove that they should be allowed to remain in the United States.

Our interviews and observations revealed that among the illegalized long-term residents we met, the practice of saving day-to-day documents as a means of preparing for any future immigration opportunities that might arise was pervasive. For example, we interviewed Manuel, whose experiences are described earlier. Manuel had not always saved documents. In fact, when he first entered the United States in the 1980s at the age of nineteen, he planned to save money, then return to Mexico to marry his girlfriend. A friend had suggested that he try to qualify for status through the Immigration Reform and Control Act (IRCA) as a Seasonal Agricultural Worker, but Manuel was not interested. He explained, "My thinking was that it was nothing more than working for a year and then returning. I decided not to do it." However, after Manuel formed a new relationship in the United States and had a child here, his perspective changed: "I began to worry about being right in the country." Manuel said that he began looking for ways to regularize his status. At the time of our interview, which occurred after the DAPA announcement but before DAPA had been enjoined, regularization seemed within reach. Manuel told us how he had prepared for just such an opportunity:

> I had a drawer where I was putting everything, I even had problems with the mother of my children because she was asking me why I was keeping so many papers. But I said, "Someday they will be useful to us." My thinking was that one day, we would be able to get legal status (*arreglar*). So I said, "Some moment [will come when] they will be useful to us." And thanks to God, right now in a few months, they are going to help us a lot [in applying for DAPA]. . . . From that time, every little thing that I

think could be proof that I have been here, I have saved. I have all kinds of papers. We suddenly give a donation and they give us the receipts and I have receipts . . . I have everything. I don't have it in order, but I know that I have it there. Yes, what I am going to do is to buy some things [like folders or organizers] to put it in order, year by year.

Manuel's practice of saving documents in preparation for a future opportunity demonstrates illegalized long-term residents' understandings of the importance that the state places on documentation, and is, in the meantime, evidence to themselves of their deservingness. The existence of this drawer full of documents enables Manuel to imagine a future moment when he would be able to regularize his status—something that almost happened with the announcement of DAPA. We were told of people keeping papers in boxes, folders, briefcases, piles, and bags, in preparation for such a future moment, and, as volunteers, we saw people bring these materials to nonprofit staff, for their review. Manuel's example of saving receipts for donations also depicts him as a generous and giving person, presumably the sort of person the United States would want as a legal resident. His description of having "everything" implies that his drawer full of records doubles as a representation of his life in the United States, the totality of the sorts of proof that immigration officials might ask to see. The fantasy of someday organizing these documents– presumably, in order to submit them to officials—further confirms Manuel's sense of deservingness, and the way he thinks he can embody the sort of disciplined subject who would have their paperwork in order.

The excess meanings conveyed by the documents that immigrant residents save are reflected in the mundaneness and the deeply personal nature of these records. People had records of their hospital stays, phone bills, rent receipts, correspondence, dentist appointments, and vaccinations. One nonprofit client even brought her pregnancy test results to the appointment. On the one hand, there was a "flattening" of such documents in that, despite their wide variety, the most significant features of these documents for immigration purposes were the dates and names, since those proved that persons were present on particular dates. On the other hand, packets of documentation were a byproduct of life in the United States, and therefore depicted illegalized residents as community members who engaged in activities—going to school, seeking medical care, working—that were not unlike those of other residents. While repurposing personal records as immigration documents might be experienced as alienating—imagine the emotions associated with learning that one is pregnant, for example—such documentation potentially made the voices and experiences of illegalized residents and their associates part of a legal record. For example, for Clara, who immigrated to the United States from Guatemala in 1991, letters from relatives in Guatemala were the only documentation of her earliest years in the United States. She related how she had saved letters from her father and others:

My father would write to me, my older brother, my oldest siblings would write to me. And all of those papers, those letters, are the very first things that I received here. I have them. Because I said, "They'll be of use to me." And I, a little bit ignorant. And my husband, "And why are you saving that?" And [I replied], "Who knows, someday, one never knows, they are going to be useful, whether for me, whether for you, whether for my oldest daughter. They are going to ask me for so much [and I'll be able to say] 'Okay I have it here.'"

Like Manuel, Clara fantasized that someday, immigration officials would ask her for evidence and she would be able to provide it; she would be prepared and would be able to show that she was the sort of person who generated the evidence that they needed. It is striking that this evidence would include letters that she described with a note of longing: those from her father and older siblings who used to write to her when she first arrived in the United States, a moment when she surely felt bereft of their company. Perhaps saving and recalling these letters was a way for her to document her family's love and support. Moreover, Clara's account of saving documents depicts her as forward-looking. From Clara's point of view, these documents could potentially be of value.

The ways that illegalized residents spoke about the documents that they saved indicated that they imagined a potential transference between persons and documents. Recall Manuel's comment that he had "everything." We witnessed numerous instances in which people walked into the offices of nonprofit staff carrying piles of documents in miscellaneous containers: a bright blue American Automobile Association tote bag, a bag from the Smart & Final grocery store, carrier bags from department stores, an agenda featuring the logo of the Mary Kay cosmetics company. I found the contrast between the importance of this documentation, which could potentially confer status, and the casualness of these bags striking. When people described their paperwork, many, like Manuel, used terms like "all" and "everything"—they seemed to imagine that these collections of documents contained everything that service providers would need (though often something, such as a document with a particular date, was missing). Indeed, my own field notes from August 2012, when DACA was new and I first saw the records that applicants brought to their appointments, convey my sense of awe:

The documentation that people are bringing in for DACA also strikes me as pretty incredible. People are bringing in their lives. In the presence documentation, e.g., through multiple school I.D.'s, you see the person growing up, going to school, getting awards, etc. I have all of these sorts of things for my kids as well. And yet, the people bringing in the documentation lack legal status. It is so weird.

My comment, "People are bringing in their lives," suggests that I too started to see documents as standing in for the person, which, in the case of DACA, meant demonstrating what it is to be a child arrival through school IDs for each grade level beginning in elementary school. My comment, "I have all of these sorts of things for my kids as well" reflects the ways that documenting presence is a way for illegalized residents to overcome the gap between their experiences and those who are legalized, showing that they exist *in the same world*, and that law should realign itself with social reality.

Documenting back to the state through such collections of records had a complex temporality: on the one hand, documents produced at earlier moments *retroactively* took on legal significance. For example, Juana Maria reported that she had registered for adult school in 1989 and had kept a copy of the registration receipt. Later, that turned out to be important proof of her entry date. Similarly, Daniela said that her practice of saving papers paid off when her daughter qualified for DACA: "It turned out that I had saved the *documento clave* [key document] that allowed her to qualify. It was the light bill. She had to show that she was present in the United States on [June 15, 2007], and it turned out that on that precise date, the exact one that they wanted, she had made a payment. And this is what helped my daughter to register for DACA." The fact that a light bill could retroactively be critical to an immigration case is evidence of the bizarre workings of immigration law. On the date when the light bill was paid, it is unlikely that either Daniela or her daughter could imagine that, years later, they would need to prove that Daniela's daughter was present on that date. And on the other hand, saving papers was an act of hope that looked toward the future. For this reason, some interviewees tried to assemble more documents than they needed, reasoning that the more evidence they had, the better their chances of obtaining status, particularly given the difficulty of knowing what might be requested of them.

Additionally, for certain cases, such as U-visa applications, applicants secure letters of support from friends, family, and coworkers attesting to their moral character. Such letters make illegalized residents socially visible by showing that they have people who can write to immigration officials on their behalf, even as these letters also articulate notions of merit held by letter writers. As a volunteer, I translated such support letters from Spanish into English, and was able to observe letter writers praising applicants for things like attending church regularly, being polite, saying thank you, acting respectfully, helping others, being a good listener, sharing experiences, giving children rides to school, cooking food for hospitalized neighbors, completing schoolwork on time, being cheerful, working hard, and taking good care of their children. This sort of praise presumably reflects the characteristics that letter writers value, regardless of official notions of merit, which do not focus on things like cheerfulness. Applicants also sometimes prepared their own written declarations, adopting language that was seemingly designed to appeal to officials' sense of compassion, or to overcome the limitations of paperwork as a means of representing experiences. For example, recall that one VAWA applicant concluded her declaration with the words,

"Everything that I have told you is true, nothing is a lie, and I lived through it in my own flesh. I hope that you have been able to read what I have written and that you have been able to understand me. I take my leave of you." This statement asserts that embodied experiences produce a kind of truth that warrants deference from those who merely read about it. Another applicant described how painful it was for her to prepare a declaration, writing, "Mr. Judge, you do not know how hard, how sad it was to write this letter. I was crying a lot as though it were happening again. Mistreatments, insults, shouts, threats." This sort of commentary insisted on the vividness of applicants' experiences, seeking to sway officials' consciences.

By putting forward community-based standards of deservingness, "documenting back" to the state was a way of striving to create conditions in which regularization would be possible. Clara, for example, took credit for saving the paperwork that had allowed her daughter to qualify for DACA. She had kept receipts over the years, and she was able to secure letters from US residents attesting to her daughter's presence. Within Clara's narrative, her daughter's successful DACA claim had resulted *both* from the opportunity to apply *and* from Clara's own preparedness in saving receipts for years before any opportunity to apply existed. After describing these efforts, Clara added, "And these are going to help me someday. I'm not giving up (*yo no me doy por vencida*). They are going to work for me as well." For Clara and the many other interviewees who insisted that "por algo me van a servir" ("they'll be useful to me somehow"), saving papers was a form of agency that, they hoped, could eventually result in status. They, like Clara, were not giving up.

The connection between hope and document collection is shown by our interview with one participant who lost hope and stopped saving papers. Antonia had been awarded withholding of deportation due to the danger that she faced in her country of origin. Unlike political asylum, withholding of deportation does not confer the ability to become a Lawful Permanent Resident (American Immigration Council and National Immigrant Justice Center 2020), so Antonia, like other interview participants, had saved papers in hopes of securing a more permanent status. She explained: "I saved all of the receipts that they gave me from what they paid me for recycling [cans and bottles]; I saved receipts for what I bought. All of that I saved, receipts where I paid rent and all of that." After being the victim of a crime, Antonia applied for a U-visa, but her case was denied. No longer hopeful, she stopped saving papers. She related, "I destroyed everything, because I said, there is no future in this. Why save papers? They are papers that are not going to be useful. So I destroyed them. I destroyed everything." Antonia's decision to destroy her collection of paperwork seemed to be a defiant act, one that rejected the state's claim to be humanitarian and that refused the subject position of supplicant. Nonetheless, when we asked her what advice she would give to others who hoped to regularize, Antonia replied,

"It would be good for her or them to save that type of paperwork. In the future, it will be useful to them."

CONCLUSION

Clara and others who saved documents in the hope that these would be useful someday contended with the paradox that they needed to appeal to *legal criteria* to qualify for status that the state could award or deny as a matter of *political will*, which is outside of the law. I have described this subject position as one of *routine exceptionality*. Immigrant residents' claims are routine in that residents navigate immigration law on a daily basis when they face requests for identity documents. These claims are exceptional in immigrants appeal to discretionary forms of relief, such as asylum or deferred action, and must show that they are exceptional in some way, such as being a child arrival for whom humanitarian considerations warrant temporary permission to remain in the United States. They likewise seek an exception to the detention and removal to which they would otherwise be subjected. As subjects who experience routine exceptionality, illegalized residents feel that they are under the state's gaze, both through the situations in which they are asked for papers, but also in that, in the long run, they may hope to file an immigration claim. Awareness of surveillance motivates residents to create the record that they would like the state to see. For this reason, many residents "document back" to the state in an anticipatory fashion, collecting paperwork that they hope to eventually be able to submit. Such evidence is a form of papereality that, immigrants hope, will have some force. Recall that Dery defines papereality as a feature of bureaucratic organizations, in which there is "a world of symbols, or written representations, that take precedence over the things and events represented" (1998, 678). Thus, residents who have been told that their lack of official authorization to be in the country takes precedence over the realities of their lives in the United States hope to flip this relationship such that their own documentation of their lives will take precedence over their lack of status. Furthermore, the declarations and letters of support that applicants secure as part of their files create opportunities to assert their own understandings of merit, according to which qualities like cheerfulness and having a strong work ethic are grounds for regularization.

Illegalized residents' abilities to attempt to sway government officials to exercise discretion favorably stems from an interdependency between the United States and illegalized residents. Even before they enter the United States, those who travel without authorization are shaped by US law, as they travel clandestinely and endure degrading conditions. This vulnerability continues within the United States, as they live in what multiple interviewees described as a cage of gold: they are able to work (often in the informal labor market) but their immigration status traps them, limiting their movement. Residents counter illegalization by acting in ways that define them as legal: they avoid checkpoints where they are subject to surveillance; some acquire false identity documents; and they identify strategies, such as family petitions, through which they can eventually seek status. Collecting documentation of daily life further counters illegalization by attempting to produce a record that would define them as legal residents. Yet, the success of such strategies depends in part on the support of advocates, whose knowledge of legal craft mediates between illegalized residents and the state.

3

Legal Craft

In July 2011, I had one of my first opportunities to shadow legal staff at the nonprofit. I arrived at 9:15 a.m., and, unsure what to do, I joined the line of clients checking in with the receptionist. Soon, an intern noticed me and unlocked a door so that I could access the office area where service providers worked. There, two staff invited me to sit in on their appointments, however, one appointment ended quickly when the client unexpectedly had to leave, and I did not want to interrupt the other appointment, which was already underway. Uncertain where to wait, I returned to the lobby, where I sat awkwardly, until an attorney who spied me there brought out a U-visa training manual for me to read in preparation for future volunteer work. In the weeks to come, I would learn to fill such empty time with volunteer tasks, and I would be given the code to access the office area instead of sitting in the lobby.

At around 11:00 a.m., a paralegal came out to invite me to observe, with his client's permission, a consultation regarding an asylum-based work permit renewal. I walked to his office, taking a seat beside him while he met with Rosibel, a Salvadoran woman in her early fifties. The paralegal reviewed the intake form that Rosibel had completed in the reception area, and asked to see her most recent work permits. Rosibel searched through a bag filled with papers, her wallet, and envelopes. Finally, she found two expired work permit cards.

The paralegal examined the cards and immediately asked Rosibel when she had first applied for asylum. She said that she had done so in the 1990s. The paralegal commented, "Then you had TPS," and Rosibel confirmed that that was the case. Her last work permit renewal was from 1995 or 1996, some fifteen to sixteen years earlier. In addition to her two expired work permit cards, Rosibel had a work permit renewal application that had been completed at the nonprofit in 1998, but which Rosibel had never mailed. It looked to me as though it had been ready to submit, with two photos of Rosibel paper-clipped to the completed form.

After reviewing these documents, the paralegal called the Executive Office of Immigration Review (EOIR), reaching their automated phone system, to check whether Rosibel had any pending court appearances, and we heard a recording state that there was no record of her A#—the "alien number" that USCIS assigns to individuals to track their records. (Later, after observing numerous consultations, I learned that when there was no record of a person's A#, that meant that they were not in removal proceedings and had not been ordered deported.)

Noting that Rosibel had moved since she had first applied for asylum, the paralegal asked Rosibel whether she had notified Immigration of her new address. Rosibel responded that she had not. Because she did not change her mailing address, she would have missed any notices that she received from Immigration officials.

The paralegal told Rosibel that he could not apply to renew her work permit because too much time had gone by since her last application, and he first needed to know what had come of her asylum application. She seemed disappointed. He then delivered some incredible news. He said that Rosibel was potentially eligible to apply for Lawful Permanent Residency through NACARA, which Rosibel at first seemed to think was the name of a service agency, like the nonprofit, rather than an immigration program. She brightened when the paralegal reiterated that she might be able to get her residency, depending on what was in her file with Immigration. He recommended doing a Freedom of Information Act (FOIA) request to find out. She agreed.

The paralegal completed the nonprofit's service contract and the FOIA request and explained to Rosibel that she should mail the request in an envelope that he had provided (it was already addressed) and that she would receive a response in approximately four to six weeks. The paralegal also told her that it was likely that her file would arrive in the form of a computer disk rather than a packet of papers, and that when she received it, she should bring it in to the nonprofit or to an attorney so that they could review it and discuss her options with her.

As Rosibel left, the paralegal advised her to take good care of her expired work permits, saying, "They are very strong proofs (*son pruebas muy fuertes*) that you may be eligible for NACARA."

After Rosibel left, I asked the paralegal how he had known that she had obtained her work permit through TPS. He said that there are two ways to tell. One is that on the card, the code "A-11" appears, in reference to the way that the individual qualified for a work permit. He said that that number refers to DED (Deferred Enforced Departure), which is what TPS became when it was extended for Salvadorans.[1] Moreover, he explained, the A#s for people who had TPS start with 094, though some may start with 095, as 094 numbers have run out.

I also asked whether it was possible that Rosibel had been called to court and ordered deported in absentia.[2] The paralegal didn't think so, because there was no record of her in the EOIR system. More likely, he said, her case was administratively closed by the asylum unit. But if it was closed, he said, it would be straightforward to reopen it, because she is likely NACARA eligible.

This consultation is an example of the legal craft through which service providers at the nonprofit navigated securitization and humanitarianism, developing a way of "seeing like an advocate" that mediated between the state's gaze and immigrant residents' experiences.[3] The long line of clients that I joined that morning demonstrates the demand for advocates' services (Eagly and Shafer 2015) while the abrupt departure of one client and the fact that Rosibel never submitted her TPS renewal application are indicative of the ways that the exigencies of daily life— perhaps a change in work schedule, lack of funds, a sick child—could prevent clients from following through with their cases. Service providers operated in a climate of uncertainty: Rosibel could not explain what became of her asylum claim and did not know that she likely could have become a resident years earlier, through NACARA. The paralegal who attended to her was nonetheless able to diagnose her case by filling in her record—the two work permits from the 1990s, an unsent work permit renewal application from 1998, the phone call to EOIR, and her verbal report that she never filed a change of address form—with his knowledge of immigration law and policy. He knew that the 1990 Immigration Act gave Salvadorans the right to apply for TPS due to the civil war in their homeland; that the 1985 *American Baptist Churches v. Thornburgh* class action suit was settled out of court in 1991, giving Salvadorans the right to apply for asylum under special rules; and that previously submitted Salvadoran asylum applications were administratively closed, to allow Salvadorans to submit new applications (Mountz et al. 2002; Hallett 2014; Blum 1991; Leiden and Neal 1990–1991). He also drew on his own technocratic expertise: the meaning of the codes on Rosibel's Employment Authorization documents, the fact that her A# began with "094," her potential eligibility for NACARA. Yet, there were still gaps: what had become of Rosibel's original application? What records did US immigration officials have in her file? The bag of paperwork that Rosibel brought in did not have the answers to these questions, so the paralegal had to seek the file itself through a FOIA request. Requesting this file was a form of advocacy, as were the paralegal's careful explanations to Rosibel about her potential eligibility for NACARA, how to mail the FOIA request, and what to do with the computer disk when it arrived. As an advocate, he sought to use the expired work permits, which were "strong proofs," to transform Rosibel from an undocumented immigrant to a Lawful Permanent Resident. Residency, he knew, would confer more rights, and greater legal security than would the work permit that Rosibel had originally sought to renew.

The legal craft that the paralegal exercised that morning was an amalgam of different phenomena, combined through the complex circumstances that shape legal advocacy on behalf of immigrant residents. Legal craft was a form of alchemy (Williams 1991) that could potentially transform persons, even as it also involved mundane bureaucratic actions, such as completing forms. In contrast to notarios and attorneys who were unscrupulous, legal staff at the nonprofit set high standards of service provision. For them, practicing legal craft required technical expertise, such as the paralegal's knowledge of the codes on Employment Authorization Documents, even as it also demanded creativity in seeing potentials, as when the paralegal saw Rosibel's possible eligibility for NACARA.[4] It also required sheer determination and effort, due to the administrative burden of applying for legal status in the resource scarce environment of nonprofit work. As they mediate between the federal government and illegalized residents, service providers strive to educate their clients regarding immigration law (Yu 2023b). Their intermediary role required seeing their clients through the eyes of the state, which compelled service providers to follow the state's standards regarding eligibility, documentation, and form completion. At the same time, as intermediaries, service providers were also committed to seeing like their clients. They strived to be empathetic, to hear the narratives their clients wanted to tell, and to understand their clients' social realities. As empathetic intermediaries who translated between the state and its noncitizen subjects,[5] service providers acted as "para-ethnographers," learning to navigate complex cultural milieus (Holmes and Marcus 2006; Marcus 2016). By pursuing not only legal but social justice, advocates were heir to decades of struggle waged by immigrant residents and their allies. Their actions carry the weight of these histories.

By "documenting back" to the state in allyship with immigrant residents, the legal craft performed by service providers influenced law. Legal craft plays this role not merely because service providers carry out "law-in-action" in contrast to "law-on-the-books," but also by putting forward arguments about membership (such as arguing that a person deserved residency), belonging (e.g., documenting someone's strong ties to the community), and social justice (e.g., that it would be a hardship for someone to be separated from their relatives) that become part of legal records, remaining to potentially be returned to in the future.[6] Of course, not all records are a form of advocacy or counter-documentation. For example, documents prepared by notarios or unscrupulous attorneys may defraud immigrant community members (Guerra 2011). However the relationship of solidarity enacted through legal craft imbues the resulting records with complex meanings. Applications and supporting documentation are prepared to secure status for individual clients, but in addition, these records document the struggles of immigrant community members in the face of increasingly securitized immigration policies. The 2011–2015 period when I carried out fieldwork at the nonprofit was a time when the Obama administration had promised a more humane approach to immigration policymaking, but had not delivered comprehensive immigration reform, and then had announced DAPA and DACA+ only to have these programs enjoined by the courts (Chacón, Coutin, and Lee 2024). The records gathered by immigrant community members and prepared by service providers chronicle illegalized residents' experiences of these processes: the family separations that they sought to overcome; the work authorization they hoped to secure; the residency or citizenship they hoped to acquire. Service providers sought pathways forward, analyzing family relationships, legal histories, and eligibility for specialized programs. They tried to discern obstacles on these paths, and to communicate whether barriers were insurmountable. And they did their best to prepare documentation that would withstand scrutiny. Through such legal craft, service providers sought to solve challenges faced by their clients.

It may seem odd to argue that the attorneys, paralegals, interns, DACA clerks, and volunteers who provide services to an illegalized population play a role in influencing law; after all, in her work on financial markets, Annelise Riles (2011, 36) refers to people who complete forms and prepare documents as "legal technicians" who do "back office work." Yet, Riles also points out that the documents they produce have power. Of a particular type of financial document known as an International Swaps and Derivatives Association Master Agreement, she writes, "The physical existence of thousands of such signed documents—transformed the feel of the question of what to do about substantive legal rules" (2011, 45). Relatedly, in the case of service providers and immigrant residents, the thousands of U-visa declarations, provisional waiver applications, asylum claims, presence documents, and completed forms likely influence bureaucratic understandings of harm, hardship, persecution, continuous presence, and other legal concepts. By navigating through an uncertain legal landscape on behalf of residents who are viewed with suspicion by government officials, service providers deploy the power of bureaucratic inscription—that is, "the social and material dynamics through which migrants are inscribed into official bureaucratic systems at various scales of government. . . . Bureaucratic inscription entails discrete—and sometimes prolonged—moments of visibility to a field of power" (Horton 2020, 3). By shaping the documentation that the state sees during such moments of visibility, service providers and immigrant residents potentially intervene within this field of power, inserting their understandings into the record. The mundane activities of form completion and document preparation therefore are politically significant (Coutin and Fortin 2023). As Riles concludes, "Hope comes from creating small opportunities for change, small spaces for reflection, and then letting those opportunities unfold" (2011, 245). Such small opportunities can be created by filling out an application form, taking a declaration, or assembling a documentation packet in ways that promote social justice for illegalized community members.

Legal craft relies not only on knowledge of law but also on para-ethnography—that is, on activities—conversations, observations, note-taking, meetings—that are not fieldwork but that nonetheless generate quasi-ethnographic understandings of social and cultural milieus, enabling service providers to adapt their work to the contexts in which it is employed (Holmes and Marcus 2006; Marcus 2016). Nonprofit staff needed to understand not only the social conditions in which their clients lived, but also the practices and thought processes of the immigration officials who would be evaluating clients' cases (Yu 2023b). To understand the latter, service providers had to rely on clues discerned at something of a distance, through meetings, conference calls, government websites, administrative guidance documents, the instructions provided on forms, and Requests for Evidence (RFEs)—that is, an official notification that additional information was needed before a decision could be rendered. Attending to such clues was akin to what Nancy Hiemstra refers to as periscoping: "this methodological approach encourages the researcher to search out cracks in barriers to studying structures of power and attempts to lay bare the violences concealed in gaps between public knowledge and restricted access" (2017, 330). By piecing together fragments of information from various indirect sources, periscoping overcomes the inaccessibility of powerful institutions, and "assembles a variety of lenses to acquire a coherent picture of elements previously illegible" (Hiemstra 2017, 329). In contrast to their distanced relationship with state officials, service providers had direct interaction with clients, and were able to learn the terminology they used to discuss immigration law, the cultural understandings that they brought into appointments, and the ways that their lives were shaped by illegalization and liminal legality, an "uncertain status—not fully documented or undocumented but often straddling both" (Menjívar 2006, 1001). Some service providers also had immigration histories and cultural backgrounds that were not unlike those they assisted. Advocates' quasi-ethnographic knowledge shaped the communication strategies, social support, and political commitments through which services were delivered. Of course, service providers sometimes became frustrated with clients who were late, unprepared, or uncooperative, as well as with the lack of technological and clerical support that generally characterizes nonprofit work. They nonetheless performed legal craft despite demanding workloads and resource scarcity.

To explore legal craft, this chapter examines the forms of archival advocacy practiced by legal staff and volunteers at the nonprofit. Situated as intermediaries between illegalized residents and the discretionary state, service providers learned to navigate a challenging administrative environment, diagnose their clients' legal opportunities (or lack thereof), deploy technocratic expertise on their behalf, translate between formal policies and their clients' understandings, and marshal the power of papereality. They did so in a context shaped by securitization, even as the state's need to demonstrate administrative grace created opportunities to pursue social justice.

THE CONTEXT OF SERVICE PROVISION

In August of 2012, the nonprofit was scrambling to provide services to dramatically increased numbers of clients as DACA, which had been announced only sixty days earlier, went into effect (Boehm 2020). Attorneys and paralegals had had to hire and train new staff, determine how to screen potential applicants for eligibility, and develop new information sessions, even though application forms and instructions would not be available until the first day of the program. Deprioritizing my research goals, I joined in the volunteer effort, and became caught up in the general feeling of being overwhelmed. My field notes recorded a dream I had at the time:

> I dreamed that I had gone in to [the nonprofit] to volunteer and that someone had given me an intake form and asked me to complete an application. I went to a computer but in my dream had a hard time figuring out whether to use my laptop or one of their computers. Finally, I was sitting in a room with long desks and many computers, like the computer lab [on my campus], but the tables were made of wood and there was light streaming in one of the windows. Sitting at the computer and looking at the intake form, I struggled to complete the DACA application. I couldn't figure out which words in the applicant's name were the last name (since some people have two last names), or whether the birthdate had been written Month/Day/Year, as in English or Day/Month/Year, as in Spanish. Then, in my dream, I remembered being told to ask the applicant such questions, but where was the applicant? I realized that I had been supposed to go get the applicant and have him (it was a guy) with me while I filled out the form. So I walked out to the reception area and called out the person's name. When he came forward, we went together to go back to the room where I had been working on the application, but I couldn't find the room. I kept opening doors and looking in and trying one computer after another, but I couldn't find the one I had been using previously. I was worrying about my laptop as well, because I had left it plugged in somewhere and couldn't find it either. I kept wandering and wandering, and then I woke up.

When I told one of the attorneys about this experience, she said, "That's definitely a stress dream!" Apparently, legal staff at the nonprofit had been having their own stress dreams for weeks.

While the launch of the DACA program was unusual, the challenge of providing services in an uncertain and shifting legal landscape was not (Lakhani 2013). Over the years that I carried out fieldwork and volunteer work at the nonprofit, I witnessed multiple legal changes: the Morton memos, the rollout of DACA, reinterpretations of what it meant to be "inspected and admitted," a new provisional waiver program, a proposal for and then failure to pass comprehensive immigration reform, the influx of unaccompanied minors in 2014 coupled with increased services for this population (Galli 2023), state and local efforts to mitigate the impacts of federal policies, and the announcement and then enjoining of DAPA and DACA+ (Wadhia 2011, 2015; Abrego 2018b; Juarez 2017; Tepeli 2013; Elias 2013; Pham and Van 2019; and Chacón, Coutin, and Lee 2024). In the years that followed, the Trump administration attempted to further reshape immigration priorities by curtailing opportunities, revising forms, reducing the number of refugee admissions, forcing asylum applicants to remain in Mexico, banning admissions from certain majority Muslim countries, and imposing border restrictions as a public health measure (Pierce, Bolter, and Selee 2018; Schmidt 2019;

Rosen 2022). President Trump rescinded DACA, but this rescission was enjoined, with the result that current DACA recipients can renew deferred action but no new DACA applications can be approved (Rosenbaum 2023; Aranda et al. 2022). The Biden administration reversed a number of Trump-era immigration policies, but instituted further restrictions on asylum (Cuic 2022; Garrett and Sementelli 2023). Court battles over these policies continue. In the meantime, avenues for legal relief for long-term undocumented residents remain much as they were at the time of my fieldwork: family visa petitions, U-visas, VAWA cases, SIJS, TPS, and DACA renewals, and asylum, along with naturalization for Lawful Permanent Residents. A few, such as Rosibel, were eligible for earlier forms of humanitarian relief, in a kind of time warp, and service providers occasionally identified people who had unknowingly already gained US citizenship when a parent naturalized. All too often, though, illegalized residents were ineligible for any form of relief.

This context of heightened pressure for status, restricted opportunities for regularization, and the launch and demise of new programs exacerbated illegalized residents' vulnerability to notario fraud, further complicating service providers' work. Notario fraud occurs when people who are public notaries take advantage of the fact that in many Latin American countries, "notarios"—the Spanish term for "notary"—have considerable legal expertise (Cossman 2023). It was not unusual for clients to tell nonprofit staff that they had paid a supposed attorney or notario thousands of dollars to submit paperwork on their behalf, but that they had no copies of what had been submitted. Staff then had to submit FOIA requests to obtain these clients' immigration files. Having to wait for the results added to service providers and residents' sense of uncertainty. Staff regularly encountered people who were ineligible for relief but who had applied through a notario and been ordered deported in absentia. At a public presentation on immigration law that I attended, a nonprofit attorney tried to educate his audience about these risks, asking them, "What is a notary?" After hearing a few answers, the attorney pointed out that in the United States, a notary is someone who can witness legal signatures. "How long does someone have to study to be a notary?" he then asked. Again, there were guesses. "Six hours," he told them. "Whereas an attorney has to go to law school for three years. This is the deception that the notario performs. The notario tells someone, 'I'm going to apply for asylum for you. And then we will apply through the law of ten years'"—referring to cancellation of removal, which requires ten years of continuous presence within the United States. But, he continued, it is very hard to win asylum, and it is hard to win a cancellation case.[7] "So be careful," he concluded; "it is better to live your life in peace, though undocumented, than enter into deportation proceedings." In contrast to the approaches adopted by notarios, legal staff at the nonprofit had their clients sign contracts that outlined costs and services, gave clients copies of completed applications, spent time to educate clients about immigration law, and provided honest assessments, even when there was no opportunity to regularize their status.

Service providers' work was also complicated by the suspicion with which authorities regarded their clients' cases (Colomé-Menéndez, Koops, and Weggemans 2021), a factor that added to their administrative burden. Service providers had to spend time asking clients the many security-related questions on immigration forms, and had to develop expertise in criminal law in order to determine whether clients were eligible for relief. At a training on the TPS renewal process, for example, a paralegal showed volunteers and interns how to distinguish between felonies and misdemeanors on police reports. On countless occasions, I witnessed service providers telling clients with criminal convictions that they were ineligible for relief unless they were able to reopen their criminal cases and obtain a different outcome; expungements did not count for immigration purposes. The unlawful presence bars also posed obstacles (Lundstrom 2013). Children who were undocumented did not accumulate unlawful presence; however, when they turned eighteen, unlawful presence began to accrue, potentially subjecting them to bars on reentry. I witnessed one case in which a woman who was gaining lawful permanent residency wanted to petition for her eighteen-year-old son, but it would take three years for the visa to become current. If he remained in the United States for those three years, then he would be subject to a ten-year bar on reentry; however, if he left the country while waiting for the visa to be current, then he would be able to reenter as a Lawful Permanent Resident, but he would be separated from his family for three years. Because of the securitization of immigration law, which punished presence in the country, this family faced a difficult choice. Officials' attitude of suspicion also shaped service providers' documentation strategies. For example, a service provider who was completing a naturalization application for a Lawful Permanent Resident expressed concern that an official had failed to stamp her client's passport following a trip outside of the country. The official's error made it appear that this resident had been outside of the United States longer than was actually the case, potentially disrupting his continuous presence. She had to seek additional documentation of his travel dates. The provider also told me that for naturalization applications, she photocopies every page of clients' passports so that their travel histories can be examined by US officials. If someone allows their passport to lapse, then this passport-less period creates a gap that officials can view with suspicion.

Service providers also had to contend with uncertainty, a psychological cost of administrative burdens. Their clients did not always have all of their records, so service providers submitted FOIA requests on their behalf and then waited (sometimes months) for records to arrive. Immigrant residents did not always understand their own histories. For instance, some said that they had spent time in jail or prison, but they did not know what they had been convicted of, so service providers advised them to obtain their court records. One nonprofit client, Marcia, hoped to become a Lawful Permanent Resident through her US citizen husband.[8] Her ability to do so hinged on whether she had been "inspected and admitted" when she first entered the United States. If so, she could adjust her status in the United States, and if not, she would have to seek a provisional waiver of the presence bars. Yet, when she entered the United States, she was a nine-year-old child who was asleep in a car, and she had no evidence of having been lawfully admitted. Moreover, Marcia had DACA but did not have a copy of her DACA application, which had been prepared somewhere other than at the nonprofit, and it was not clear how her entry had been described in her DACA application. Luckily, as a DACA recipient, at that time, she was eligible for advance parole, so if she could travel outside of the country to visit an ill relative and reenter, then she would have a lawful admission that would make her eligible for adjustment. Before advising Marcia about any of these options, the service provider asked her to get more information about her original entry, her DACA application, and the medical situation that her relative was experiencing.

In advising clients, service providers also faced uncertainty about the state of the law and how officials were processing applications. I observed one appointment in which the service provider repeatedly used the phrase "a veces"—"sometimes," as in "sometimes they ask for more evidence." It struck me that when confronted with legal uncertainty, in which sometimes one thing happens and sometimes another, one has to prepare for multiple possible outcomes. When confronted with unclear areas of policy—what evidence of completing educational requirements would be required for a DACA renewal?—service providers sometimes opted to overdocument. They also had to contend with the possibility that the law could change in the future. For instance, in 2013, legislators contemplated eliminating the sibling category of family petitions, so that year, I noticed service providers telling clients who hoped to petition for a sibling that they should do so as soon as possible, before the law changed (see Wong 2017). In 2012, as DACA was being launched, I reflected, "I feel like I'm in the vortex of current forces shaping immigration policies in the US. For years, people have been debating the DREAM Act, local versus federal immigration control, and comprehensive immigration reform. And now DACA is actually happening, though it is not clear what 'DACA' actually is or whether it will last."

Service provision was also shaped by conditions of work in the nonprofit sector. Attorneys and paralegals had to do their own photocopying, computers were sometimes slow, and there were frequent interruptions as attorneys and Board of Immigration Appeals (BIA)–accredited representatives had to answer questions and review others' work. While they approached their work with great empathy for immigrant residents, they also managed a heavy caseload, leading to frustration if clients were late for appointments or did not bring requested documentation. The nonprofit was part of a network of immigrant rights groups, so legal staff could collaborate and consult with supportive colleagues at other organizations.[9] Their work was shaped by funding constraints, as they had to rely on grant funding, donations, and fees (set at rates designed to be affordable for their clients and lower than those of private attorneys). Staff tried to strike a balance between (a) serving large numbers of clients, which meant focusing on routine cases, and (b) taking on a leadership role by representing those with complex cases who could not afford to hire private attorneys.[10] Legal staff sometimes formed close relationships with clients, and found it rewarding when they felt that they made a difference in people's lives. For example, at one legal meeting, an attorney shared a story about a seemingly impossible situation in which the visa for a client's child became current only a few days before he would turn twenty-one and lose eligibility. The attorney and her client worked feverishly to arrange flights and the necessary appointments, and the client's son was able to report to Immigration with the visa in hand only minutes before midnight on the last day. This situation was extreme, but the fact that legal staff shared this story demonstrates the value that they placed in overcoming the odds stacked against their clients. To do so, they had to understand the possible pathways through which illegalized residents could gain status, as well as the obstacles that they would encounter along the way.

DIAGNOSING A CASE

I came to think of the process through which service providers determined whether someone was eligible to apply for legal status as "diagnosing a case." Just as medical professionals assess individuals' health by consulting their medical histories and symptomology, so too did service providers evaluate clients' legalization prospects through studying their records and questioning them about their immigration histories. By using the term "diagnosis," I do not mean to pathologize nonprofit clients by suggesting that being undocumented is akin to an illness. Rather, I highlight how service providers' efforts resembled a diagnosis in that these staff members used their expertise to make sense of clients' histories and to identify courses of action that could improve their legal condition. By assessing their clients' eligibility, service providers took on some of the learning costs faced by illegalized residents. To do so, legal staff had to "see like a state," considering how officials would view their clients records, *and* "see like an advocate," who could identify opportunities. In essence, service providers compared clients' accounts of their immigration histories to the known pathways to legal status, the obstacles along these pathways, and possible strategies for surmounting barriers. I witnessed this diagnostic process repeatedly, as I sat in on consultations that often lasted an hour or more, in which those who hoped to gain work authorization, permanent residency, or citizenship for themselves or a relative met with a service provider. The legal and technical expertise involved in diagnosing a case is extensive. Though my own understanding of immigration law grew over time, I rarely could anticipate what service providers would tell their clients.

Within this process of diagnosis, a "case" is akin to a pathway that could potentially lead to legal status but that might also result in either deportation

A Dispute Pyramid: The General Pattern
No. per 1000 Grievances

Court Filings	50
Lawyers	103
Disputes	449
Claims	718
Grievances	1000

FIGURE 4. Example of a Dispute Pyramid. Reproduced from Miller and Sarat's (1980–1981, 544) research regarding grievances and civil legal disputes in the United States during the 1970s. Permission to reprint this figure granted by Austin Sarat.

or the status quo. Sociolegal studies scholars have pointed out that "disputes"— arguments, grievances, or disagreements between two or more parties—do not arise automatically, rather, they only exist if someone raises a complaint in a forum that leads to litigation or some other action designed to resolve the dispute (Merry 2012; Mather 2021; Mather and Yngvesson 1980–1981). In order to raise a complaint, a person must first conclude that they have been wronged and must attach blame to someone else (Felstiner et al. 1980–81). Moreover, complainants have multiple forums in seeking redress; for example, they can "lump it"—that is, they can opt to live with the issue; they can seek informal resolution (e.g., by gossiping about the matter, in order to shame the offender into compliance); they can pursue mediation (either formally, through some sort of arbitration, or informally, through a respected community member or third party); or they can file a formal grievance in court (Miller and Sarat 1980–1981; Kritzer 2011). Research suggests that there is a "disputing pyramid": the bottom of the pyramid represents the most common response (lumping it), while the top (a court case) is the least common (Galanter 1983; Sarat 1985).[11] The vast majority of disputes never result in formal legal action (see Figure 4).

Similarly, an immigration "case" does not exist automatically, but rather has to be constructed, either by the government initiating a removal process or by an illegalized resident, family member, or potential entrant filing a petition. As well, as noted in chapter 2, many immigrant residents live *as though* they have a pending case in that they assume an anticipatory administrative burden, collecting evidence in preparation for a future immigration opportunity. When service providers "diagnosed a case"—my terminology, not theirs—they were determining whether there were any claims already pending, what happened to them, and what legal opportunities might be available for individuals at the present time or in the future. In sociolegal terms, service providers were deciphering whether the person had, perhaps unknowingly, already moved up the pyramid by filing a claim, and if not, whether it was a good idea to do so or to continue to "lump it" by not applying for anything. Service providers referred to the appointments in which they performed this assessment as a "consultation" or "consulta" and they spoke of specific cases according to the type of relief a client sought (for example, an asylum case, a DACA case, a U-visa or VAWA case, a family petition). They also sometimes referred to cases, and form preparation appointments, by the number of the form that they were completing on behalf of their client—for example, an "I-90" was an appointment to prepare a green card renewal form. In addition to general consultations, there were consultations for specific legal actions, such as a naturalization consultation or a provisional waiver consultation. Service providers therefore played an important role in identifying the sorts of immigration cases that their clients could pursue. And, sadly, service providers often had to tell individuals that they "had no case" in that they were not eligible to apply for anything.

An example of diagnosing a case can be seen when, in 2011, a young couple, Ana Maria and Rodolfo, came in for a consultation, along with their four-year-old son, who seemed quite nervous. Ana Maria related that their son had confused this appointment with a visit to the doctor's office and was afraid of getting shots, an analogy that struck me as apt. The family had traveled from some distance in order to learn whether Ana Maria, who was a US citizen, could petition for Rodolfo, her husband. "My sister fixed [her papers] here and so I don't want to go anywhere else," Ana Maria said.

The service provider gave them the nonprofit's service contract to sign, and opened a document on their computer in order to take notes while I and a legal intern observed. I captured the service provider's dialogue with Ana Maria and Rodolfo in my notes, translated from Spanish to English (and with a few minor changes to preserve confidentiality):

"When did you get married?"

"In 2005."

"And have you had other family petitions or immigration transactions (tramites)?"

"No, none."

"Neither of you?"

"No."

"And when you were minors, did anyone file a petition for one of your parents?"

"No, no one."

"Do you have other relatives in the United States?"

"Yes," Rodolfo said, "My brother."

"Only your brother?"

"Yes."

"And how did you enter the United States?"

"Illegally (ilegal)."

"Ilegally?"

"Yes."

"And were you ever detained?"

"No. Well, they stopped me at the border. But it wasn't a detention. They only held me for thirty minutes and they sent me back to Mexico."

"Did you say you were Mexican?"

"Yes, exactly."

"When was that?"

"In '98."

"And did you ever enter with false documents?"

"No, never."

"Were you ever arrested?"

Rodolfo explained that once, he had been briefly detained by the police for a minor infraction. He completed the classes that they told him to take. The service provider suggested that he obtain the record of whatever he was charged with so that he would know the details. The service provider also asked them whether they had ever reported being victims of a crime—they had not—and whether this was their first marriage—it was.

After taking a few notes, the service provider said that the problem that they faced was that it was "very complicated" for Rodolfo to qualify for a family petition. Ana Maria could petition for him, but in order for him to use the petition, he would have to leave the country. Then, he would face a ten-year bar on reentry due to having lived in the United States without legal status. He would have to submit a petition for a waiver to reenter earlier than 10 years. The provider thought they had a possibility of being granted such a waiver. They would have to show that it was a hardship for Ana Maria to have Rodolfo out of the country, and that the hardship was more than a normal separation. The provider also explained that if Rodolfo were ever in removal proceedings, he should apply for cancellation of removal, because he had more than 10 years in the United States and could argue that his son would experience a hardship if he were deported.

Rodolfo said that he very much appreciated getting the information, as it is important to have accurate information, and there are many people who are trying to give people false hope. He added that it is good to know what their options are. After they left, the provider commented to me that it was sad that they traveled such a distance to get bad news.

This example demonstrates how a legal case is diagnosed. The service provider's repeated questions about whether anyone had filed a petition for Rodolfo or whether, as a child, he might have been included in a petition filed by his parents, or perhaps someone had petitioned for Ana Maria and included him as her husband, were likely designed to determine if he could qualify for 245(i), a provision of immigration law that that allows those who have been lawfully admitted to adjust their status in the United States instead of at a US consulate outside of the country. People who had a petition pending prior to 2001 are "grandfathered in" for 245(i) eligibility. The provider also asked about Rodolfo's mode of entry, because if he had been inspected and admitted, by traveling on a tourist visa, then he would have qualified to adjust his status without leaving the country. But, if he had entered with false documents, claiming to be a US citizen, then he would have been permanently barred, so the provider asked about that. As usual, arrests and Rodolfo's prior immigration history were also relevant, because criminal convictions or returning following a deportation could also permanently disqualify him. Because Rodolfo was seemingly ineligible for 245(i), he would have to travel outside of the United States for consular processing, and because he had been in the United States without status for more than one year, he would then trigger a ten-year bar on reentry. In 2013, the United States established a "provisional waiver" program, in which a person in Rodolfo's situation could apply for a waiver of this bar *before* leaving the United States. But in 2011, when this consultation took place, that program did not exist, so if Rodolfo left for consular processing, he would have to wait outside of the United States to learn whether he would qualify for a waiver (Gomberg-Muñoz 2017). The service provider outlined both this option and the possibility of seeking cancellation of removal if he were ever in proceedings. Neither of these options seemingly struck Rodolfo or Ana Maria as promising.

Deciphering individuals' previous immigration histories—such as whether a petition had ever been filed for Rodolfo—was key to diagnosing a case, and service providers relied on multiple sources of information to do so. Most fundamentally, they asked clients for information, often posing questions about key matters in multiple ways, as occurred in the above example ("And have you had other family petitions or immigration transactions (*tramites*)?" "Neither of you?" "And when you were minors, did anyone file a petition for one of your parents?") Service providers also gleaned information from an intake form that clients completed in the reception area, documents that they brought to their consultations, the nonprofit's own client database (if the person had been seen there previously), and the Executive Office of Immigration Review's automated case information system (recall that the paralegal who assisted Rosibel contacted this system to learn about her immigration history). When providers were missing key records, they advised clients to submit a FOIA request or to obtain copies of any criminal records. To interpret the information that they received, service providers drew on their knowledge of immigration law. In another consultation that I observed, a client told the service provider that her father had become a citizen through asylum, but the provider concluded that he actually had obtained citizenship through the 1986 Immigration Reform and Control Act's amnesty program. Afterwards, I asked how she reached this conclusion, and she explained that when she learned that her client's father was in the US in the early 1980s, she knew that he could have qualified for amnesty, as one had to be present on or before 9/1/1981 to be eligible (see Chishti and Kamasaki 2014). He would have applied for amnesty in 1987 or

1988, then he would have had to be a resident for five years, and then he would have been eligible to naturalize. According to his daughter, he became a citizen in 1996, which matched that timeline.

While people who sought consultations usually had a specific question, such as whether Rodolfo could qualify for a spousal petition through Ana Maria, service providers also screened them for other remedies. Providers asked them about their family relationships, whether family members had legal status in the United States, how they had obtained it, and their ages at the time. Sometimes, people learned that they could be included in someone else's case. As occurred in Ana Maria and Rodolfo's consultation, service providers explored 245(i) eligibility by inquiring about how clients had entered the country and whether anyone had ever filed a petition on their behalf. They also explored any previously submitted applications, as sometimes, having applied for TPS or asylum at an earlier date made an individual eligible for relief through NACARA. If people were victims of crime and had collaborated in an investigation (e.g., by reporting the crime to the police), they could potentially apply for a U-visa, which is why the service provider had asked Rodolfo if he had been a crime victim. Individuals who were abused by their spouses could self-petition through VAWA, and trafficking victims could seek T-visas. Providers also explored criminal convictions, whether clients had been ordered deported, and clients' entries and exits from the country, as these could potentially make someone inadmissible or trigger a bar on reentry. And, of course, when clients were seeking a specific remedy, such as DACA, naturalization, or a provisional waiver, providers screened them for eligibility for these opportunities.

Two additional examples of consultations illustrate how screening played out in practice. Jasmina, a forty-year-old from El Salvador who had obtained lawful permanent residency through NACARA, was about to naturalize, so she approached the nonprofit to learn whether she could petition for her sisters, nephews, and husband. The service provider asked her about these relatives' entry dates, departures, statuses held, parents' status, criminal convictions, and whether family members were victims of crime. Based on her answers to these questions, the service provider advised Jasmina that her sisters would face a ten-year-bar due to having been in the United States without status for more than a year. If her mother were to become a Lawful Permanent Resident and enter the United States, then her sisters would have a "qualifying relative" (an LPR or USC [US citizen] spouse or parent) and become eligible for a waiver, and her nephews could potentially be included in their cases, but those were long-term strategies. Her husband, however, was in a different situation. Because Jasmina had obtained residency through NACARA, he was eligible to be included in her case and could become a Lawful Permanent Resident without a spousal petition, as long as he had lived in the United States for at least seven years. The provider advised her to have her husband schedule his own consultation, and Jasmina left, happily promising to do so. What Jasmina had originally imagined as a family petition became an extension of her NACARA case.

Iván's consultation had a different outcome. Iván, who was undocumented, and his wife Sandra, who was a US citizen, approached the nonprofit in 2013, to learn whether they could qualify for a provisional waiver. Both were from Mexico. Again, the service provider asked a series of screening questions. Had they ever come in for a consultation before? When did Iván first enter the country? How long had Sandra and Iván been married? How long had they been together? Did they have children? What were their children's ages? Had they been previously married? Had Iván been convicted of any crimes? Had Iván been apprehended at the border? What had happened? Was he fingerprinted? Had he returned to his country? When? Why? How had Sandra naturalized? Had anyone petitioned for Iván previously? Had either of them been victims of crimes? What about their children? Had their children been the victim of any crime? Based on their answers to these questions, the provider delivered some devastating news. Iván had lived in the United States without lawful presence for more than one year, which meant that he was subject to the ten-year-bar, which could potentially be waived. But unfortunately, Iván had left the country in 1999 to visit an ill relative, triggering this bar, and had reentered before the ten years had elapsed. As a result, the service provider explained, he became permanently barred. He could petition for a waiver to the permanent bar, but only after leaving the United States and remaining away for ten years. More optimistically, because it was 2013 and immigration reform proposals were being discussed, the provider suggested that future reforms could potentially include people in Iván's circumstances. Sandra and Iván left, planning to return to the nonprofit if a new opportunity arose.

The last step in diagnosing a case was delivering the diagnosis, several examples of which have already been presented. For service providers, this was a critical moment, one that enabled them to use their expertise to identify possible pathways forward, empower clients through legal education, and, if they were ineligible for any remedies, warn them about the risks of notarios and those attorneys who were unscrupulous. For example, the service provider cautioned Iván and Sandra to avoid notarios who might tell them that they qualify for something but in reality would just take their money and worsen their situation. Service providers at the nonprofit took care to explain immigration law, presenting advantages and risks so that their clients could make informed choices. In so doing, service providers helped to reduce the learning costs of administrative burdens. To give one more example, Elena, who was undocumented, and Armando, her US citizen husband, approached the nonprofit for assistance because they had filed a petition nine years earlier through a legal office (perhaps a notario?) and had never learned what became of it. Based on the time that had elapsed, the provider advised them that it likely had been cancelled. But, he said, "You have options." He explained that Elena was likely eligible for DACA (at the time of this appointment, DACA applications could still be submitted), that DACA recipients can apply for advanced parole if there is an emergency in their country of origin (which was true at the time of this appointment), and that reentering the country on advanced parole gives people a lawful entry, making them eligible for 245(i). Elena and Armando could either resubmit the spousal petition and apply for a provisional waiver or they could pursue DACA, advanced parole (if applicable—he took care to state that that was only an option if there were an actual emergency), and the spousal petition without needing a waiver. The provider explained how to restart the visa process, if that is what they opted to do, as well as the next steps if they wanted to pursue DACA. Such detailed advice allowed Elena and Armando to evaluate their options. "You have given us hope," Armando commented.

TECHNOCRATIC EXPERTISE

Service providers' abilities to "give hope," when that was possible, depended on their technical knowledge of immigration law and bureaucracy, knowledge that was employed not only in diagnosing a case, but also in completing immigration forms and assembling application packets, thus reducing the compliance costs of administrative burdens. To advocate for their clients, service providers had to understand and anticipate "how 'state work' is done through technical legal devices" as officials process applications for immigration status (Riles 2011, 87). They needed to know which forms to use for different immigration opportunities, what additional forms (e.g., application for a fee waiver) might be needed for individual circumstances, which questions on the forms were tricky, how officials might interpret answers, the material requirements of form completion (e.g., what colors of ink were acceptable), how much supporting documentation to provide, how this material should be organized, what to do with information that did not fit in the space provided in a form, whether it was acceptable to leave blank spaces, and how to read the notices, cards, and certificates that officials issued to nonprofit clients. Such technocratic knowledge also had to align with service providers' understanding of immigration law (such as what "continuous presence" means), the workings of other relevant bureaucratic systems and agencies (e.g., schools, the Internal Revenue Service, courts, police, registries of vital records in other countries), and their clients' lives and circumstances. Yet, though technocratic knowledge was employed on a routine basis and involved repetitive and tedious work, it also enabled creativity, as service providers had their own style in completing forms; they continually had to resolve challenges that arose when someone's life circumstances defied assumptions behind the forms (e.g., a client who was unhoused did not have an address); they had to anticipate how officials might use forms in the future (e.g., inconsistent answers in different forms could be considered indications of fraud); and documentation packets needed to be organized. Providers expressed satisfaction when forms were complete, applications were signed, documentation was assembled, and the application was handed to the client. Technocratic expertise was both mundane and extraordinary.

I learned about service providers' technocratic expertise from observing appointments, chatting with providers regarding their work, and being trained to perform routine legal tasks, such as filling out DACA applications and TPS renewals, always under the supervision of an attorney or BIA-accredited representative. I found even these straightforward procedures challenging, as I recorded in my field notes:

> In thinking about completing TPS renewal forms as a volunteer, I realized how even the simplest of procedures is somewhat complicated. It seems that preparing one of these renewal applications requires the following steps: entering the client database, pulling out the previous application, populating the renewal form, doublechecking the information to see whether there are any changes (e.g., in address, marital status, number of children), printing out the application, completing and printing out the work permit renewal application (which also has to be updated with changes), copying and enclosing the previous EAD (employment authorization document, aka work permit), giving the applicant a copy of the application form (stamped "COPY"), double-checking the completed forms against the intake form and reviewing everything one more time to make sure there are no mistakes, enclosing the application forms and photocopy of the work permit in an envelope, addressing the envelope, filling out the money order (if available) or including instructions on how to fill out the money order, and enclosing the money order in the envelope as well. Oh, and completing a green "certified mail" form and handing that to the applicant as well.

While completing such tasks, service providers were cognizant that their clients' applications could be viewed as suspect by the officials who reviewed them, so service providers tried to anticipate and counter suspicion. A key focus, as alluded to in the field note excerpt that I just quoted, was ensuring consistency within and across applications. At one appointment, for instance, I observed a service provider who was meeting with a client to prepare a naturalization application. From the code on her green card, the provider realized that this client had previously applied for asylum, so he reviewed her asylum application to ensure that information reported there—such as membership in any groups—would also be included in her naturalization application. These applications needed to be consistent, or, if there were errors in the earlier application, they had to be explained, since officials would have access to both forms. On another occasion, I observed as a paralegal prepared a family visa petition for a man who was petitioning for his wife and her daughters from a previous relationship. In reviewing the daughters' birth certificates, the paralegal asked the man's wife if she realized that there was a ten-month delay between the date of birth of one of her daughters and the day that the birth was registered. The paralegal related that such delays sometimes lead US immigration officials to request more documentation of the relationship. She therefore asked if they could submit additional evidence, such as school records showing that her daughter lived with her, or her baptismal certificate. The couple agreed to locate the baptismal record. Documentation countered suspicion, as service providers employed their knowledge on how rights work in practice.

The mundane yet critically important nature of technocratic expertise was evident as service providers assisted illegalized residents in completing immigration forms. Experienced providers knew which questions on application forms were most likely to generate errors. For example, at a training on how to complete TPS renewal applications, the presenter warned participants that on the I-821 (TPS) form, the applicant had to list the date when they entered the United States for the *first* time, but that the I-765 (Employment Authorization Application) form asks for the date of *last* entry. These may be different dates, he noted, if the client had left the country after they entered for the first time. The presenter also advised trainees that the most common reasons that TPS renewals were rejected included sending the wrong application fee, failing to sign the money order, submitting an unsigned form, and forgetting to check the box for "renewal." We were also warned not to leave questions blank; instead, we were to write "not applicable" or "N/A"; otherwise, forms could be returned as incomplete.[12] Questions about social security numbers were especially tricky, as it is common for illegalized residents to use false social security numbers to work, a practice that could lead to accusations of fraud (Horton 2015). Providers noted that it was possible to simply write, "No valid number issued," and thus avoid unnecessary disclosures. Providers also had developed strategies for calculating the length of clients' absences from the country, as required in the naturalization application. As previously discussed, I observed one form preparation appointment in which an individual's passport was missing a reentry stamp, something that could potentially lead an official to conclude that he was outside of the country longer than he claimed. The service provider asked him if he had traveled with anyone else, and when he said that his wife had accompanied him, she suggested bringing in his wife's passport to obtain the missing travel date. Providers also prepared forms in ways that were designed to withstand the rushed conditions in which officials reviewed applications. One provider told me that he always set the font on bold so that the information that was entered would stand out from the form itself, making it easily visible.

Providers' expertise in forms was matched by their knowledge of evidentiary requirements. Providers' approach to documenting cases was shaped by their awareness that officials could respond with an "RFE"—a "Request for Evidence," thus further delaying case outcomes. After observing an appointment where the forms and supporting documentation for a family visa petition were prepared, I asked the service provider how she had decided how much evidence to submit. She explained that she provides more documentation for any matter that is potentially ambiguous, such as when the petitioner's income level is only slightly above the minimum required. The nonprofit's policy, she added, was to ask clients for three years of tax records or check stubs, even though that exceeded minimum requirements. Over multiple appointments, I was able to see how service providers assessed documents' evidentiary value, selecting from the multitude of papers that clients brought to appointments and requesting additional evidence when needed. Official documents from companies or government agencies were preferred over letters from friends or coworkers, but the latter were useful for documenting character, hardship, and that a marriage was genuine rather than fraudulent. To prove presence, applicants needed records with their name, address, and date, for every 3–4 months over the period being documented. Relationships were documented through official certificates (such as marriage, birth, or adoption), but in the case of suspect relationships (e.g., marriages, children born out of wedlock), nonprofit clients were asked to provide cards or letters that family members had exchanged, photos of the wedding and of shared activities, and documents that had both individuals' names (such as shared bank accounts or rental agreements). State scrutiny of people's private relationships could be experienced as invasive and dehumanizing (León 2020). Even pregnancy was a form of documentation, as having a child together was seen as evidence of a marriage's validity (Abrams 2007). Documentation was carefully reviewed by providers before it was submitted. My field notes recorded my conversation with one service provider about how he assessed bank statements:

> After she [the client] left, I asked the DACA clerk whether the content of the bank statements mattered for the purpose of the application. What was important about them? Simply the date and the person's name? Or did the activity on the account matter? He explained that there needed to be account activity in order to show that the individual in question was present. It also mattered whether the bank account was in one person's name or multiple people's names. If the DACA requester was not the only person listed on the bank account, then it would be difficult to show that the activity on the account was the requestor's. He also pointed out that if there were any questionable transactions, such as a purchase of marijuana (an example that he noted one of the attorneys who was no longer with the organization used to give; hypothetically, I assume, given that most people probably do not pay for marijuana out of their bank account)[13] then that could be a problem. He mentioned as well that once, someone provided a copy of their enrollments or transcripts from an after school program to support their DACA claim, and that this documentation also had a comment that the person was suspected of being in a gang, so it could not be used after all.

As this field note excerpt demonstrates, providers assessed documents not only for their evidentiary value but also to determine whether they would reveal harmful information that clients were not required to disclose.

An example of how technocratic expertise played out over the course of a single appointment is provided by a paralegal's meeting with Sandra, a US citizen, originally from El Salvador, who looked to be in her fifties and who was petitioning for her daughter. According to my field notes (which have been edited for clarity):

The appointment began when [the paralegal] asked Sandra, "Did you bring the documents that I asked for?" Sandra said that she had. She took out a large manila envelope and began pulling out birth certificates, marriage certificates, and divorce certificates. . . . Her daughter, [for whom] she was petitioning, was married, plus she had other children, plus there was her own birth certificate. Soon, [the paralegal's] desk was covered with birth certificates. He asked for her naturalization certificate, and she took out what looked like a leather-bound certificate holder, opened it, and carefully removed the naturalization document. I wondered whether she was proudest of this document and therefore had purchased this cover or whether that is something they gave out to everyone at her naturalization ceremony.

This process went on for quite some time. The paralegal would ask for a particular document, and she would search through multiple manila envelopes as well as through the large purse that she carried. "This purse is my filing cabinet," she joked. At one point, she had to go to her car to look for a document that he requested.

As he collected these documents, the paralegal put them in an order that was only apparent to him. Then he began to review them with her. He announced that even though they always include the petitioner's birth certificate in a family visa petition, despite the fact that it is not required, he was not going to do so in this case. The reason was that her second surname on the birth certificate did not appear on any of her other documents. Including the birth certificate could introduce discrepancies that would then have to be explained somehow.

As the paralegal began to prepare the case, he did a skeletal translation of the documents, then and there. But, in further examining these documents, he noticed a delay between Sandra's daughter's birth in the 1970s and the date that the birth was registered in the early 1990s. He indicated that from Immigration's point of view, such a delay could suggest fraud, so they might request additional proof of her relationship with her daughter. Sandra reacted with surprise. "Then what should we do?" she asked. "There isn't anything that we can do," he responded. "We will have to see if that is how they react." Sandra explained that it was because the municipal building burned down during the Salvadoran civil war. Everyone had to replace their birth certificates.

The paralegal turned to me and said that Sandra's daughter's entire birth certificate would have to be translated word-for-word, due to this delay in registration and asked whether I could do this translation. I had my laptop with me, so I said I would be happy to do so, and I asked whether it would be good to document the reason that they had to replace the birth certificate. I googled the name of her town and "incendio" [fire] but didn't find anything. I tried other terms, like "bombardeo" [bombing] and "destrucción" [destruction] also without success, but then the paralegal found the text of a law that was referred to in the birth certificate.[14] He printed it out as well.

While they continued filling out forms and preparing the case, I translated the birth certificate, proofread the translation, added the "translator's certificate" and then emailed it to the paralegal. He printed it so that I could sign the translation. I then asked about the text of the law. He said that this needed to be translated as well. "The whole thing?" I asked. "The whole thing," he confirmed. So I started on that, and got through about a page and a half before I had to go pick up my children from daycare. I found the law itself fascinating. It was approved in 1992, and was intended to address the problem of Salvadorans having emigrated, including to other countries, due to the violence, and then returning and needing birth certificates and other documents. It was also intended to allow for the recreation of birth certificates that were destroyed during the civil war.[15]

This extended example demonstrates the multifaceted nature of technocratic expertise. Sandra brought many documents to this appointment, so many that she left some in her car rather than carrying them in her purse, which she compared to a filing cabinet. The paralegal appraised these for their evidentiary value, selecting those that would support her case. To do so, he drew on his knowledge of how officials would potentially read these documents, noting that the inclusion of Sandra's second surname on one document but not others and the delayed registration could be viewed signs of fraud. In identifying these issues, he employed his knowledge of naming practices in El Salvador as well as Salvadoran law regarding the replacement of records destroyed during the civil war. He also knew that US immigration officials would want a full rather than skeletal translation of the certificate with the delayed registration date, and a full translation of the relevant law. The paralegal practiced legal craft in a way that was designed to address uncertainty, noting that "We will have to see if that is how they [officials] react." However, though the paralegal said that there was nothing that he could do, in fact, he went to great lengths to proactively defend against accusations of fraud. On other occasions, I witnessed providers searching the California vehicle code to identify the violation that appeared in clients' records, explaining how school transcripts worked to DACA applicants, suggesting ways that clients who had not submitted taxes could work with the IRS to do so, and locating housing resources for a client with housing insecurity. Thus, while their technocratic expertise focused on immigration law, providers often developed at least rudimentary knowledge of myriad other systems that impacted their clients.

Technocratic expertise informed the last step in document preparation, namely assembling an application packet. It seemed to me that there was an art to this final step. The form and supporting documentation had a neat appearance and the order in which documents were placed constructed an implicit evidentiary narrative.[16] For example, while assisting an attorney who worked on U-visa cases, I was asked to review a set of files to put documents in the following order, as I noted on a Post-it:

G-28 (Notice of Entry of Appearance as Attorney or Accredited Representative)

Passport

Order of removal, if any

I-918 (Petition for U Nonimmigrant status)

I-912 (Request for fee waiver)

Birth certificates of children, if any

Letters re abuse & therapy

Diplomas and awards

918 Supplement B (U Nonimmigrant Status Certification)

Police report

Restraining order, court docs, if any

G-28s (for children, if they are part of case)

I-918 (for children)

Supplement A's for children (Petition for Qualifying Family Member of U-1
Recipient)

With this ordering, the file puts forward the following sort of narrative, as I summarized in my field notes: "This person is being represented by So-and-so, an attorney. Here is proof of who the person is and the person's prior immigration history. The person is now applying for a U-visa and is requesting a fee waiver. The person has these kids, and suffered substantial harm to the degree that the person needed therapy. The person is a good person—has gone to classes and won awards. The person collaborated with the police as shown by this certification. The crime that the person suffered is documented in this police report, and led to particular legal actions. The children also are included in the case and are seeking status as dependents of a U-visa applicant." In assembling a packet, a service provider also had to be attentive to practicalities, such as using a bracket to keep documents together, ensuring that the applicant's name and A# were on the back of photos in case they became separated, and highlighting important information so that it would not be missed. Providers, I noticed, much preferred to submit applications through the mail rather than online (which was starting to become an option), as printing out a hard copy gave them another chance to review the packet prior to submission. As applications were submitted, service providers hoped that their legal craft had been sufficient to sway officials to approve their clients' cases.

CONCLUSION

Legal craft is honed in the climate of securitization and humanitarianism that characterizes immigration law. To "see like an advocate," providers mediate between the state, which views applicants skeptically, as potential security risks who may be submitting fraudulent materials (Barbero 2019), and clients, who articulate their own understandings of deservingness. Suspicion and uncertainty create heightened evidentiary standards, making forms and supporting documentation enormously important. Yet, while providers discern clients' immigration histories and possible paths forward by relying on preexisting records and clients' verbal accounts, there are still gaps. Providers fill in these gaps by drawing on their own expertise in law and immigration bureaucracy. This coupling of records and expertise enables service providers to make sense of clients' records, weigh their options, and assemble application packets. To develop their legal craft, service providers act as para-ethnographers, deciphering officials' practices and ways of thinking. Unlike adversarial legal proceedings, where opponents confront each other in court, much of the legal work that I observed took place at some distance from officials, as service providers submitted applications by mail or online. Through webinars, conference calls, administrative guidance documents, and the RFEs that officials submitted in response to applications, providers could identify patterns in the ways that officials processed applications. Likewise, as they interacted with clients, service providers learned about their lives and legal knowledge. Providers learned the terminology through which clients discussed their immigration histories, the details that they were likely to remember, and the ways that clients' life circumstances, such as working in low-income jobs and speaking English as a second language, may have shaped their capacity to pursue immigration remedies.

Legal craft sought to activate papers' power to transform people. Recall that in bureaucracies, papereality—the representation of reality in documents—can take precedence over the people and events that are represented (Dery 1998). The archival advocacy practiced by service providers is a way to harness the power of papereality in order to make applications so compelling that officials will confer residency, citizenship, or temporary status, such as DACA or a U-visa, on nonprofit clients. Legal craft seeks to take charge of bureaucratic inscription, writing illegalized residents into bureaucracies in ways that will benefit them. Therefore, although completing forms and assembling documentation packets is mundane and tedious, these processes also perform the kind of transformational work that Patricia Williams (1987, 430) refers to as alchemy: "the making of something out of nothing." Instead of being defined by "nothing," as people who are *undocu*mented, *un*authorized, an *absent* presence, *non*existing, illegalized residents become "something," such as DACA recipients, U-visa holders, Lawful Permanent Residents, citizens. Documenting back to the state is a powerful process, one that not only can transform individuals but also, cumulatively, can potentially alter the terms through which legal concepts such as hardship, presence, and good moral character are understood. Sometimes, legal craft involves a sort of time warp as when NACARA eligible individuals are able to apply for residency under the rules that were in effect in 1997, when NACARA was passed, or when people qualify for 245(i) because someone petitioned for them years earlier. But time travel can move forward as well as backward, in that the goal of most applications for legal status is to bring about a future reality in which immigration status ceases to be a barrier to life opportunities. In most instances, such changes occur only on an individual level, leaving the broader system of immigration law and policy intact. Yet advocacy is an expression of hope, one that, to again quote Patricia Williams (1987, 430), strives to "breathe life into a form whose shape had already been forged by society." The nature of this form is the subject of the next chapter.

4

Otro mundo es posible
(Another World Is Possible)

In fall of 2014, I had the opportunity to travel to Artesia, New Mexico, with nonprofit staff to join a group of volunteers supporting women and children who had been detained crossing the US-Mexico border. I went as a volunteer rather than a researcher. There had been a so-called "surge" in the number of Central American children who were migrating to the United States,[1] and to house them, the US government had opened what it called "family residential centers"—basically, detention facilities—in remote locations where few legal services were available.[2] In response, advocacy groups organized volunteers who would travel to these centers for one or more weeks at a time to provide legal counseling and representation. I was invited to accompany several nonprofit volunteers from Los Angeles for one week, even though I was not an attorney. After returning, I wrote a short personal reflection:

[The trip to] Artesia was great, though intense . . . . There were about fifteen people in the volunteer group that I was part of, and two of us were not attorneys—the rest were. We got to the detention center early each morning and spent all day meeting with detained women, who were there with their children. There was a single trailer dedicated to legal assistance, so that is where we had to stay, except for going to the restrooms or walking to the "court" trailer or to an asylum interview (which I didn't do—only the attorneys went to Credible Fear Interviews).[3] All of the women and kids we met with seemed to be sick, due to being confined, and some of the kids had stopped eating due to depression. The meeting space was divided into cubicles, a general room (where kids were playing and the TV was on) with tables and chairs, and a partitioned area which was the only space where we could use cell phones for personal calls. So not too much privacy during conversations. Of course, there was also an ICE official overseeing this trailer. Some of the detained women spoke indigenous languages, in which case it was hard to assist them (unless they also spoke Spanish). I was able to help out with initial intakes, CFI [Credible Fear Interview] prep, and bond hearing prep, and I also attended a morning court session to take notes for the attorneys, so I was able to see what video court is like. Every evening, the legal volunteers met, plus after that meeting, we spent time writing and upload-ing notes, scanning and printing documents, updating files, etc. So very long days.

While we were meeting with the detained women and their children, Disney movies were playing in the background—particularly, the movie "Frozen," but in Spanish. Several of us noted the irony of hearing the song, "Let it go," in that particu-lar setting. The kids were also given coloring sheets and crayons to entertain them-selves. I noticed that they seemed to be really good at coloring within the lines—probably they have had a lot of practice. I don't know what else they get to do while they are there.[4] Some of them had also gotten good at folding the coloring sheets into paper airplanes or origami of some kind. One of the volunteer attorneys that I traveled with was given a flower made out of folded coloring sheets. The kids were all ages, from a baby crawling on the floor to teenagers, but mostly, they seemed to be pretty young (like between 3 and ten years old).

In what kind of world are people who are fleeing violence and poverty kept in isolated detention facilities where, were it not for legal volunteers, they would have little chance of being informed about or exercising their legal rights? How did it come about that children—including babies—are detained as though they pose a security risk? How is it that legal proceedings where detainees' credibility is assessed take place in a video court trailer? How did the provision of crayons, col-oring paper, and Disney movies come to constitute humanitarian care in a context where people are ill, depressed, and at risk of being deported? Why does detainees' ability to seek asylum depend on first passing a "credible fear interview" carried out under these adverse conditions? How did a detention facility come to be called a "Family Residential Center"?

The answers to these questions lie within the securitization-humanitarianism nexus that generates application forms with pages of security-related questions, makes deferred action the only possible remedy for undocumented youth who grew up in the United States, and leads presidential candidates to promise to send troops to the US-Mexico border. The legal rights of those who are undocu-mented are limited by their legal status, which positions them as foreigners (and potentially a threat) and gives federal authorities discretion to decide whether they can stay in the United States. As has been discussed earlier in this book, legal grounds to remain in the United States are quite limited. Illegalized residents have to prove that they have a well-founded fear of persecution, qualify for a fam-ily petition, or are eligible for relief through narrowly tailored programs, such as U-visas. They have no right to a court-appointed attorney; illegally obtained evi-dence can be employed against them; they may be detained until their hearing;

and those apprehended near the border must first pass a credible fear interview, such as those that took place at the Artesia facility. Illegalized residents' efforts to assert their rights take place in a context shaped by public fantasies of immigrants as a monstrous other (Sati 2020).[5] For illegalized residents, law becomes another obstacle in the series of travails they have faced journeying to the United States. Excessively high evidentiary standards, the three- and ten-year bars on reentry, the scarcity of high-quality low-cost legal services and other factors[6] often prevent the limited formal rights that are afforded to illegalized residents from being recognized in practice. Notions such as "administrative grace" suggest that the US government sees any relief awarded to illegalized residents as generous. Relief, however temporary or precarious, depicts the United States as a caring nation, even as restrictive measures such as Family Residential Centers are touted as humanitarian.

Scholar-activists who have participated in the immigrant rights movement have argued that because immigration law provides scant relief and is often deployed *against* illegalized residents, it is better for justice struggles to focus on broader social change than a specific piece of legislation (Abrego and Negrón-Gonzales 2020). For example, Martinez et al. (2020, 9) argue for policy reforms that advance "*collective* freedom," not only for immigrant youth, but also for their families and for all who experience racism, exploitative labor practices, police brutality, homophobia, and other forms of repression.[7] In their analysis, US citizenship alone is unlikely to deliver liberation, given that many US citizens are disadvantaged due to their race, gender, sexual orientation, or other sources of marginalization. These scholar-activists contend that crossing borders without authorization should be viewed not as "illegal," but rather as a "courageous, dignified decision to cross borders to care for one's family" (Martinez et al. 2020, 33). Likewise, these scholars insist that immigrant residents should have the agency to define their own futures, and they reject narratives of deservingness that exclude some members of their communities. For example, scholars who contributed to the edited volume *We Are Not Dreamers* reject the narratives that suggest "being undocumented is a monolithic experience" and that define those who deviate from mainstream norms as undeserving (Abrego and Negrón-Gonzales 2020, 16.) Relatedly, Alvarado, Estrada, and Hernández (2017) critique the criminalization of immigrant communities and delineate ways that the US policies fueled migration from Central America. Yet, instead of entirely discarding rights, these scholar-activists seek to broaden them, drawing connections between the immigrant rights movement and the struggle for Black liberation (Martinez et al. 2020) and fighting for "the day that undocumented immigrants' dignity, humanity, and rights are recognized, regardless of their immigration status" (Valdivia 2020, 143).

These scholar-activists' theorization of rights as predefined in ways that limit their utility and are therefore in need of expansion speaks to socio-legal debates over the utility of law as a means of pursuing justice. During the 1970s, critical legal scholars, whose aspirations to achieve social justice through the courts had repeatedly been thwarted, argued that the notion that law was politically neutral was a myth (Kairys 1998). They suggested instead that legal outcomes are shaped by power relationships, and that because many interpretations of the law exist in the legal record, judges can find legal rationalizations for desired outcomes. Furthermore, feminist scholars have argued, law reflects the experiences of the relatively elite white men who wrote most law and decided most legal cases (Levit and Verchick 2016).[8] Such approaches suggest that "rights" can only deliver limited benefits, and do not enact transformational visions of justice.[9] Yet, some critical race theorists have argued that rights are important both substantively and symbolically, and that instead of rejecting rights as a focus of activism, it is better to force law to deliver the justice that it promises. For example, Patricia Williams (1987, 424) insists on rights' importance, writing that "rights are to law what conscious commitments are to the psyche. This country's worst historical moments have not been attributable to rights-*assertion*, but to a failure of rights-*commitment*. From this perspective, the problem with rights discourse is not that the discourse is itself constricting, but that it exists in a constricted referential universe." Critical race scholars have denounced racism as one such constriction. For example, Devon Carbado and Cheryl Harris (2011) note that, according to the US Supreme Court, "appearance of Mexican ancestry" is a permissible legal ground for suspecting people of being undocumented.[10] Therefore, the right to freedom from unwarranted search or seizure in immigration enforcement is not extended to those who appear Mexican. Relatedly, Miriam Ticktin points out that recognizing rights promotes democratic inclusion in ways that humanitarian exceptions do not. She observes that the "logic of exceptionalism creates and privileges non-rights-bearing, apolitical, nonagentive victims The goal of a more radical political project, therefore, requires that we think about how to bring the borderline situations—these victims, dealt with as exceptional—into a democratic political community and, ultimately, how to have a system in which borderlines do not exist" (2005, 350).

There are at least two ways that illegalized residents' and nonprofit service providers' actions and discourse speak to the arguments put forward by undocumented scholar-activists and to sociolegal debates over the utility of rights. First, residents and their allies insist that legal rights are key to justice, even as they also seek to redefine rights such that immigrant residents and their similarly situated peers gain legal recognition. In their view, rights matter procedurally in that residents should be treated with care and respect, and substantively in that defining rights in ways that eliminate differences based on citizenship status repositions immigrant residents as community members rather than outsiders. This position is akin to that of Patricia Williams, who advocated for "an expanded frame of right-reference" (1987, 426) contending that "rights-assertion has been limited by delimiting certain others as 'extrinsic' to rights-entitlement" (1987, 424).

Second, by treating nonprofit clients with respect and empathy, service providers *prefigure* ways that the state could recognize rights. The notion that social change can come about through prefigurative politics—that is, by acting in ways that bring future worlds into being—is an alternative to the more instrumentalist understandings of how activism secures rights (Coutin 1993). According to instrumentalist notions, movement actions are tools to bring about *future* change, not forms of change in and of themselves (Jenkins 1983). In contrast, those who practice prefigurative politics act in accordance with the values they seek to affirm, and in so doing, create change in the here and now and for the future. They may adopt consensual decision-making practices, adhere to community agreements, repurpose public streets, and build multiracial communities. Though prefigurative practices generally do not focus on law or the state as a policy target, Cohen and Morgan (2023, 1054) have suggested that some social movement participants "use legally inflected tools and forms to enact in the present, and anticipate for the future, their own desired understandings of legality—understandings that exceed what is officially available to them now." Cohen and Morgan use the term "'prefigurative legality' to describe efforts to use the language, form, and legitimacy of law to imagine law otherwise" (2023, 1054). When nonprofit service providers treat illegalized residents with respect, empathize with their concerns, inform them about legal rights and opportunities, and advocate for their social visions to become realities, service providers and their clients are prefiguring a legal order in which law would be a source of support rather than an obstacle to be overcome. In so doing, they put forward a theory of documentation according to which the residue of residents' daily lives—the check stubs and letters that Sonya saved, Manuel's drawer of receipts—makes them socially visible in ways that, in their view, powerfully counteract illegalization. Recall Laura's observation, quoted in chapter 2, that "papers speak."

This chapter explores the world that could be brought into being by expanding the frame of rights reference in accordance with these strategies. To do so, the chapter analyzes the vision of justice put forward by illegalized residents and their allies, how legal craft gives life to legal rights, and what state practices might look like if the worlds that residents and allies imagine came into being.

ENVISIONING SOCIAL JUSTICE

In January 2015, my research assistant Gray Abarca met with Isabel, a thirty-eight-year-old woman from Mexico, in a Los Angeles park, where Isabel's young son and daughter played while Gray recorded an interview. Gray had met Isabel at one of the nonprofit's DAPA information sessions. At the time of the interview, DAPA had not yet been enjoined and Isabel was planning to apply, though she had some concerns about the fact that she had been apprehended when she first entered the United States. She nonetheless hoped to qualify, so that she could live in the

United States without fear of deportation and could work without being turned away due to lacking papers. Gray asked her what she would like to communicate to US immigration officials if she had the opportunity to do so. This was her reply:

> Well, that they try to—I know that everyone, as I see it, well everyone sees what will benefit them and fights for their ideals—that is, the good as well as the bad. And it is valid for everyone to struggle for what they believe in. But also that they should give an opportunity, well, to benefit the country and to benefit other people, because the fact that one is an immigrant does not mean that one is bad, and sometimes, due to certain people or certain situations that happen with immigrants, they judge every-one and they close the doors to those of us who want to get ahead, who want to strive, who want something good for ourselves and for our family. So, that they don't judge [us] only because some people cannot accomplish what they think [they should], and for them, everyone pays, that they be a bit more open, and that they consider our situation because many times, we do not come here just because we want to. When one goes through—I at least I crossed the border and Immigration caught me several times, and it was something that was very difficult. But my desire to struggle, and my desire to get ahead and to change my life made me go on and withstand humilia-tion, withstand being detained, withstand that the [border] patrol captured me, and nights in the desert walking, but it is that we come with these desires, and sometimes we forget, because believe me, motivation doesn't last, and it is difficult, it is difficult, because on top of that, they close many doors to us. So it is like they are putting us down, but also one has to prepare oneself, one has to demonstrate to the country and to these persons and one can and that one has the desire to belong to this country. But in the best way.

In this passage, Isabel shares several components of what she imagines as a more just world. In the world that she describes, officials would not judge all immigrants based on the actions of a few; immigrant residents would be able to contribute to society; officials would be understanding of the fact that if people endure hard-ships to immigrate, then it is because of their strong desire to change their lives. In this world, doors would be open instead of closed and immigrant residents would be supported rather than further harmed. Isabel felt that it was important for immigrant residents to counter pathologizing narratives by demonstrating their capabilities and desires, and, in fact, she seemed to see the interview as an opportunity to do so. She concluded by thanking us for doing the study, saying that we would be able to provide everyone with information about the type of circumstances that immigrant residents experienced.

Nonprofit clients' visions of a more just world can be gleaned from both explicit statements, such as Isabel's comments about what Immigration officials should know, and their denunciations of the injustices that they had experienced. As Alonso Bejarano and colleagues (2019, 12) argue, theory is produced not only in academic circles but also by those "who are deeply engaged in resisting injustice and fostering reform and who are struggling to make sense of their experience."

The Introduction to this book presented Aimee Cox's notion that narratives produced by people who are deemed a social problem are "inherently political," even when speakers do not explicitly delineate their politics. Cox contends that such narratives "shapeshift" existing institutions. She explains, *"Shapeshifting* most often means shifting the terms through which educational, training, and social service institutions attempt to shape young Black women into manageable and respectable members of society whose social citizenship is always questionable and never guaranteed, even as these same institutions ostensibly encourage social belonging" (Cox 2015, 7;). Likewise, scholar-activists who have been at the forefront on the immigrant rights movement have challenged the "DREAMer" narrative of high-achieving, Americanized immigrant youth to instead "assess how these claims of 'deservingness' exclude the people that are supposed to benefit from such a movement" (Monico 2020, 105; Pavey and Saavedra 2016). Similarly, Isabel's discussion of what she would like to tell US Immigration officials shapeshifts government institutions, arguing that currently these agencies judge people unfairly, limit opportunities, cause harm, and prevent social inclusion. Like Isabel, many interviewees adopted a collective tone, speaking as "we" and "us," and even described the accounts that they shared during interviews as a "testimonio" or "testimony," a mode of speaking in which one person's account stands in for a collective group. Reyes and Curry Rodriguez (2012, 525) describe *testimonio* as follows:

> A first person oral or written account, drawing on experiential, self-conscious, narrative practice to articulate an urgent voicing of something to which one bears witness. Presented at times as memoirs, oral histories, qualitative vignettes, prose, song lyrics, or spoken word, the *testimonio* has the unique characteristic of being a political and *conscienticized* reflection that is often spoken. . . . The objective of the *testimonio* is to bring to light a wrong, a point of view, or an urgent call for action.

By speaking collectively about personal experiences, interview participants brought to light immigration-related injustices, while prefiguring the alternative worlds that they sought to bring about.

Interviewees' visions of a more just world were *transnational* in that these visions contemplated changes within their countries of origin. Most fundamentally, interviewees with close relatives who remained outside of the United States hoped that their families would be safe there. Juana Maria, whose account in chapter 2 of hiding her name in her clothing in case she died while en route to the United States, told us of her prayer for the safety of her children in El Salvador: "Give me patience, Lord. Take care of my children. I beg you, Lord, that nothing will happen to my children where I have left them." Likewise, Magdalena who had immigrated to the United States from El Salvador, described the horrors of the Salvadoran civil war. She recalled hiding under her bed while the soldiers were at her house, and that she repeatedly heard neighbors crying out, "Don't take me! Not my son! Don't take him!" Gang and police activity continued to be a concern for interviewees with relatives outside of the United States. On a more mundane level, interviewees wished that it were easier for them to obtain documents from their countries of origin, and to correct errors. During a focus group interview, Gloria, whose journey to the United States was described in chapter 2, shared a story about how difficult it was for her to obtain her birth certificate from El Salvador in order to get advanced parole to visit her ill father. She had given the original to US immigration authorities as part of her pending NACARA case, and she could not easily obtain another copy, as the registry book where her birth was recorded had disappeared. Listening to Gloria's story, Patricia, another focus group participant, commented, "Sometimes one's own country makes things difficult." Daniela, whose practice of saving documents was described in chapter 2, was from Mexico and needed Mexican identity documents in order to open a bank account in the US, since she did not have US identity documents. But she could not get them. She explained, "I had to call the Mexican consulate and go to the Mexican consulate, but I couldn't get it because my family members lived far away from any city. We lived on a *rancho* so it was very far away for my family members; they cannot get my [birth] certificate. And it was very, very frustrating to me, because the consulate made it difficult. *Exegían ellos mucho, pues.* [They required a lot.] My birth certificate, my passport." In the end, Daniela and her husband opened a bank account in the name of their daughter, who was born in the United States.

Interviewees' visions of a more just world also emphasized the *ability to be with family members*. In fact, interview participants often view legal opportunities through a *collective* rather than individual lens (see also Martinez et al. 2020; Abrego and Negrón Gonzalez 2020). For example, Adriana, who immigrated to the United States from El Salvador and gained lawful permanent residency through a spousal petition, was considering naturalizing in order to petition for her siblings. Likewise, Nelson, a Lawful Permanent Resident, sought to naturalize to help his wife (who had TPS) obtain residency more quickly, as she urgently wanted to travel to her country of origin but was afraid to do so on advance parole. Nonprofit clients also sought to reunite with geographically distant family members, whether through acquiring the ability to travel internationally so that they could visit relatives in their countries of origin, or through petitioning for relatives to immigrate to the United States legally and rejoin them there. Recall Arnulfo's great frustration, discussed at length in chapter 2, over being separated from his wife and children from the 1980s to 2003, when he obtained residency through NACARA, and then for years while he waited for family petitions to become current. Arnulfo described the suffering that his family endured due to this lengthy separation that, in his view, served no purpose:

> It was very difficult for both of us [Arnulfo and his wife] because I have been here for many years. Sometimes I would go [to El Salvador to visit] every two years. There

was a period when eight years went by without me being able to see her. Only letters and phone calls, very difficult for both of us. My son grew up and he met me when he was already big. Because one of the times that I visited, she became pregnant with him, and another time, the last two [children]. And always working hard to support my family and to live this life that, for me, is not normal, but due to love for my children, I have worked for them to be able to study.

In this passage, Arnulfo highlights the abnormality of a life characterized by the emotional deprivation of family separation. Indeed, one of interviewees' key criticisms of DAPA was that it did not recognize that people who did not have children who were US citizens or Lawful Permanent Residents also had a need for family unity.

In the alternative world that nonprofit clients envisioned, *opportunities to regularize one's status* would be plentiful and affordable, with transparent processes, reasonable requirements, and outcomes that were both swift and predictable. Recall Arnulfo's great frustration, discussed in chapter 2, over the fact that his son, who was a beneficiary of a family visa petition that Arnulfo had filed, was forced to remain in El Salvador for a psychological evaluation. Arnulfo commented further:

> I think they [Immigration officials] would have to be a little more conscious. . . . Because they ask for some requirements that one cannot fulfill. Because for that information that they ask for, a letter of support [the sponsorship letter that accompanies family petitions when the petitioner's income is below the qualifying threshold], not every person wants to give all that information; they want to help one but the information that is requested is very sensitive. Now with the time that we are living [through], there is general distrust. It is very difficult to find a document or someone who can help one. . . . They should not ask for so many exaggerated things where it is very impossible.

Arnulfo's contention that US immigration law established requirements that were impossible to meet, particularly in a context in which immigrant residents did not trust the US government, was echoed by other participants. Juana Maria noted that immigration-related fees were too costly and that it was difficult to meet evidentiary requirements, Ramona struggled to find affordable legal assistance before the nonprofit took her case, and, regarding her efforts to get a tourist visa to travel to the US, Adriana commented, "$125 they charge you to go to ask for a visa.[11] That is not so they give it to you. There, in the United States Embassy in El Salvador. It's only so that they give you all of the information, so that they tell you, 'You do not qualify.'" She added that if she had the opportunity to speak to Immigration officials, she would tell them that "They aren't clear. They aren't clear. And they are asking for too much, too much information, and they are taking advantage [by] charging people too much." For Nelson, a central complaint was the slow pace of immigration transactions. He commented, "Well, sometimes the process is delayed not because they can't do it, but rather it could also be that they have very few employees. And I think that it would be one of the principal bases, to have adequate personnel to move the millions and millions of petitions that Immigration has."

Interview participants uniformly *rejected illegalization*, stressing their own law-abidingness and socially positive activities. On the one hand, such comments suggest that it is legitimate for the government to exclude those with criminal convictions. For example, Estéban, who immigrated to the United States on a tourist visa, said that US immigration officials should "give opportunity to the people who deserve them. Who have not violated the laws here, of the United States. Like crimes, significant violations of the law." On the other hand, some interviewees criticized US immigration law's categorical approach to convictions. Emilia, who had a minor shoplifting conviction that had prevented her from applying for status, said that those with convictions deserved "a second chance or even a third one. There are those who have so many years here." Furthermore, some theorized, subsequent good behavior can overcome the stain of an arrest or conviction. In one provisional waiver consultation that I observed, Jose Miguel, a Guatemalan man in his thirties, told the service provider that he had been convicted of a crime, deported, and prohibited from reentering the United States for ten years. After serving time in prison and spending ten years outside of the country, Jose Miguel had reentered, married a US citizen, and gotten a job. From his point of view, he had done what was required: "Cumplí todo," he said, "I did everything." To Jose Miguel, documenting his family ties, work history, and compliance with immigration and criminal penalties ought to confer status, an understanding that prefigured a more just future in which convictions would not be treated as a permanent stain on someone's records.

Interview participants' rejection of illegalization also *disputed the characterization of their own entries into the United States as illegal or criminal*, a perspective that resonates with immigrant activists' assertion that they were "unapologetic" about having immigrated to the United States (Abrego and Negrón-Gonzalez 2020; Martinez et al. 2020). Interviewees insisted that hard work and educational or familial achievements conferred deservingness. For instance, Manuel, whose workplace injury had led to unemployment, said that he would like to tell US immigration officials, "that the majority—perhaps not everyone, but the majority of us come to work and it is not true that we are taking jobs from Americans, because unfortunately, they are not accustomed to work in the harvest, or in sewing, or in parking." Such comments played into respectability politics by depicting those who weren't working as undeserving (and suggested that farm work, the garment industry, and service sector positions are "immigrant" jobs), but these comments also push back against illegalization. As Martinez et al. acknowledge, "Our struggle for liberation is fraught with ambiguity and contradictions as we live and work within the very system that we criticize and seek to transform" (2020: 23; see also Sati 2020). To push back, residents claimed to be what scholars have called a Super Citizen, that is, "the idealized figure of the naturalized citizen who, in the eyes of local state representatives, personifies a combined potential to become a political, economic, and cultural asset to the nation-state, and should develop her/ his own aspirations accordingly" (Badenhoop 2017, 411). Interviewees were speaking back to the state in what they understood to be its own language.

As interviewees denounced illegalization, they also envisioned *exiting the in-between* status that they had held. As one Lawful Permanent Resident who was hoping to naturalize commented, "[We are] half way up the tree; we are in the middle of the street. We cannot vote for our president or for whomever is going to be in charge." Recall that some interviewees described living in a "cage of gold," in which they could access jobs that paid more than in their countries of origin, but they were trapped in the United States. For interviewees, leaving this cage would mean living without fear, being able reunite with family members, voting, and no longer being vulnerable to notarios who swindled them out of money and legal opportunities. When asked what it would mean for her to obtain residency, Sonya replied, "For me, it would mean happiness! Yes, because with residency, I would be able to go about more freely." Similarly, Adriana described how she felt upon becoming a resident, "One is no longer with the fear that always, they are always keeping records on one, that one does not have papers." Interviewees dreamed of things that many (but not all) residents who are not illegalized may take for granted, such as the ability to travel, access health insurance, go to college, and grow professionally. Arnulfo, for example, described his joy at becoming a resident and being able to travel by plane, instead of making difficult journeys by land: "Go fly, now you can fly! And the first thing to do is to fly to my house, to see those who I love most in my life: my children, my wife, my mother. It had been so long! It was beautiful what I felt, because I had felt like a prisoner, because I could not leave."

In sum, interview participants imagined that in an alternative world, they would be *treated with respect and dignity rather than suspicion*. Some imagined that with status they would be able to achieve the American dream, whereas others were more critical of the "opportunities" the United States had provided. Arnulfo, who lived in a trailer, commented that he had left El Salvador due to poverty, adding ironically, "And look where I am today!" Arnulfo's wife, who was also present during the interview, was more optimistic, saying that "where one door closes, another one opens," but Arnulfo replied, "That saying doesn't really apply to our situation." Arnulfo's comments draw attention to the tremendous toll of living in the United States for decades without legal status or with only precarious status. Indeed, participants noted ways that the US government created the very conditions that make people ineligible for status. Dora, for example, pointed out that those who used public assistance for their US-born children were then condemned for taking benefits, but also they were denied work authorization, which made it impossible to support their families without applying for assistance. Dora commented, "It is frustrating because they require things of you on the one hand,

and they don't help you on the other. So you remain as though in a cage of gold, one could say, stuck." One way that interview participants tried to leave this cage was by applying for status.

GIVING LIFE TO LEGAL FORM

The legal craft practiced by service providers sought to make illegalized residents' visions a reality, thus *prefiguring an alternative legal world that would not treat undocumented people as a national emergency* (García Cruz 2020). Nonprofit staff tried to help clients obtain required documentation from their countries of origin, enable family members to be together, expand legalization opportunities, counter illegalization, support claims of deservingness, and treat clients with respect. In so doing, they practiced the form of legal alchemy that, as noted in earlier chapters, Patricia Williams (1987, 430) referred to as striving to "breathe life into a form whose shape had already been forged by society." The complex advocacy practiced by service providers indicates what law could become in an alternative world in which policy would focus on care rather than suspicion, support rather than securitization.[12] In this alternative world, rights to presence, status, refuge, relationships, and indeed to law itself, would come to life, rather than being unfulfilled promises.

Service providers' abilities to prefigure alternative legal orders were shaped by their complex positionalities. Many were of immigrant backgrounds themselves, giving them familiarity with their clients' life circumstances, and many empathized politically with their clients' visions for justice. Nonprofit staff sought to provide a low-cost, reliable legal service to large numbers of immigrants and in ways that were legally responsible and that also informed clients of their rights. Nonprofit staff distinguished themselves from private attorneys who charged more, from notarios who were unethical, and from some other nonprofits that did not have their level of legal expertise. At the same time, to provide effective legal service, advocates had to view cases from the point of view of the state as well as from clients' points of view. As intermediaries, service providers had to ask questions that were on immigration forms or request additional evidence that officials might want. From clients' perspectives, service providers were not only allies and advocates but also gatekeepers. For their work to be efficient, service providers needed clients to comply with their own procedures, which could be part of the administrative burden experienced by those seeking services (see e.g., Robinson et al. 2023). Nonprofit clients often had to attend a charla, be screened, stand in line, and then wait to be seen. There were also delays, as attorneys stopped to answer interns' questions or to review their work, and clients often had to obtain additional records before their paperwork could be finalized. While I focus here on how client services prefigured alternative legality, it is important to note that the nonprofit was also involved in broader legal and social justice campaigns, such as a pathway to citizenship for TPS holders, expanding eligibility for provisional waivers, passing the DREAM Act, achieving comprehensive immigration reform, raising wages for immigrant workers, and supporting day laborers.

A key facet of service providers' prefigurative legality was *demonstrating empathy* in ways that addressed the psychological costs of applying for legal status. Immigration law contends with deeply emotional and potentially traumatizing circumstances, as Véronique Fortin, who at the time was my research assistant, reflected in her field notes: "Law is much more embedded in sentiments than one would think, although the law needs to preserve this image of disconnection with passions . . . This emotional side of the law, for me, goes beyond the politics of the law (as meant by the critical legal scholars, for example). The law is fraught with emotions, but love and sentiments are taboo for the law."[13] Yet, despite this taboo, service providers responded to clients with compassion and support. For example, as a client who was petitioning for her sibling told a long story about her financial challenges and lack of experience with technology, the paralegal who was assisting her nodded sympathetically instead of interrupting to focus on the case. Similarly, in another appointment, I observed a nonprofit client tell a service provider the backstory for each of his criminal convictions, even though she only needed to know what they were. After her client left, I pointed this out to the provider, and she responded that she felt that it was appropriate to let people tell their stories. On more than one occasion, I saw providers waiting patiently while clients made phone calls to get additional information for their cases, or checked in with employers to determine their availability for future appointments.

Such patience and support were critical to overcoming system avoidance. For clients, the nonprofit was a safe space but also potentially frightening, as it was where they confronted the possibility and impossibility of gaining status. I was reminded of the degree to which nonprofit clients elicited such emotions when I observed Rogelia's appointment to prepare a naturalization application, and we had an opportunity to chat while her attorney stepped out to make photocopies. I later noted the following in my field notes:

> Rogelia commented to me that it was very cold. I was surprised because when I had been outside earlier, it had been hot. "It is nerves," Rogelia remarked. She touched my arm. "Feel how cold I am." Indeed, her hand was quite cold. I wasn't sure why she was so nervous about this appointment, but I guess a lot was at stake. She thought that this was the appointment at which her naturalization paperwork would be submitted. So I imagine that if she had been told that she was ineligible, she would have been very disappointed.

Service providers tried to reassure clients in the face of such anxiety. For example, one provider told me of a U-visa recipient who called regularly to ask what papers she should keep in anticipation of her application for residency in a few years. The provider had told her many times to keep everything with her name and address on it, yet it seemed that she was still insecure. The provider told me that she was especially patient with this client.

To maintain their empathetic relationship with clients, service providers attempted to distance themselves from the state. For example, when posing uncomfortable security-related questions, they often apologized in advance, or stated that the questions were necessary. One intern told her client, "I need to ask you some questions to make sure that there will not be any problems in your application," thus mitigating the questions' offensiveness. Likewise, when a nonprofit client who was hoping to naturalize told a paralegal that he had paid child support, stating, "I've always been there for my kid, always," the paralegal relayed that he would most likely need proof of what he had done, as the official would probably want to see it. This statement displaced the need for proof onto the official rather than the paralegal. To speak with clients using terms with which they were familiar, service providers learned how to translate between their clients' terminology and more formal legal categories. For example, at one training, attorneys instructed clerks how to answer a question about their clients' manner of entering the United States. The attorneys stated that when clients say that they entered "por el cero" (through the hills) then that meant, "Entry without Inspection," or EWI. If they said that they entered with a "visa," then that would be a B-2 tourist visa. If they entered with "el permiso" (the permit), then that is an I-94 visa that only covers a particular entry. And if they said, "por la línea" (through the line), then that meant that they were "inspected and admitted."

Two key areas in which providers had to translate between clients' understandings and those of the state were kinship and securitization. As was discussed in chapter 1, one of the few ways that illegalized residents can regularize their status is through a relationship to a Lawful Permanent Resident or US citizen spouse, parent, or child, so numerous conversations between providers and their clients focused on kinship. A common perspective on the part of nonprofit clients was that only relatives who were in the United States, or only marriages that were formed in the United States counted for immigration purposes. Such perspectives reflect the importance of borders in illegalized residents' lives, and the ways that they thought officials would view their relationships. Service providers frequently had to inform their clients that when completing immigration forms, they needed to list *all* of their children, regardless of where they lived, and that marriages that took place outside of the United States were considered valid in this country. Clients were sometimes concerned that aspects of their personal histories were legal liabilities. Immigrant residents who had work permits and social security numbers but who were unemployed sometimes feared that US officials would consider them lazy and deny their cases. For instance, a DACA recipient who was applying for a renewal expressed concern that she was not using her social security number.[14] In response, a DACA clerk assured her that this was not an issue. Another nonprofit client feared that she would be disqualified for DACA due to her poor health, a factor that the service provider insisted would not be taken into account. Such concerns reflect long-standing public stereotypes of immigrants as people who commit crimes, use public benefits, and bring diseases into the country (Chavez 2013).[15] Yet, even while they questioned their own eligibility based on these stigmatizing discourses, nonprofit clients also seemed to think that remedies were more accessible than was actually the case. For example, nonprofit clients sometimes thought that a provisional waiver could pardon them for a conviction, that spending money on an attorney would enable them to gain status even if they appeared to be ineligible for remedies, and that the amount of time that they had lived in the United States would qualify them for status. In correcting these misconceptions, attorneys and paralegals sought to help clients avoid deportation.

Service providers also prefigured alternative legalities by attempting to *equip illegalized residents with tools and knowledge* that could improve their chances of acquiring status, whether immediately or in the long run. I observed that numerous consultations and document preparation appointments had an educational component in which the service provider explained technicalities of immigration law and procedure. For example, Gladys, a previous TPS recipient, had allowed her TPS to lapse. She hoped to either qualify for a family visa through her mother, who was about to become a US citizen, or to get a new work permit. The service provider explained that for the visa, Gladys would face a ten-year bar on reentry as she was not 245(i) eligible, and that once one loses TPS there is no way to get it again, by reapplying. Furthermore, he pointed out, a work permit is a secondary benefit that results from the primary benefit of having TPS. If TPS is lost, then one cannot just apply for a work permit. There is no such thing, he said, as just renewing the work permit itself, unrelated to the primary status. Service providers also took the time to inform their clients about what to expect during interviews with officials, how long procedures might take, what questions they might be asked, next steps in their cases, and so forth, attempting to demystify legal processes. For instance, I observed one appointment at which the provider asked his client whether she had a valid social security number. After she replied that she had used someone else's number, the provider told her, "I would like to give you some advice. If you go to an interview with Immigration and they ask you whether you have a valid social security number, you should just say 'No.' Otherwise you are giving them more information than you need to answer the question, and that could cause other problems for you." Significantly, this provider did not tell his client to misrepresent information, which would have been unethical, but rather only to be circumspect about revealing information unnecessarily.

As advocates, legal staff at the nonprofit sought to *reduce the administrative burden* of document preparation. They regularly provided detailed information to their clients regarding how to take key steps in their cases, such as how to get fingerprints or where to seek police reports. Generally, the nonprofit charged a flat rate for its services, so the agency did not receive additional payment for providing such a high level of services. Furthermore, legal staff sometimes took actions on behalf of clients even when they considered the odds of success to be low. For example, when staff were approached by a parent whose son had become ineligible for a family petition because the US consulate had scheduled his appointment after he "aged out" by turning twenty-one, they decided to advocate for this family with the consulate. Service providers sometimes provided socio-emotional or educational support, though of course they did not attempt to act like counselors. I observed one appointment in which a provider was meeting with a U-visa recipient and her son, both of whom were adjusting their status. As evidence of her son's presence in the United States, the U-visa recipient had brought copies of his school records, which unfortunately showed that he had low grades. Though the grades did not affect this young man's case, the legal worker spent a few moments discussing how to consult with a school counselor at school, find out whether the teachers were paying attention to her son, and advocate on behalf of his right to get a good education. On another occasion, I was present when an attorney met with a DACA client who was twenty-two years old and had not completed high school. When the attorney asked her about the GED, she commented that she was stupid and could not pass certain subject areas. The attorney immediately shifted to providing educational support, informing her that the nonprofit could help her find a location to retake the GED exams. She then shared her dream of becoming a nurse, telling us, "I want my parents to be proud of me. I want them to see me walking across the stage with my cap and gown to get my nursing certificate." This sort of support and encouragement was consistent with the nonprofit's advocacy goals.

By prefiguring an alternative legal order in which official law would be interpreted in an empathetic fashion, legal processes and outcomes would be transparent, and administrative burdens would be reduced, nonprofit staff sought to give life to legal form, making noncitizens' rights under US and international law "real" (De Graaw 2016). Their legal work was informed by their clients' visions of an alternative world in which families would be together, and residents who were born outside of the United States would be recognized members of society and be treated with dignity rather than suspicion. As mediators between the state and illegalized residents, service providers offered a glimpse of what the state could become in an alternative, more just world. What would it be like if such an alternative world became reality?

JUSTICE AND ACCOUNTABILITY

Illegalized residents' visions for a more just future and the ways that service provision at the nonprofit prefigured an alternative legality suggest ways that the securitization/ humanitarianism nexus that is currently at the heart of US immigration law and policy could be replaced with a focus on justice and accountability.[16] Such a focus would analyze inequities with an eye toward future remedies for immigrant residents. Immigration scholars have argued that US involvement in creating the conditions that lead people to immigrate makes the United States accountable to immigrant residents.[17] For example, after detailing US intervention in Guatemala, El Salvador, and Honduras, Willman (2017, 49) pleads, "We must address the thousands of people seeking safety within the United States. This requires that the United States accept the immigration consequences resulting from its policies." The United States is also complicit in the harm that illegalized residents suffer while traveling to the United States. The legal scholar Lori A. Nessel (2022, 1571) points out that "refugee law is premised on the notion of a binary relationship between the home country (who has breached its obligation to protect its own citizen) and the host country (who may now be obligated to offer surrogate protection). Increasingly, however, multiple nations play a role in creating danger for refugees." Furthermore, if living and working in the United States *is* a form of membership—what some have called "jus domicili" (Bauböck 2003; Bauder 2016; Kaufmann 2019)—then it does not make sense to view illegalized residents as suspicious "aliens" or outsiders, as is the case within a securitization/humanitarianism framework. Finally, to the degree that the plenary power doctrine makes US immigration law, in a sense, "extralegal," then it could be argued that the charge of criminality applies more to the US government than to illegalized residents. Recall Marco Saavedra's poem, quoted in the Introduction, which asks, "What if the illegal is you?" (Saavedra, in Martinez et al. 2020, 78). Saavedra and colleagues elaborate, "The problem (and indictment) of the undocumented illegal immigrant is a metaphor for the country. If I was never illegal, then that cornerstone on which lay the foundation for our way of life is folly. If I was never illegal, then, perhaps the economy, the international politics, multinational corporations and their unmatched revenues were never legal" (Martinez et al. 2020, 78).

Making justice and accountability, rather than security and humanitarianism, the goals of US immigration law would refocus policy on *care*, which can be defined as "a relational set of discourses and practices between people, environments, and objects. . . . Theorized as an affective connective tissue between an inner self and an outer world, care constitutes a feeling with, rather than a feeling for, others. When mobilized, it offers visceral, material, and emotional heft to acts of preservation that span a breadth of localities: selves, communities, and social worlds" (Hobart and Kneese 2020, 2). Likewise, scholar-activists writing from a positionality of undocumentation have emphasized the importance of care: "Maybe the process itself can be our end, being and becoming a beloved community" (Martinez et al. 2020, 81). While "care" and "humanitarianism" might seem synonymous, they have distinct features.[18] Unlike humanitarianism, which distinguishes those who are deserving of assistance from those who are not (Cabot 2019), care is grounded in mutuality and interdependence (Cohen et al. 2022). Furthermore, care includes immigrant residents within the group that should experience security, whereas humanitarian approaches often distinguish those who deserve care from those who are considered security risks. The American Academy of Pediatrics provides an example of including immigrant residents in the group that deserves care. In 2019, it issued a policy statement, asserting that "the United Nations Convention on the Rights of the Child, endorsed by the American Academy of Pediatrics (AAP) but not ratified by the US government, is an internationally recognized legal framework for the protection of children's basic rights, regardless of the reasons children migrate" (Linton and Green 2019, 3). Providing such protection would mean rejecting or reforming policies that harm residents.[19] Indeed, within a care framework, the focus on interdependence redefines immigrant residents, citizens, and government actors as part of a single community. In such an approach, distinctions based on legal status would disappear or be minimized, as "caring like a community" would replace "seeing like a state."[20]

While it may seem far-fetched to imagine the US government approaching immigrant residents—especially new arrivals—as members of a shared community that is deserving of care, the reality is that the US government *is* capable of demonstrating care, as shown by its relationship with more elite sectors of society. For example, scholars have argued that alongside formal social benefits programs such as Aid to Families with Dependent Children (AFDC) (US Department of Health and Human Services n.d.), there exists a "hidden welfare state" (Howard 1997) that delivers financial benefits to middle and upper income citizens through tax breaks for things like medical expenses, college tuition, Individual Retirement Accounts (IRAs), and interest on mortgages (Howard 1993; Faricy 2011). Tax breaks, scholars argue, are indirect forms of government spending in that the government is losing income that it otherwise could obtain through taxation. Moreover, taxpayers qualify for deductions more or less automatically, when they submit their tax returns. According to Faricy (2011, 8), "these programs are on 'autopilot' since any taxpayer who qualifies can claim them and there is no annual review process." In contrast to programs that run on autopilot, another researcher noted, in welfare programs that are designed for the disadvantaged, "recipients are treated relatively poorly. Eligibility criteria and benefit levels vary considerably from state to state, and administrative hurdles are often high. Receipt of welfare is stigmatizing and at times dehumanizing" (Howard 1993, 418). The government demonstrates care for wealthy people by enabling them to easily obtain financial benefits without having to demonstrate that they are "deserving" to a caseworker who has the discretion to approve or deny their petition. Furthermore, unlike welfare programs, which have been heavily racialized through public condemnation of recipients as "welfare queens" (Gilman 2014), hidden or indirect spending programs are neither stigmatizing nor associated rhetorically with race or ethnicity (Callaghan and Olson 2017). The ease of accessing hidden welfare and the lack of stigma are likely due to the fact that "the vast majority of tax expenditure programs accrue more money to the wealthiest and most financially secure citizens while offering nothing to the poorest" (Faricy 2011, 82; Faricy 2015). Indirect social spending is one way that the US government demonstrates care for its wealthiest residents.

What would immigration law and policy look like if the US government cared for immigrant residents in this fashion instead of viewing them as undeserving outsiders who posed security risks? In such an alternative world, asylum seekers would be admitted to the United States and provided with food, shelter, medical care, and assistance rejoining family members.[21] Regularization opportunities would be widespread and relatively automatic, much as the tax breaks described above run on "autopilot."[22] With legal status, immigrant residents would be able to travel internationally and visit family members in their countries of origin. To counter family separation, visas for close relatives would be available without backlogs, permitting relatives to travel legally.[23] Convictions would not automatically make people ineligible for status—rather, residents with strong ties to the United States would be able to remain in the country, just as citizens who are convicted of crimes do (Hing 2007). Evidentiary burdens would be lessened so that documentation requirements are reasonable, and applicants for status would be given the opportunity to explain discrepancies in their records.[24] Work authorization would be widely available to immigrant residents, as it is currently for citizens. Deportations would decline and detention facilities could be closed or repurposed.[25] To address the root causes of out-migration, US foreign policies would be evaluated for their potential to displace people from their home communities. Efforts to fortify US borders could be replaced by opportunities for cultural exchange. Protection, appreciation, and support could become the hallmark of US government relationships with immigrant residents. This alternative world would in many ways be consistent with undocumented and immigrant scholar-activists' vision of justice, a vision that connects multiple social struggles:

> Another system of social relations is possible. Freedom, while a long road, is possible . . . . Legal struggles for rights are not the only recipe for overcoming structured inequality. Rather, we should be fighting to restructure the classist and racist structures of our economy, government, and institutions to protect human dignity and freedom. (Martinez et al. 2020, 38)

Clearly, current immigration policies are far from these visions of an alternative possible world. As I write, legislation to provide military aid to Ukraine is being coupled with increased border enforcement and restrictions on asylum seeking. Proposed changes to immigration policy include ending a humanitarian program that gives temporary status to nationals from Ukraine, Nicaragua, Cuba, Venezuela, Afghanistan, and Haiti; increased use of ankle bracelets for people (including children) who are awaiting court hearings; closing down the border if particular levels of unauthorized crossings are reached; and raising the bar that entrants must meet during credible fear interviews (PBS News Hour 2023). Addressing foreign wars and border enforcement in the same bill defines immigration as an urgent risk to US security, even though the people who are entering the United States without authorization are not part of an organized force that poses some sort of military threat. Furthermore, temporary programs such as DACA are stalled due to court action and may be halted altogether (National Immigration Law Center 2024). Meanwhile, Texas has characterized immigration as part of "transnational criminal activity" and has been busing new arrivals to other parts of the United States (Office of the Texas Governor 2023). Using language evocative of extermination campaigns, President Donald Trump, while running for reelection, stated that immigration is "poisoning the blood of our country" (Kurtzleben 2023). If anything, the security component of the securitization-humanitarianism nexus is intensifying, making any grants of status appear all the more undeserved. Visions of other possible worlds are more necessary than ever.

CONCLUSION

Despite the securitization/humanitarianism nexus that shapes their lives and work, nonprofit clients and service providers were able to envision and work toward an alternative world in which law would be a source of support rather than a barrier. In contrast to the rights-deficient environment of the family residential facility that I visited in Artesia, New Mexico, and the indignities associated with illegalization, nonprofit clients imagined a reality in which legalization opportunities would be more plentiful, distinctions based on legal status would fade, travel and family reunification would become possible, work authorization would be available, a criminal conviction would not be fatal to the ability to remain in the United States legally, and officials would treat residents with respect and care regardless of their mode of entry. Service providers prefigured such a world through their interactions with clients. As intermediaries between the state and illegalized residents, service providers' actions took on something of an official character—that is, service providers used legal terms, crafted application materials that addressed legal criteria, and assessed their clients' eligibility for immigration remedies. While doing so, providers delivered services in ways that took their clients' social realities into account. They listened empathetically, explained immigration law in everyday terms, spoke to Spanish-speaking clients in Spanish, kept their clients updated on the status of their cases, provided support in obtaining difficult-to-access documentation, and were nonjudgmental regarding clients' immigration and criminal records, if any. Within the context of the nonprofit's legal services, it was therefore possible to glimpse ways that the state itself could act in relation to immigrant residents. It would be possible for the US government to hold itself accountable for the role that the United States has played in immigrant residents' countries of origin. To do so, the United States could provide justice and care for those who were displaced by authoritarian regimes that it supported, by trade policies that favored US-based multinational corporations, or by illicit economies fueled by US consumption of drugs. One way to provide care would be to extend regularization opportunities to all, and to do so relatively automatically, replacing restrictive definitions of deservingness with what Isabel, who was quoted earlier, described as being "more open . . . because many times, we do not come here just because we want to."

Although it is extremely unlikely that this alternative world will be realized in the near future, the vision itself matters. Holding out other possibilities helps to denaturalize current realities, demonstrating the callousness of detaining children or holding immigration hearings by video in a trailer. Envisioning alternative possibilities helps to "breathe life into" rights, and to view immigrant residents as encompassed by rather than "'extrinsic to rights-entitlement,'" to again paraphrase Patricia Williams (1987, 424). Breathing life into rights not only redefines immigrant residents, but also shapeshifts government institutions, revealing how they currently produce undocumentation and that they could act differently. Such shapeshifting would be an important step toward the liberatory and abolitionist vision articulated by undocumented and immigrant scholar-activists who have sought to link struggles on behalf of immigrant residents with movements for Black lives, LGBTQ rights, and other social justice issues. Such scholar-activists have sought to make the United States "a place where citizenship does not dictate self-value" (García Cruz 2020, 125), and to create an opportunity "to restructure the classist and racist structures of our economy, government, and institutions to protect human dignity and freedom" (Martinez et al. 2020, 38). The voices and actions of illegalized residents, service providers, and others who have experienced undocumented realities are key to such alchemical transformations.

Conclusion

Documenting Back

In September 2023, I was invited to Amherst College to participate in a symposium at which scholars in religious studies, history, and ethnic studies compared the US sanctuary movement of the 1980s, in which congregations declared themselves "sanctuaries" for Salvadoran and Guatemalan refugees, to current sanctuary activities on the part of cities, states, and institutions in resistance to the punitive immigration policies that deport some four hundred thousand illegalized residents annually.[1] To my surprise, they were fascinated by my 1986–1988 dissertation research about sanctuary communities in Tucson, Arizona, and the San Francisco East Bay (Coutin 1993), research that I now rarely get to discuss. My own publications had become "history." As I drafted my contribution to the symposium, I revisited the materials I collected while working on my dissertation. There, I found a dusty, well-worn bound collection by Jim Corbett (1986) entitled *Borders and Crossings* (see Figure 5). At the bottom of the cover, the word "*WARNING*" appeared, underlined and in all-caps, accompanied by the statement, "The U.S. Attorney General may consider the acquisition of these papers to constitute participation in a criminal conspiracy." Although I am not aware of anyone being indicted simply for having a copy of *Borders and Crossings* in their possession, the fact is that Jim Corbett and ten other sanctuary workers stood trial on conspiracy and alien-smuggling charges in 1985–1986. Eight of the codefendants were convicted. My own copy of this collection was dated April, 1986, one month before the verdicts were delivered. Jim Corbett, a founder of the movement, who had openly assisted Central Americans in entering the United States to escape persecution, was among the acquitted, as a key piece of evidence—a photograph of him helping "Juana," a Central American refugee, cross a border fence—was deemed

117

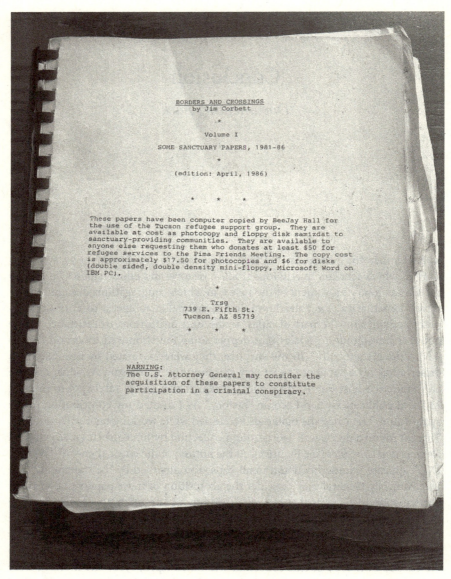

FIGURE 5. Susan Coutin's copy of the April 1986 edition of *Borders and Crossings*, obtained in 1986 or 1987 through contacts with sanctuary movement participants. Photo by author. Permission to include this image granted by Pat Corbett.

inadmissible.[2] Opening *Borders and Crossings*, I found my own handwritten notes and passages that I had highlighted, including this quote from a July 6, 1981, document that is part of the collection: "There's no way for us to take our own stand with the refugees while retaining the privileges and immunities the war machine provides us. The choice between the Kingdom of Love and the Kingdom of Money is radical; we can't serve both" (Corbett 1986, 8).

Flipping through the bound pages which are supplemented by photocopies of later writings that I inserted as they became available, I find a February 2, 1986, letter from Jim Corbett to Ruth Anne Myers, District Director of the Immigration and Naturalization Service. The letter informs Ms. Myers that Tucson sanctuary communities were assisting seven individuals (whose names were deleted from the published version of the letter) in seeking legal counsel in order to apply for asylum in Canada. Moreover, Corbett asserts in this letter, such assistance should be considered legal:

> During recent months, new ways have opened to accommodate our sanctuary services to INS administrative practice. One of these openings . . . has been the 5th Circuit Court's June 18 ruling that "by definition, a person intending to assist an alien in obtaining legal status is not acting 'in furtherance of' the alien's illegal presence in this country." (1986, 194)

Clearly, this letter was an attempt on the part of sanctuary workers to "document back" to the state by citing its own decisions and precedents. In so doing, they hoped to establish that it was lawful to provide sanctuary to illegalized refugees.[3] Indeed, in language that strikes me as defiant, given the six-month trial to which Corbett was subjected as well as the conviction of his colleagues, Corbett (1986, 193) writes this:

> We do feel that a sequence of trials will themselves result in our establishing the full legality of our sanctuary services. If the INS would like to test specific issues by initiating further jury trials, we might be able to volunteer the documentation and defendants you want, so please don't hesitate to let us know what you need for any projected future indictments. We do believe that we should be ready to put our practice of sanctuary before trial juries as often as may be necessary.

The future trials that Corbett imagined in this passage did not take place. Instead, sanctuary communities sued the US government, accusing it of discrimination against Salvadoran and Guatemalan asylum seekers, and contending that sanctuary activities were protected by the first amendment. Due to changes in the criminal laws under which sanctuary activists had been prosecuted, the lawsuit's claims regarding sanctuary's legality were dismissed, however, litigation on claims that asylum policies were administered in a discriminatory fashion moved forward (Blum 1991). In 1991, the case, known as *American Baptist Churches v. Thornburgh* or "ABC" for short, was settled out of court (USCIS 2009). The US government agreed to allow ABC class members to apply for asylum under special rules designed to ensure fair consideration of their cases, while class members who had previously filed for asylum were eligible for a de novo hearing. Moreover, as the ABC case was being litigated, Congress passed the 1990 Immigration Act, which created the new legal status called "Temporary Protected Status" or TPS, awarded to Salvadorans for eighteen months, due to violence in their homeland (Diamond 1992). In 1997, the Nicaraguan Adjustment and Central American Relief Act (NACARA) created pathways through which these Salvadoran TPS recipients and ABC class members could seek status based on the lives that they had built in the United States and the hardship that a deportation would impose. As of August 2018, just over twenty years after NACARA passed, 211,515 NACARA applications had been filed with the US asylum unit, with 184,665 grants, an approval rate of 89.1 percent (USCIS 2018a). Clearly, sanctuary workers' and Central Americans' efforts to document back to the state bore fruit.

Many of the moments that I describe in this book are a legacy of these earlier struggles. For example, TPS, which grew out of sanctuary activism, was a precedent for the DACA program that the Obama administration initiated in 2012 (Congressional Research Service 2018)—and that provoked the stress dream that I described in chapter 3. Before DACA launched, service providers asked US officials how to prepare when no application form was available, and they were told to use the TPS application form as a model. In fact, the form to apply for TPS is "I-821" and the form to apply for DACA is "I-821D," so these two forms follow the same numbering system. Some of the organizations that provide legal services to immigrant communities today—including the nonprofit with which I was collaborating—supported Central American asylum seekers during the 1980s. The imagination and determination that led Jim Corbett and colleagues to write to US officials insisting on the legality of sanctuary and on Central Americans' need for asylum can also be seen in the letters of support written by relatives and coworkers of those seeking status today. Interviewing someone to develop an asylum declaration, which I did as a volunteer with the 1980s' sanctuary movement, is not unlike preparing a U-visa application, which I have described here. In both cases, applicants must recount painful experiences while structuring their narrative around legal criteria. Central American asylum seekers, sanctuary activists, immigrant residents, and service providers have all struggled against restrictionist policies in which political considerations and immigration laws have become fused. The asymmetries in knowledge, power, and resources that led Central American refugees and solidarity workers to challenge US authorities in the 1980s by creating sanctuaries are also faced by illegalized residents today. And just as Jim Corbett and colleagues collected the writings that make up *Borders and Crossings* out of faith in the power of documentation, so too do illegalized residents collect drawers and boxes of receipts, check stubs, and other records in hope of being able to apply for status, and so too do service providers complete forms and assemble supporting documentation as a form of advocacy. And, then as now, the interdependency between the US state and illegalized residents, coupled with the need to legitimize draconian policies by demonstrating "administrative grace," makes the state vulnerable to the moral force of illegalized residents' documentation practices (Abarca and Coutin 2018). Indeed, according to legal scholar Patty Blum, one reason that the US government opted to settle the *American Baptist Churches v. Thornburgh* case was the onerous and potentially embarrassing discovery process to which the state was being subjected.[4] Papers have force.

One way to understand *On the Record*, and the ethnographic research on which it is based, is as a means of documenting back. By writing this book, I hope to intervene in the securitization-humanitarianism nexus, not by proving that illegalized residents are in fact "deserving," but rather by rejecting the notion that the ability to work, study, be with one's family members, vote, travel, feel at ease, and pursue the myriad activities of daily life should be conditioned on deservingness or legal status. Ethnography requires keeping records, such as the *Borders and Crossings* volume that I kept from my dissertation research, but also field notes, interview transcripts, and miscellaneous documents, thoughts, and observations, forged at specific historical moments, in conversation with interlocutors, colleagues, students, and one's own potential future self who will turn back to these records at a moment of writing (Strathern 1999). If one is conducting research from a position of solidarity and allyship, then ethnographic records reflect this position, and are a form of witnessing constructed through accompaniment and advocacy. Martinez et al. write, "Approaching ethnography as a form of witnessing has implications beyond the ways in which ethnographers write. The practice of ethnography is fundamentally transformed when seen through the eyes of a witness" (2020, 24).[5] Such positionality does not mean that records are inaccurate; on the contrary, being positioned alongside and within solidarity movements forces an ethnographer to strive even harder to convey experiences in ways that will "document back" to multiple audiences, including interlocutors themselves, by representing realities in ways that interlocutors recognize. And of course, undocumented and immigrant scholar-activists are themselves documenting back through their scholarship and advocacy work (Abrego and Negrón-Gonzalez 2020; Martinez et al. 2020).

Furthermore, ethnography has the potential to intervene in the historical and social conditions within which research takes place. The legal anthropologist Carol Greenhouse (2011) has pointed out that, as neoliberal policies gutted impoverished communities around the United States and internationally, ethnographers responded, perhaps unconsciously, by producing ethnographies of community. Likewise, as illegalized residents are being repressed in both dramatic and mundane ways (Menjívar and Abrego 2012), ethnography that documents both the repression and the institutional apparatus responsible for it is a means of denaturalizing existing power relationships in favor of alternative possibilities. By "documenting back," perhaps ethnography, however flawed, can serve what Corbett described as "the Kingdom of Love."

BRIGHT LINES AND BLURRED BOUNDARIES

As I draft this concluding chapter, the 2024 presidential election campaign is underway and immigration has once again emerged as a hot button issue. Conservatives accuse the Biden administration of having "open border policies" (Office of the Texas Governor 2024) while advocates and even some USCIS staff complain that although Biden had the opportunity to reform Trump's heavily anti-immigrant policies, little has changed (Reidman 2023). While it has become common in the current political context for the "same" events—elections, pandemics, wars—to be perceived completely differently by political opponents, it is striking that escalating numbers of detentions and deportations, as well as policies that seem designed to deter asylum seekers, are characterized by conservatives as an "open door."[6] One way to understand these competing perceptions is through the bright lines and blurred boundaries created by the securitization-humanitarianism nexus. This nexus distinguishes sharply between US citizens and noncitizens, treating the latter as racialized outsiders who are undeserving and whose very existence within US borders is highly suspicious.[7] As, within this framework, they are deemed potential security risks, noncitizens—especially those who lack legal status—are heavily scrutinized, through fingerprinting, criminal record checks, security-related questions on immigration forms, and a high evidentiary burden. Any grant of status, however temporary or precarious, to such allegedly suspect persons appears at best an act of generosity and, at worst, evidence of an "open door" as rights become phantom-like (Chacón, Coutin, and Lee 2024), blurring the boundaries between "legal" and "illegal" actions on the part of officials. In other words, the bright line that the securitization-humanitarianism nexus draws between citizens and others makes law blurry, as the officials who are charged with enforcing the law take actions that, whether dramatic (physical punishments in detention facilities; see Cho, Cullen, and Long 2020) or mundane (losing someone's EAD renewal application), violate substantive and procedural legal norms.

The plenary power doctrine is at the heart of the securitization-humanitarianism nexus. I have argued that in addition to being a legal doctrine cited in Supreme Court cases, plenary power shapes illegalized residents' daily lives by defining them as "outsiders" over whom the United States as a sovereign nation can exert its political will, rather than as community members to whom the government owes accountability. Furthermore, the category of outsiders is racialized, such that illegalized residents are seen as foreign, nonwhite, and potential threats. Recall Justice Field's language in the Chinese Exclusion Act case, stating that Chinese immigrants exhibited: "differences of race. . . . They remained strangers in the land" (*Chae Chan Ping v. United States*, 595). In contrasting racial "differences" with whiteness, Justice Fields asserts what legal scholar Daniel Morales (2024) describes as "the settler colonial mindset . . . that views US territory as the exclusive and inviolable, God-given birthright of European colonists and their descendants." The plenary power doctrine enables the political branches of government to regulate immigration policy in accordance with foreign and other policy objectives, even as these branches' political will is to be tempered by administrative grace when noncitizen subjects are seen as especially deserving. To be seen as deserving, illegalized residents have to slot themselves into a limited set of narratives, according to which evidence of their years of presence, meritorious behavior, the hardship that a deportation would pose, relationships with US citizens, exceptional circumstances, and law-abiding behavior convinces officials that they qualify for status. Aspects of their lives that do not fit these narratives, such as their close relationship to a grandparent or their positive behavior following a conviction, are not "seen" by the state. Plenary power, which defines noncitizens as outsiders and potential security risks, takes mundane and diffuse forms, compelling illegalized residents to collect documents as potential evidence for a future legal case, subjecting them to scrutiny at checkpoints within US territory, and exacting slow violence as residents live with uncertainty regarding their futures. Asymmetries between the US officials who can exercise discretion and the illegalized residents who are subject to their will make immigration policy both hyper-legal (illegalized residents are aware that they could be apprehended at any time) and extralegal (officials faced fewer legal constraints on their actions than in other areas of law). While other countries that are immigrant destinations have also adopted restrictive policies, the United States' reliance on the plenary power doctrine is exceptional. As immigration law scholar Jennifer Chacón (2023, 13) observes:

When it comes to the regulation of migration, U.S. constitutional law largely remains frozen in the nineteenth century, particularly in its treatment of national sovereignty as absolutely trumping individual rights. This archaic conception of state sovereignty places the United States out of step even with other postcolonial states when it comes to recognizing the rights of migrants. State power over migrants is (at least formally) acknowledged to have some limits in international law, and in many jurisdictions around the world.

Examining the asymmetrical relationship between US authorities and undocumented residents contributes to studies of administrative burdens. First, attending to this relationship demonstrates that administrative burdens are established not only through policy but also through hierarchies of legal subjectivity. The plenary power doctrine defines noncitizens as subjects who have limited constitutional rights but who, on limited grounds, can appeal to authorities' discretion by applying for legal status. There is a high evidentiary burden associated with being positioned legally as both suspect and a supplicant. Second, because US immigration law potentially subjects undocumented residents to removal, immigration relief is a policy *exception* granted begrudgingly, sometimes as a matter of "grace." Study-ing the administrative burden of seeking policy exceptions complements research on the costs of qualifying for programs extended to targeted populations. Third, my analysis of documentation practices identified the strategy of assuming an anticipatory administrative burden by saving paperwork in order to "document back" to the state in the event of a future legalization opportunity. The political implications of this anticipatory administrative burden are mixed. On the one hand, assuming this burden is a sign that learning, psychological, and compli-ance costs can arise even before a person initiates an application, but on the other, documenting back is also a way to resist illegalization.

The administrative burdens of seeking legal status are exacerbated by the fact that, within current immigration law and policy, existing immigration remedies are insufficient when faced with the realities of international movement. Reme-dies that focus on individual deservingness ignore the role of the United States in contributing to the conditions that displace people from their homelands. These conditions include international intervention in political processes and civil con-flict, such as US support for authoritarian regimes during the Salvadoran and Guatemalan civil wars or tacitly supporting a military coup in Honduras (Kino-sian 2017). Likewise, foreign trade agreements have displaced agricultural work-ers from their land, leading them to migrate (Martin 2004), while US demand for drugs has fueled narcotrafficking (Felbab-Brown 2017). Instead of making citizens in Latin American countries more secure, repressive anti-gang policies have contributed to escalations of violence. Given these hardships, the expecta-tion that new arrivals and illegalized residents will have the financial resources, evidentiary record, and community connections to convince the very govern-ment that helped to oust them from their homelands that they meet narrowly tailored grounds of deservingness is unrealistic. Furthermore, as officials treat illegalized residents as a suspect population, the evidentiary bar for a favorable exercise of discretion is high.

For illegalized residents, occupying the subject position of being legally outside but socially and physically inside the United States creates what Barbara Yngves-son and I have elsewhere termed an "impossible reality" (Coutin and Yngvesson 2023), where what cannot be true (that they belong in the United States) and what must be true (that they belong in the United States) intersect. Illegalized residents live a form of "routine exceptionality," in that on an ongoing basis, they are excep-tions to law, subject to authorities' political will. The impossibility of occupying this insider/outsider subject position bleeds into the challenge of documenting a prohibited existence. Their experiences of undocumentation—that is, of being compelled to live without identity documents, give them what Linda Tuhiwai Smith referred to as a "knowing-ness" of the state and of tactics of governance (Smith 2012). This knowing-ness enables them to document back to the state, devising strategies that can potentially change not only their immigration status but also the criteria according to which status is allocated. I have argued that illegalized residents' insistence on living according to their own visions of membership is a form of resistance. Yet, persisting despite prohibitions and defying legal uncertainty by moving forward with life plans takes an emotional and physical toll. Recall Diana's terror that she would be apprehended by immigration authorities; Emelia's description of how stress over her immigration status manifested itself in pain in her feet; and a VAWA applicant's account of how writing a declaration caused her to relive abuse: "Mr. Judge, you do not know how hard, how sad it was to write this letter. I was crying a lot as though it were happening again." Some interview participants used the metaphor of living in a cage of gold to convey the ways that they were trapped by US immigration law and policy.

For nonprofit clients, documentation could potentially compel legal reality to change in accordance with the social reality of their lives. Recall that bureaucracies are characterized by what Dery (1998, 678) calls, "papereality," in which paperwork can "take precedence over the things and events represented." By collecting the records that are the residue of everyday life, working with advocates to assemble the documentation that makes up an immigration case, and applying for status, illegalized residents can strive to use their social existence as insiders to transform their legal nonexistence as outsiders. In other words they can attempt to use processes of bureaucratic inscription to their advantage, to inscribe themselves in the ways that they want. Of course, as noted earlier, legalization opportunities are scarce, so there are many who are not eligible for existing remedies. But archival advocacy—marshalling the power of papers in support of more just outcomes—can be an embodied and emotional experience. Ramona, a focus group participant who had self-petitioned through VAWA, described how she successfully marshalled such evidence:

> One had to have, as they say, "some evidence." Good evidence, that was not false. I had to ask for letters from the neighbors who knew me. I had to go to a domestic violence class and get letters from the counselor. And that was very difficult but not impossible. . . . And I had to pay. Each time that I met with the counselor, I had to pay five dollars. Sometimes I left owing it, but the next time that I went, I had to bring it. And I did that for two years. And when I went to Immigration, I had to bring that letter, that I was attending those classes. And I did it, as though it were a pastime that I had. That's how I felt. I didn't feel that it was a burden, I was doing it like something to do. . . . And when I got it [a residency card], I'm going to tell you and you are going to laugh. I shouted like a crazy person, "I AM A RESIDENT!" And I was at home. "I AM A RESIDENT!" Like a crazy person. That's how I shouted.

In this passage, Ramona narrates her own creativity in treating the counseling sessions that she had to attend as a pastime, rather than a disciplinary process imposed on her by a court, as well as her pride in making regular five dollar payments, despite financial difficulties. What stands out to me in this passage is her joyful exclamation, "I AM A RESIDENT!" She celebrates that she beat the system, overcoming mistreatment from her husband and obtaining residency.

Access to high quality, affordable legal services is critical to illegalized residents' documentation efforts, making the nonprofit's work especially valuable. As I have detailed, service providers operated in a context characterized by high-demand, scarce resources, and an entrenched network of notarios and unscrupulous attorneys who sought to defraud immigrant residents (Shannon 2009). Serving illegalized community members required overcoming both system avoidance, due to community members' distrust of US authorities, and unwarranted system engagement, when notarios or unethical attorneys encouraged people to submit applications when they were not eligible, potentially leading them to be deported. To build trust, service providers had to see like an advocate, understanding the realities of their clients' lives as well as how their cases would likely be viewed by US officials. Providers acted as para-ethnographers, crafting a legal practice that met the needs of the community they served. They also learned how to navigate immigration bureaucracy, diagnosing their clients' cases through the narratives and documentation that they presented, and using their technocratic expertise to complete forms and assemble supporting documents. The suspicion directed at immigrant residents has increased the administrative burden of service providers' work, a burden that grew even further during the Trump administration (Herd et al. 2023; Heinrich 2018).

By deploying documents as a means of seeking status, either by filing a claim or by saving documents for a possible future immigration reform, illegalized residents practiced alchemy, attempting to transform nothing (undocumentation, nonexistence, illegality, lack of rights) into something (legal status, a dignified life, membership, rights-based claims). For the US government, papers were a means of drawing bright lines, in that identity documents could distinguish those with authorization from those who were unauthorized. But, like Smaug's underbelly,[8] the evidentiary requirements that the state imposed on illegalized residents were a source of vulnerability in that they enabled residents to "document back" to the state, attempting to mobilize "administrative grace" in their favor. Moreover, as applicants filed immigration claims, their visions of deservingness and social justice became part of the record. Even though illegalized residents' legal cases were, of necessity, structured around existing legal criteria, other meanings crept in. For instance, I translated one declaration that addressed officials by saying, "You are very important people in my life and in my children's lives," and concluded, "I hope that you will have compassion and understanding, as whether or not I am able to stay in the country depends on you alone." Such statements attempt to position officials as caring persons who can exercise discretion favorably if they so choose, potentially shapeshifting government from seeing like a state to caring like a community. The applications and records gathered by illegalized residents and their allies are a form of counter-documentation of times when politicians' promises to illegalized residents were unfulfilled. But, by striving to activate papers' power, illegalized residents and service providers prefigured alternative worlds, in which membership boundaries would blur, eliminating or reducing distinctions based on status, making promises meaningful. Ethnography, too, can play a role within such alchemical processes.

ETHNOGRAPHY AS A MEANS
OF DOCUMENTING BACK

In September 2014, in my fourth year of conducting volunteer work and observations at the nonprofit, I was finding it more difficult to write about my experiences. In my field notes, I reflected as follows:

> I am taking fewer field notes because my role at [the nonprofit] has increasingly become that of a volunteer. At the same time, I still learn new things every day. It is striking though how routine being there has become. I used to feel a tremendous sense of responsibility any time I myself performed a service involving one of their clients, however now I am simply striving to be of service. Of course I am still conscientious but I think my sense of confidence that I know what I'm doing has increased.

In contrast, my field notes from July 2011, when I was first embarking on this project, describe the décor, procedures that I was seeing for the first time, terminology that I was learning (e.g., I wrote that "people use the term 'a clean case' to describe straightforward cases that shouldn't be controversial for immigration officials"), and my own fumbling efforts to figure out what roles I would take on as a researcher who was committed to supporting the organization through volunteer work. In the classic anthropological sense, throughout my time at the nonprofit, I was both an outsider (a researcher who was there to collect data) and an insider (committed to performing service as a volunteer alongside other volunteers and nonprofit staff). However, the legal context that I was operating in gave these outsider/insider roles additional meanings that are not always part of ethnographic projects. As an outsider, I had to be careful not to record information in a way that violated attorney-client confidentiality or disrupted staff members' work. As an ethnographer, I avoided knowing things like social security numbers, A#'s, or addresses, even though as an insider, I had to record such confidential personal information on immigration forms, while also following the nonprofit's procedures and preparing paperwork to the best of my ability, always under the supervision of an attorney or BIA-accredited representative. I was continually aware that if I made a mistake in filling out a form and if no one caught it, I could be responsible for someone's case being delayed or denied. Like other service providers, I was assisting illegalized residents in documenting back to the state.

The notion that ethnography is a means of critiquing policy directions and suggesting alternatives is not new (Reed-Danahay 2016). George Marcus argued that the notion of anthropologist as a witness and potential activist "emerged in anthropology through the 1990s in the ways that anthropologists think about what they do as still disinterested independent parties in scenes that strongly push them toward flimsier pleas of detachment or disinterestedness based on professional norms or encourage them to abandon these in favor of explicit activist or advocate roles" (Marcus 2005, 36). Marcus cites ethnographic studies of violence, social suffering, and trauma as examples of such work (e.g., Daniel 1996; Kleinman, Das, and Lock 1997; Robben and Suarez-Orozco 2000). Relatedly, as previously noted, Carol Greenhouse has argued that during the 1990s, anthropologists who carried out ethnographic studies the United States strived to be relevant by documenting inequalities in particular communities and calling for social change at a moment when the welfare state, if it ever existed, was being dismantled. She writes, "U.S. community studies are always in some sense 'about' federal power (or its lapses) even when the books are overtly addressed to other concerns" (Greenhouse 2011, 17). Numerous scholars have argued that ethnography is a form of witnessing what Nancy Scheper-Hughes referred to as "the ordinary lives of people often presumed to have no history" (Scheper-Hughes 1995, 419).[9] Such work of documentation potentially takes on political implications, even when hierarchies are so entrenched that researchers find it disingenuous to suggest policy recommendations (Abu El-Haj 2023).

Although the notion that ethnography serves as a form of witnessing is not novel, the practice of "documenting back" through paralegal ethnography presents a new twist. The commitments that I took on as a "paralegal ethnographer" who assisted in performing legal tasks while also shadowing staff and observing appointments have shaped the ethnographic account that I have presented in this book. Most fundamentally, like other service providers, I entered into this project with a normative focus in that I was committed both to supporting individuals' efforts to secure status and to promoting social and legal change that would advance immigrants' rights. The empathy that I felt with clients and service providers spilled over into my field notes. For example, one of my earliest sets of field notes, from July 2011, reflect on an appointment that I observed between a service provider and a nonprofit client I referred to as T-E:

> One version of his life appears in the file. His entry date, his asylum application, the NACARA application, a cancellation application. All very orderly. And behind all of that is the life of the individual—who knows what was going on when he submitted these applications . . . , what was at stake for him personally in the outcome of the case, what his family situation was like, who urged him to apply or not apply, what he thought he was doing, where he worked.

In this passage, I focused both on the written file that would be apparent to US officials and on what they would not see, namely, the personal circumstances that shaped T-E's decisions about applying for status. Empathetically, I was committed to documenting the ways that these circumstances had shaped the legal record. My notes record a brief conversation between the service provider and T-E, whose asylum claim was based on working in a pharmacy during the Salvadoran civil war, and being compelled to give medicine to combatants:

> [The provider] told T-E that according to the margin notes written by the officer who interviewed him about his asylum claim, he had said that he never worked in a pharmacy or sold medicine. T-E said that he had understood the officer to be asking whether he sold drugs, and he said that he had said that he didn't, thinking that the officer was asking him about being a drug dealer. "Did you have an interpreter for the asylum interview?" [the provider] asked. He said that he hadn't.

My commitment to documenting injustices led me to record what struck me as an unfair situation; namely, being held accountable for statements delivered to officials without an interpreter; a matter that the provider, who asked about interpretation, noticed as well.

As a paralegal ethnographer, I gained experiential knowledge of immigration bureaucracy and could view procedures such as completing a form or preparing a declaration from the inside out. I not only asked about and observed procedures— I had to learn how to contend with slow computers, a crowded photocopy machine, the fact that illegalized residents had difficulty remembering their previous addresses, the discomfort of posing accusatory security-related questions, and the secondary trauma of repeatedly hearing about domestic violence and other crimes. Of course, experiential knowledge is precisely what good ethnographers often seek, as they try to immerse themselves in social contexts (Geertz 1973). Yet, as a paralegal ethnographer, my own actions also took on legal significance, First, I signed documents as the interpreter or the preparer. The translations that I and others prepared enabled a document to become part of someone's immigration file, thus making it part of the record. As Véronique Fortin and I have observed, "Translations were links in power-laden bureaucratic chains, potentially conveying applicants' voices, enabling their social worlds to become visible, and inserting documents from their countries of origin into the documentary record" (Coutin and Fortin 2023, 26). Second, completing forms and assembling documentation packets (which I only ever did under supervision of an attorney or BIA-accredited representative) helped individuals to legal status. Third, the field notes and interview transcripts that I generated as an ethnographer document the experiences of service providers and illegalized residents during a historical moment when advances in discretionary opportunities such as provisional waivers and deferred action were overshadowed by increased border enforcement and the continual postponement of comprehensive immigration reform. Fourth, I have produced an ethnographic account that documents legal violence and advocates replacing the securitization-humanitarianism nexus with an ethic of care.

A central component of the experiential knowledge that I gained as a paralegal ethnographer was learning about ways that papers have power. The documents that illegalized residents brought to appointments, the declarations that they prepared, and the forms that service providers and residents completed were never "just paper"; rather, these documents had alchemical potency. They could permanently ban people from the United States; serve as a key piece of evidence, as when the light bill became the *documento clave* in Daniela's daughter's DACA case; or transform an illegalized resident into a Lawful Permanent Resident, as when Jasmine's husband turned out to potentially be NACARA eligible. The work that I did writing field notes and carrying out interviews was not all that different from the tasks I performed as a volunteer when I met with people to fill out forms or write out a declaration. In both cases, I questioned people, took notes, and wrote out their answers. Nor were my own records "just paper." As an ethnographer, I am deeply invested in the value of documentation for research purposes. The records that ethnographers accumulate during research enable the ethnographer to produce the analyses that they eventually publish. As Jean Jackson observed, based on her interviews with anthropologists regarding their field notes, "fieldnotes may be a mediator . . . They are a 'translation' but are still en route from an internal and other-cultural state to a final destination" (Jackson 1990, 14). Field notes recorded what I had observed, translating experiences into written text, while also serving as a vehicle to eventually produce an ethnographic account.

Like an immigration file, this book references and thus assembles other documents, including immigration forms, field notes, interview transcripts, miscellaneous records viewed or collected during research, news articles, policy reports, website text, letters, and academic publications. In a sense, a published ethnography is a collection of papers (though they appear in snippets) and therefore is not unlike the *Borders and Crossings* collection that Jim Corbett assembled. An ethnography contributes to the historical record by documenting a specific context and moment, and, as a "collection" that references other documents, is also an archive of sorts. Much as a birth certificate references an external event—a birth—and constitutes this event as a legal phenomenon, the creation of a new legal person, appearing in a chain of documents (it is given a number and place in a book of birth certificates, and it cites other documents, such as the ID of people who testify regarding the birth) (Pearson 2021; Mitchell and Coutin 2019), so too does an ethnography document social contexts, constitute these contexts as part of a broader ethnographic record, and become part of a chain of documentation.

As a form of advocacy, I hope that my own ethnographic account, much like field notes, is "en route" in that it reflects the realities that I documented even as it gestures toward alternative possibilities. A central goal of this book has been to document the limitations of what the state sees. I have strived to make context, structure, and history visible and thus demonstrate the inequities of current policies. For example, throughout the book, I have referred to those who are seeking status as "immigrant residents" or "illegalized residents" in order to draw attention to the state policies that produce illegality, as well as to the fact that these people actually live in US communities. By doing so, I hope to denaturalize and historicize categories such as "immigrant" as well as the citizen–noncitizen distinctions that undergird US immigration law. The material from interviews details the hardships, such as traveling through difficult terrain, being separated from family members, and living with uncertainty, that are caused by US immigration policy. Instead of arguing that, within current frameworks, illegalized residents are actually deserving, an approach that would reinforce these frameworks, I have detailed participants' own visions of social justice, visions in which opportunities to regularize one's status should be widely available. My observations of the legal craft practiced by service providers highlight the many obstacles, such as the paucity of legal opportunities, high evidentiary requirements, and lack of resources, that make it challenging to seek and obtain status. In essence, much as documentation takes precedence over the things that it represents, I hope that by detailing the broader context that the state does not "see," my own ethnographic account will contribute to formulating policies that are responsive to the circumstances of immigrant residents' lives.

Documenting back through ethnography is collaborative work. Recall that Linda Tuhiwai Smith described "researching back" as a collective act that involved "a recovery of ourselves" (Smith 2012, 8). Similarly, as a paralegal ethnographer, I developed close working relationships with nonprofit staff and other volunteers, and took on roles within the legal services that they performed. While carrying out both volunteer and research activities (which were often one and the same), I was responsible for observing the ethics and policies of the nonprofit. These included treating people with respect, providing support within one's areas of expertise, providing high quality service, advocating in ways that advanced social justice, and deferring to those with greater expertise (namely, attorneys and BIA-accredited representatives). There were occasions when I had to choose between my role as a volunteer and as an observer, such as when I was shadowing a service provider and someone stopped in to ask me to perform a task. Due to my commitment to the organization, I prioritized the need to provide service over the information that I would learn by continuing to shadow the provider. Nonprofit clients who participated in interviews seemed to see the interview as a way to collaborate in efforts to change policy. As I noted in chapter 4, many participants adopted a collective voice, speaking for immigrants or Latinxs as a group, and referring to their accounts as a "testimonio." By talking to me, they were also talking back to scholarship about their communities, particularly to the taken-for-granted nature of nation-state boundaries (Khosravi 2018). Their insistence on the need for transnational justice, opportunities to regularize, family reunification, collective benefits, and dignity have informed my analysis throughout. Lastly, as I discussed in the Introduction, I collaborated with students who joined the project as research assistants, writing their own field notes, conducting some of the interviews, and coauthoring publications (Abarca and Coutin 2018; Coutin and Fortin 2015, 2021, 2023; Coutin, Richland, and Fortin 2014). I am also indebted to the many colleagues with whom I discussed this project. The ethnographic account that I present here reflects these collaborations and conversations.

Interweaving legal and ethnographic craft produced a documentary layering such that the actions that I took as a legal volunteer and as an ethnographer were shaped by commitments to stance-taking and to accuracy. Thus, just as the declarations that I prepared and the forms that I completed had to be truthful, so too did I strive to produce field notes that accurately conveyed my experiences at the nonprofit. Yet, there was a normative element to both field notes and to my work as a volunteer in that in both cases, I was trying to document individuals' lives and the workings of US immigration law, both to aid people in obtaining status (as a volunteer) and to promote more just social policies (as an ethnographer). Indeed, as Véronique Fortin and I have argued, "instead of being a source of bias, advocacy is deeply intertwined with accuracy, as translators bear witness to the facets of immigrants' lives that are recorded in documentation" (Coutin and Fortin, 2023, 35). Furthermore, just as service providers' legal craft prefigured the alternative worlds that providers sought to bring into being, so too did my own work as an ethnographer strive for such a world. During interviews, when people spoke of hardships that they had endured, I expressed empathy, and I did not hesitate to convey my own ethical and political commitments, thus attempting to demonstrate in small ways the care and support that I wished would characterize US policies. For example, during a focus group interview, when Juana María said, "We came [to the United States] illegally [mojados]. I came illegally [mojada]," I immediately responded, "Like the majority [of people,]" thus trying to demonstrate my own awareness that entering the United States "mojada," as Juana María put it, was normal and understandable. Likewise, when Arnulfo told me that he had fled El Salvador during the civil war to avoid being kidnapped or killed, but that he could not qualify for asylum because he had no proof that he was in danger, I commented sympathetically, "Many people suffered without having documentation of a direct threat, but they fled anyway." My hope is that cumulatively, the work that illegalized residents, service providers, activists, academics, and allies perform to document policy failures and opportunities will move law in new directions.

LOOKING AHEAD

In January 2024, as I began drafting the concluding section of this chapter, I noticed a "UCI News" email in my inbox. Every day, the communications staff at my campus, the University of California, Irvine, compile and send out links to news stories in which UCI faculty have been quoted or cited. Scrolling through the headlines, I saw, "Immigration emerges as key 2024 election wedge issue for

Trump, vulnerability for Biden." My colleague Louis DeSipio, a political scientist, had been quoted:

> "Biden's on a tightrope with this issue," DeSipio said. "It's the first time in quite a while that Democrats have had this level of internal division over immigration." . . . DeSipio said Trump, both during his presidency and in the years since, has "captured the fear of the change that was coming to the country" with migration over the past few decades and amplified it. (Hutzler 2024)

As I clicked on the link, I felt sad. I was aware that whenever immigration is a campaign issue, news media cover politicians' anti-immigrant statements as well as their calls for stiffer enforcement. Such rhetoric and policy proposals are painful for immigrant residents (Sati 2020), who may feel attacked and whose relatives may very well have to traverse stiffened border enforcement to enter the United States. Recall Isabel's comment, quoted in chapter 4: "Sometimes, due to certain people or certain situations that happen with immigrants, they judge everyone and they close the doors to those of us who want to get ahead." Interviewees such as Isabel felt they had to defend themselves against negative accusations.

The article in which Louis DeSipio was quoted turned out to be from *ABC News*. In it, journalist Alexandra Hutzler (2024) reported that as governors of border states had been sending busloads of immigrants to so-called sanctuary states, concern that immigrant residents were destabilizing local communities and the nation more generally had grown. I thought to myself that a key source of chaos was the decision to put new arrivals on these buses, upending their efforts to reach relatives, and then discarding them on city streets, often without support or services. The article described President Biden's shift on immigration. When he first took office, in 2021, he advocated comprehensive immigration reform, but in 2024, Hutzler wrote, he was working with Republicans on a bill that would restrict asylum access in exchange for increased aid for Ukraine in its war with Russia. Some Democrats, Hutzler reported, had criticized Biden for reneging on his earlier commitments to immigrant residents even as Biden's opponent, former President Trump, increased calls for mass deportations, and Republicans called the immigration issue "Biden's border crisis." Immigration appeared to be a losing issue for Biden, as the director of the nonprofit Immigration Hub stated in this piece: "You're not going to win by out-Republican[ing] the Republicans."

The dynamics that undergird the securitization-humanitarianism nexus that I have analyzed in this book help to explain the current historical moment, in which both the Republicans and the Democrats appear to be competing to be seen as the party that can control the US-Mexico border. From 2011, when I began this project, to 2024, when I am finalizing the manuscript, the primary forms of immigration relief that have been proposed or implemented have been discretionary executive actions that are, by definition, temporary, as they can be changed by subsequent presidential administrations. These discretionary measures, which allow

US officials to claim that immigration law is being "enforced in a strong and sensible manner" rather than "blindly" (Napolitano 2012, 2), include DACA in 2012, the Provisional Waivers in 2013 (USCIS 2018b), and DAPA and DACA+ in 2014. Such "humanitarian" gestures are difficult to sustain. DACA has been challenged in court, and no new applications are being approved, while DAPA and DACA+ were enjoined in 2015. The comprehensive immigration reform promised by both the Obama and Biden administrations has not materialized. Meanwhile immigration policies that treat immigration as a security issue have proliferated, from the rise in deportations during the Obama administration to reductions in refugee admissions, "remain in Mexico" policy, family separations, Title 42, and the dismantling of asylum protections during the Trump administration, to what human rights organizations are calling Biden's "asylum ban"—namely, the rule that only those who have applied for an appointment through a Customs and Border Patrol app (which is very difficult to navigate) or who have been denied asylum elsewhere can apply for asylum in the United States (Human Rights Watch 2023; International Rescue Committee 2023). Not surprisingly, some immigrant activism has turned away from the narratives of deservingness that limit policy discourse to instead advocate for abolitionist approaches, such as not one more deportation (NDLON 2013), removing ICE activity from local jurisdictions (ICE Out of LA!, n.d.), and citizenship for all (e.g., Voces de la Frontera, n.d.). Such transformative advocacy "documents back" expansively, employing social media, political theatre, civil disobedience, and scholarly publications. Such approaches not only strive to alter what the state and public see by narrating context and history, but also to make state violence visible. The state not only *sees* but *is seen* through accounts of curtailed futures, family separation, and physical deprivation.

I am tempted to conclude with policy recommendations that are informed by my research. For example, I could recommend passing an immigration reform bill that, as interview participants envisioned, would dramatically expand opportunities for people to regularize their status in the United States. I could recommend that, in light of US roles in displacing immigrant residents from their countries of origin, applicants for these regularization opportunities be presumed to qualify simply on the basis of being present in the United States.[10] I could recommend that, when documentation packets contain minor discrepancies (for example, in the spelling of names or in dates of birth), applicants be granted the benefit of the doubt—for instance, by being permitted to submit an explanation for the discrepancies. I could recommend that after living in the United States for a certain period of time—say, five years—people would become ineligible for deportation. I could recommend that, following a criminal conviction, an immigrant resident be permitted to demonstrate that their equities in the United States outweigh any harm caused by the crime for which they were convicted. I could recommend that legal distinctions associated with immigration status be lessened or erased, such that people would be able to work, travel, marry, study, and vote in the United

States, whether or not they have work authorization, a pending application for status through a relative (which sometimes requires remaining unmarried), permanent legal status, or citizenship.[11] I could recommend dismantling the border enforcement apparatus, repurposing detention facilities for socially positive uses, and providing social support to asylum seekers. I could recommend grounding immigration policy in caring like a community rather than seeing like a state.

Much as I would like to make these recommendations—and indeed, I do advocate for the measures just listed as each would make a difference in the lives of immigrant residents—the reality is that changes to immigration policy alone will not address the violence and deprivation that produces mass displacement (Khosravi 2018). Addressing those conditions would begin with changes in foreign and economic policy. In the meantime, illegalized residents have imagined alternative possibilities in which justice would be administered transnationally, families could unite, rights would accrue in ways that generate collective benefits, regularization opportunities would be plentiful and easy-to-navigate, and illegalization would be erased, enabling immigrant residents to exit the liminal domain in which they are currently situated, and to be treated with respect and dignity. Likewise, the legal craft practiced by nonprofit service providers prefigures a world in which immigrant residents would be treated with empathy, legal options would be explained, residents would be empowered to make informed decisions, and rights would become real. Most fundamentally, caring like a community would help to make these alternatives a reality. As Hobert and Kneese observe, "It is precisely from this audacity to produce, apply, and effect care despite dark histories and futures that its radical nature emerges. Radical care can present an otherwise, even if it cannot completely disengage from structural inequalities and normative assumptions regarding social reproduction, gender, race, class, sexuality, and citizenship" (Hobart and Kneese, 2020, 142). At a moment when long-term residents must cope with continued uncertainty, when asylum seekers are prevented from reaching safety, and when even an allegedly pro-immigrant president appears willing to shut down the border, presenting an otherwise seems like a worthy endeavor.

NOTES

INTRODUCTION

1. All names of individuals encountered in research are pseudonyms.

2. Some law enforcement agencies are reluctant to issue certifications for U-Visa cases (Gill 2013; Lakhani 2014).

3. Mental or psychological harm can be more difficult to prove than physical harm, yet both matter. According to the USCIS website, "The U nonimmigrant status (U visa) is set aside for victims of certain crimes who have suffered mental or physical abuse and are helpful to law enforcement or government officials in the investigation or prosecution of criminal activity" (USCIS, 2024h). The definition of Extreme Cruelty that allows a spouse to self-petition under the Violence Against Women Act includes psychological abuse (see USCIS 2024b).

4. Enriquez, Vazquez Vera, and Ramakrishnan (2019) analyze the racial politics of driver's license access.

5. The documents that illegalized residents are able to obtain vary. For example, California legislation that allowed unauthorized residents to apply for drivers licenses has been criticized for favoring documentation that Mexican residents have but that may not be available to those of other nationalities (Enriquez, Vazquez Vera, and Ramakrishnan 2019).

6. In the early days of the US republic, free white persons who had resided in the country for two years were eligible to naturalize (Schneider 2001); criteria that left out many groups, including enslaved Black Americans, those who were not white, Chinese laborers who were denied entry through the 1882 Chinese Exclusion Act, Japanese persons through the "Gentleman's Agreement" in 1907, and those whose actual or imputed behavior was deemed politically or morally undesirable (Ngai 2004; Calavita 2020; Haney-Lopez 1996).

7. Scholars have also characterized immigration policy in the United Kingdom as "British exceptionalism," in reference not to plenary power but rather to the ways that the UK deviates from EU policies. Zotti explains, "The assumption that the UK can (no longer) be

a country open to immigration—despite its quite successful history of integration and multiculturalism—is based on a more composite notion of exceptionality that draws, among others, on the country's insular nature—with the supposedly self-evident corollary of a 'more finite' inhabitable space than continental nations—the assumedly unique and fragile balance of social mores and constitutional practices ensuing from having been physically and politically separated, albeit not isolated, from Europe and the rest of the world, as well as Britain's supposed Anglo-Saxon identity" (2021, 69, citations omitted).

8. During the first Trump administration, immigration processes became less predictable and forms changed more frequently, making it more difficult for service providers to familiarize themselves with processes (Moynihan, Gerzina, and Herd 2022).

1. SECURITIZATION, HUMANITARIANISM, AND PLENARY POWER

1. Krajewska draws attention to the ways that, in the United States, requests for identity documents are fueled by the notion that immigrants are a suspect group: "terrorism and illegal immigration are the primary drivers of identity policing schemes" (Krajewska 2017, 214).

2. Jane Lilly López, who has written about mixed-citizenship couples, observes that one of her study participant's "experience of governmental rejection and family separation is as central to US immigration policy as family reunification" (2022, 1).

3. There is a parallel between (a) the expansive influence of convictions versus the way immigration opportunities are limited by eligibility criteria, and (b) the ways that state agencies collaborate with each other while remaining opaque to the public. In their study of child welfare systems, Edwards et al. observe, "State and nonstate agencies coordinate with each other relatively smoothly for the application of social control, that is, through mandated reporting or compliance monitoring, but with opacity, hostility, and suspicion when interacting with subjects of intervention" (2023, 215).

4. See Pineda (2021) for a discussion of ways that civil rights activism challenged the white supremacy of the US state. Pineda writes, "The critical practices of seeing like a white state suggest *seeing like an activist* as an important alternative starting point" (2021, 18).

5. For an account of the temporality of migration procedures in the United Kingdom, see Anderson (2020).

6. Torpey observes that "people have also become dependent on states for the possession of an 'identity' from which they can escape only with difficulty and which may significantly shape their access to various spaces" (2000, 4).

7. The notions of deservingness that underlay such criteria prioritized middle-class and heteronormative notions of merit such as advancing in the workplace, furthering one's education, and having children, even though job and educational opportunities were often denied to illegalized residents. Similarly, Edwards et al. (2023) note that in child welfare cases, parents are evaluated according to such standards.

8. During the COVID-19 pandemic, electronic signatures became possible, and there has been litigation over denying applications due to leaving blank spaces on forms (USCIS 2021c).

9. "USCIS recognizes that at least some degree of hardship to qualifying relatives exists in most, if not all, cases in which individuals with the requisite relationships are denied admission" (USCIS 2024d).

2. ROUTINE EXCEPTIONALITY

1. Sovereignty also pertains to relationships between states, enabling the United States to ignore the ways that US foreign policy contributes to migration to the United States. I thank Pooja Dadhania for this point.

2. Likewise, Enriquez observes that for couples who were seeking to legalize through marriage, "immigration policies crept into the most personal and private corners of their lives" (2020, 2).

3. In fact, Kitty Calavita's (1990) research regarding IRCA's employer sanctions provisions suggests that the fact that employers might accept false identity documents was anticipated and tolerated, as long as the documents were plausible.

4. I discuss the relationship between asylum and work authorization more extensively in Coutin (2000).

5. Keyes (2012) discusses the limitations of narratives of deservingness that underlie distinctions between "good" and "bad" immigrants.

6. And it is possible that she was right, if the offense was considered serious enough or if she had falsely claimed to be a US citizen.

7. See Enriquez (2020) for a detailed account of how couples who are filing a spousal petition document their relationship in order to prove that it is valid. In this documentation process, couples strive to meet officials' expectations of marriage, such as having a meaningful ceremony and combining one's finances.

3. LEGAL CRAFT

1. For details of this history, see Coutin (2011).

2. Koh (2017) discusses in absentia removal orders and other forms of removal that occur in the "shadows" of immigration court.

3. I also discuss the notion of "legal craft" in Coutin (2020). And, for an account of seeing like an activist," see Pineda (2021).

4. See also Pineda (2021) regarding the political imagination entailed in seeing like an activist.

5. See Galli (2023) regarding this intermediary role in legal representation of unaccompanied minors.

6. The distinction between law-on-the-books and law-in-action originated with Roscoe Pound in 1910. See Calavita (2016) for a discussion of the influence of this distinction on law and society scholarship.

7. For an account of how officials are to view cancellation cases, see Shibley and Holt (2022).

8. See Gomberg-Munoz (2017); León (2020); López (2022); and Enriquez (2020) for accounts of the challenges of spousal petitions.

9. Kawar (2011) analyzes the formation of a field of immigrant rights lawyering in the United States and France.

10. Yu (2023a) discusses the dilemmas created by these competing goals.

11. Albiston, Edelman, and Milligan (2014) suggest that a "dispute tree" is a better metaphor than a pyramid.

12. In the case of Vangala et al. v. USCIS et al., the government was sued for rejecting forms that contained blank spaces. A 2021 settlement agreement gave rejected applicants an opportunity to reapply (USCIS 2021c).

13. At least, doing so was probably not likely at the time that I carried out my research.

14. See "Ley Especial Transitoria" (1992).

15. See Mitchell and Coutin (2019) for a discussion of birth certificates as immigration documents.

16. Matthew Hull made a similar point in his study of documentation practices in Pakistan. Hull writes, "meanings of memos, petitions, and plans are transformed when they are placed in or 'on' (as Pakistani bureaucrats put it) a file" (2012, 116).

4. *OTRO MUNDO ES POSIBLE* (ANOTHER WORLD IS POSSIBLE)

1. Providing background about the conditions that forced these individuals out of their countries, including, most prominently, US intervention in Central America, Abrego concludes, "Central American migrants are not the crisis, they merely reveal to us the crises that nation-states do not want us to see" (2018a, 225).

2. The detention center in Artesia was eventually closed (Caldwell 2014). Visitors were not permitted to take photographs of the facility, however the volunteers Stephen and Clio Reese Sady created an artistic rendering; see Reese Sady (n.d.).

3. For these detainees, a "credible fear interview" was the first step in the process of seeking asylum. For an overview and critique of the credible fear interview process, see Augustine-Adams and Nuñez (2021).

4. For a review of the literature on detention center conditions, including the lack of appropriate educational opportunities for detained children, see Edyburn and Meek (2021).

5. For example, President Donald Trump said of immigrants, "These people are very aggressive: They drink, they have drugs, a lot of things happening" and "It's the blood of our country; what they're doing is destroying our country" (LeVine and Kornfield 2023). Similarly, during the August 23, 2023, Republican presidential primary debate Florida governor Ron DeSantis stated, "I'm not going to send troops to Ukraine, but I am going to send them to our southern border" (S. Sanchez 2023).

6. For example, detention center conditions are often abusive and seem designed to force people to accept deportation rather than fighting their case (Dreisbach 2023).

7. As well, Jane Lilly López (2022) critiques US immigration policy for its individualistic focus, noting that eligibility is evaluated at an individual level, even though families are affected by outcomes.

8. For instance, many legal decisions rest on what could be expected of a "reasonable" person, but what is reasonable to one sector of society may appear far-fetched or unreasonable to another (Martin 1994).

9. An example of such a limited framework is that international law asserts that individuals have the "right" to leave their countries, but there is no "right" to enter other countries, so the right to leave is not all that meaningful (Guild and Stoyanova 2018). For a discussion of debates over rights, see Hunt (1990). And for an analysis of the value of rights struggles even when litigants do not prevail in court, see McCann (1994).

10. Carbado and Harris (2011, 1549) refer to these cases as "undocumented," not only because they concern the unequal legal status of noncitizens but also because these cases have been largely overlooked by legal scholars who study criminal procedure, race, and the Fourth Amendment.

11. The $125 rate is based on Adriana's memory of her own experience. Current rates are posted on the US State Department website.

12. Similarly, Edwards et al. argue for a new child welfare system, "built on supports rather than suspicion, and on offering assistance to rather than placing burdens on families" (2023, 227).

13. Fortin noted that her thoughts were inspired by the work of Nicholas Kasirer (2006, 28): "Love relationships may elicit poetical enthusiasms elsewhere, but lawyers seem to sense that order in the family depends in part on their own dispassionate use of language to explain law's discipline over sentiment."

14. Sarah Horton (2015) studied the "economy of document exchange" (56) and found that "a set of unspoken moral principles appeared to structure the exchange: 'Good papers' must not be left 'idle,' just as the work histories associated with valid Social Security numbers must not be left 'blank' *(blanco)*" (59).

15. For example, during the Bracero Program, workers were fumigated with DDT when they entered the United States (Mize 2016).

16. Dauvergne (2020, 98) notes that this nexus has become a global phenomenon, as polices developed by the United States and other so-called "settler" societies are exported: "global immigration politics are defined by those states that are sought after immigration destinations and that have the capacity to defend—legally, politically, militarily and rhetorically—their borders."

17. And, of course, the very land to which they immigrate previously belonged to others. In critiquing binary notions of property as "owned" or "not owned" by particular individuals, Nicholas Blomley notes, "settlers access land through a relation with indigenous societies, the original holders of the land, although on highly unequal terms" (2019, 39).

18. Ticktin (2019, 139) points out, "While care is absolutely central to humanitarian government, these forms of care do not produce and protect society (or the social) but rather a concept of universal 'humanity' enshrined in the individual human body. . . . This form of care is restricted to the temporal present. Beyond that, no promises are upheld, no long-term human condition supported, no vision of the future elaborated, and this is precisely because it is based on the logic of medical emergency." For a review of anthropological engagement with humanitarianism, see Ticktin (2014).

19. De Trinidad Young and Wallace (2019, 1171) analyze the mix of integrative and exclusionary policies across US states, concluding that "both integration and decriminalization are necessary for achieving health equity."

20. See Asad (2023) for examples of policy changes—like expanding Affordable Care Act eligibility to all—that would minimize distinctions based on legal status.

21. For a description of the health-care needs of those who enter the United States as refugees, see Pace et al. (2015).

22. Hiroshi Motomura (2010) provides an account of how regularization opportunities could be expanded.

23. See Obinna (2020) for a discussion of family visa wait times and recommendations for improvement.

24. Heinrich (2018) describes the administrative burden created by viewing immigrant residents and their children with suspicion, especially when it comes to access to birth records.

25. For calls to end immigration detention, see Boaz (2021); Rosenbaum (2021); and Ybarra (2021).

CONCLUSION: DOCUMENTING BACK

1. The papers from this symposium will appear in Barba and Gonzalez forthcoming.

2. A copy of this photo can be seen in Medvescek and Wiley (2019).

3. The US sanctuary movement of the 1980s distinguished between political refugees, who were fleeing persecution and civil war and whose lives would be at risk if they returned to their countries of origin, and economic immigrants, who were fleeing poverty or seeking opportunity. Sanctuary movement assistance focused on the former (Coutin 1993).

4. Blum writes that "extensive discovery was pursued by the Plaintiffs regarding the claims of unlawful denial of asylum and withholding of deportation. The INS was required to produce thousands of pages of documents; many other document requests for INS offices throughout the United States were outstanding, and several depositions of government officials also were taken. It was anticipated that dozens of others would be taken over the next months" (1991, 352).

5. Martinez et al. (2020) suggest that these transformations include vulnerability, a commitment to documenting collective memories, and attending to affect.

6. See ICE (2023); Sacchetti (2023); and AILA (2024) for statistics regarding enforcement trends.

7. Even US citizens have been deported (Stevens 2011) or had their status challenged (Rosenbloom, 2013).

8. In *The Hobbit*, when Bilbo Baggins views the bejeweled underbelly of the dreaded dragon Smaug, he thinks to himself, "Old fool! Why there is a large patch in the hollow of his left breast as bare as a snail out of its shell!" (Tolkein 1966, 216).

9. Ruth Behar's (1996, 5) characterization of anthropology as a "fascinating, bizarre, disturbing, and necessary form of witnessing" is true of ethnography more generally. See McGranahan (2020) for an account of the importance of hope within such work.

10. See also Galli (2023) for a discussion of the notion that granting status to Central American youth would be a form of reparation for US involvement in Central American civil wars.

11. Another problem with the family petition process is that it creates inequities between relatives who have status and those who do not. Laura Enriquez notes that "current policies place too much pressure on families, disrupting family relationships and changing family formation processes. By requiring citizen partners and children to petition for their undocumented family members, we reproduce inequality within and among families" (Enriquez 2020, 167).

REFERENCES

Abarca, Gray Albert, and Susan Bibler Coutin. 2018. "Sovereign Intimacies: The Lives of Documents within US State-Noncitizen Relationships." *American Ethnologist* 45 (1): 7–19.

Abrams, Kerry. 2007. "Immigration Law and the Regulation of Marriage." *Minnesota Law Review* 91 (6): 1625–1709.

Abrego, Leisy J. 2018a. "Central American Refugees Reveal the Crisis of the State." In *The Oxford Handbook of Migration Crises*, edited by Cecelia Menjívar, Marie Ruiz, and Immanuel Ness, 213–228. New York: Oxford University Press. https://doi.org/10.1093/oxfordhb/9780190856908.013.43.

———. 2018b. "Renewed Optimism and Spatial Mobility: Legal Consciousness of Latino Deferred Action for Childhood Arrivals Recipients and their Families in Los Angeles." *Ethnicities* 18 (2): 192–207.

Abrego, Leisy J., and Sarah M. Lakhani. 2015. "Incomplete Inclusion: Legal Violence and Immigrants in Liminal Legal Statuses." *Law & Policy* 37 (4): 265–293.

Abrego, Leisy J., and Genevieve Negrón-Gonzales, eds. 2020. *We are Not Dreamers: Undocumented Scholars Theorize Undocumented Life in the United States*. Duke University Press.

Abu El-Haj, Thea Renda. 2023. "Against Implications: Ethnographic Witnessing as Research Stance in the Lebanese Conflict Zone." *Comparative Education Review* 67 (2): 231–250.

Aguirre, Adalberto. 2008–2009. "Immigration on the Public Mind: Immigration Reform in the Obama Administration." *Social Justice* 35 (4): 4–11.

AILA (American Immigration Lawyers Association). 2024. "Featured Issue: Immigration Detention and Alternatives to Detention." December 16. https://www.aila.org/library/featured-issue-immigration-detention.

Albiston, Catherine R., Lauren B. Edelman, and Joy Milligan. 2014. "The Dispute Tree and the Legal Forest." *Annual Review of Law and Social Science* 10: 105–131

Alonso Bejarano, Carolina, Lucia López Juárez, Mirian A. Mijangos García, and Daniel M. Goldstein. 2019. *Decolonizing Ethnography: Undocumented Immigrants and New Directions in Social Science.* Duke University Press.

Alvarado, Karina O., Alicia Ivonne Estrada, and Ester E. Hernández. 2017. "Introduction: U.S. Central American (Un)Belongings." In *U.S. Central Americans: Reconstructing Memories, Struggles, and Communities of Resistance,* 3–35. University of Arizona Press.

Álvarez Velasco, Soledad. 2009. "Transitando en la clandestinidad: Análisis de la migración indocumentada en tránsito por la frontera sur mexicana." *FLACSO: Boletín Migrante Andino*: 2–10.

American Baptist Churches v. Thornburgh, 760 F. Supp. 796 (N.D. Cal. 1991).

American Immigration Council and National Immigrant Justice Center. 2020. "The Difference Between Asylum and Withholding of Removal." October. https://www.americanimmigrationcouncil.org/sites/default/files/research/the_difference_between_asylum_and_withholding_of_removal.pdf.

Anderson, Bridget. 2020. "And About Time Too . . . Migration, Documentation, and Temporalities." In *Paper Trails: Migrants, Documents, and Legal Insecurity,* edited by Sarah B. Horton and Josiah Heyman, 53–73. Duke University Press.

Annobil, Jojo. 2009. "The Immigration Representation Project: Meeting the Critical Needs of Low-Wage and Indigent New Yorkers Facing Removal." *Fordham Law Review* 78: 517–540.

Aranda, Elizabeth, Elizabeth Vaquera, Heidi Castañeda, and Girsea Martinez Rosas. 2022. "Undocumented Again? DACA Rescission, Emotions, and Incorporation Outcomes among Young Adults." *Social Forces* 101 (3): 1321–1342.

Artero, Maurizio, and Elena Fontanari. 2021. "Obstructing Lives: Local Borders and their Structural Violence in the Asylum Field of Post-2015 Europe." *Journal of Ethnic and Migration Studies* 47 (3): 631–648.

Asad, Asad. 2023. *Engage and Evade: How Latino Immigrants Manage Surveillance in Everyday Life.* Princeton University Press.

Augustine-Adams, Kif. 2005. "The Plenary Power Doctrine After September 11." *UC Davis Law Review* 38 (3): 701–745.

Augustine-Adams, Kif, and D. Carolina Nuñez. 2021. "Sites of (Mis)Translation: The Credible Fear Process in United States Immigration Detention." *Georgetown Immigration Law Journal* 35 (2): 399–430.

Bach, Robert L. 1978. "Mexican Immigration and the American State." *International Migration Review* 12 (4): 536–558. https://doi.org/10.1177/019791837801200405.

Badenhoop, Elisabeth. 2017. "Calling for the Super Citizen: Citizenship Ceremonies in the UK and Germany as Techniques of Subject-Formation." *Migration Studies* 5 (3): 409–427.

Barad, Karen. 2007. *Meeting the Universe Halfway: Quantum Physics and the Entanglement of Matter and Meaning.* Duke University Press.

Barba, Lloyd, and Sergio Gonzalez, eds. Forthcoming. *Sacred Refuge: New Histories of the U.S. Sanctuary Movement.* New York University Press.

Barbero, Iker. 2020. "A Ubiquitous Border for Migrants in Transit and Their Rights: Analysis and Consequences of the Reintroduction of Internal Borders in France." *European Journal of Migration and Law* 22 (3): 366–385.

Barbero, Maria V. 2019. "Semi-legality and Belonging in the Obama era: The Deferred Action for Childhood Arrivals Memorandum as an Instrument of Governance." *Citizenship Studies* 23 (1): 1–18.

Bauböck, Rainer. 2003. "Reinventing Urban Citizenship." *Citizenship Studies* 7 (2): 139–160.

———. 2005. "Expansive Citizenship—Voting Beyond Territory and Membership." *PS: Political Science and Politics* 38 (4): 683–687.

Bauder, Harald 2016. "Possibilities of Urban Belonging." *Antipode* 48 (2): 252–271. https://doi.org/10.1111/anti.12174.

Bean, Frank D., Georges Vernez, and Charles B. Keely. 1989. *Opening and Closing the Doors: Evaluating Immigration Reform and Control.* Urban Institute.

Behar, Ruth. 1996. *The Vulnerable Observer: Anthropology that Breaks Your Heart.* Beacon Press.

Blomley, Nicholas. 2019. "Precarious Territory: Property Law, Housing, and the Socio-Spatial Order." *Antipode* 52 (1): 36–57.

Blum, Carolyn Patty. 1991. "The Settlement of *American Baptist Churches v. Thornburgh*: Landmark Victory for Central American Asylum-Seekers." *International Journal of Refugee Law* 3 (2): 347–356.

Boaz, Matthew. 2021. "Practical Abolition: Universal Representation as an Alternative to Immigration Detention." *Tennessee Law Review* 89 (1): 199–259.

Boehm, Deborah A. 2020. "Documents as Unauthorized." In *Paper Trails: Migrants, Documents, and Legal Insecurity*, edited by Sarah B. Horton and Josiah Heyman, 109–129. Duke University Press.

Borrelli, Lisa Marie, and William Walters. 2024. "Blood, Sweat and Tears: On the Corporeality of Deportation." *Environment and Planning C: Politics and Space.* https://doi.org/10.1177/23996544241232325.

Bosniak, Linda. 2006. *The Citizen and the Alien: Dilemmas of Contemporary Membership.* Princeton University Press.

Bosworth, Mary. 2012. "Subjectivity and Identity in Detention: Punishment and Society in a Global Age." *Theoretical Criminology* 16 (2): 123–140.

Bowling, Ben, and Sophie Westenra. 2020. "'A Really Hostile Environment': Adiaphorization, Global Policing and the Crimmigration Control System." *Theoretical Criminology* 24 (2): 163–183.

Brayne, Sarah. 2021. *Predict and Surveil: Data, Discretion, and the Future of Policing.* Oxford University Press.

Cabot, Heath. 2019. "The European Refugee Crisis and Humanitarian Citizenship in Greece." *Ethnos* 84 (5): 747–771.

Calavita, Kitty. 1990. "Employer Sanctions Violations: Toward a Dialectic Model of White-Collar Crime." *Law & Society Review* 24 (4): 1041–1070.

———. 1992. *Inside the State: The Bracero Program, Immigration, and the I.N.S.* Routledge.

———. 1998. "Immigration, Law, and Marginalization in a Global Economy: Notes from Spain." *Law & Society Review* 32 (3): 529–566.

———. 2016. *Invitation to Law and Society: An Introduction to the Study of Real Law.* 2nd ed. University of Chicago Press.

———. 2020. *US Immigration Law and the Control of Labor: 1820–1924.* 2nd ed. Quid Pro Books.

Calavita, Kitty, and Valerie Jenness. 2013. "Inside the Pyramid of Disputes: Naming problems and Filing Grievances in California Prisons." *Social Problems* 60 (1): 50–80.

Caldwell, Alicia A. 2014. "U.S. to Close Immigration Detention Center in Artesia." *Santa Fe New Mexican*, November 18, 2014. https://www.santafenewmexican.com/news/u-s-to-close-immigrant-detention-center-in-artesia/article_056a06ab-6044-5f04-950f-822b22779462.html.

Callaghan, Timothy, and Adam Olson. 2017. "Unearthing the Hidden Welfare State: Race, Political Attitudes, and Unforeseen Consequences." *Journal of Race, Ethnicity and Politics* 2 (1): 63–87.

Carbado, Davon W., and Cheryl I. Harris. 2011. "Undocumented Criminal Procedure." *UCLA Law Review* 58 (6): 1543–1616.

Chacón, Jennifer M. 2010a. "Border Exceptionalism in the Era of Moving Borders." *Fordham Urban Law Journal* 38: 129–153.

———. 2010b. "A Diversion of Attention: Immigration Courts and the Adjudication of Fourth and Fifth Amendment Rights." *Duke Law Journal* 59: 1563–1633.

———. 2012. "Overcriminalizing Immigration." *Journal of Criminal Law and Criminology* 102 (3): 613–652.

———. 2015. "Producing Liminal Legality." *Denver University Law Review* 92 (4): 709–768.

———. 2019. "Immigration Federalism in the Weeds." *U.C.L.A. Law Review* 66: 1330–1393.

———. 2023. "Legal Borderlands and Imperial Legacies: A Response to Maggie Blackhawk's The Constitution of American Colonialism." *Harvard Law Review* 137 (1): 1–22.

Chacón, Jennifer M., Susan Bibler Coutin, and Stephen Lee. 2024. *Legal Phantoms: Executive Relief and the Haunting Failures of Immigration Law*. Stanford University Press.

Chae Chan Ping v. United States, 130 U.S. 581 (1889).

Chang, Aurora. 2011. "Undocumented to Hyperdocumented: A Jornada of Protection, Papers, and PhD Status." *Harvard Educational Review* 81 (3): 508–617.

Chang, Robert S. 2018. "Whitewashing Precedent: From the Chinese Exclusion Case to Korematsu to the Muslim Travel Ban Cases." *Case Western Reserve Law Review* 68: 1183–1222.

Chavez, Leo. 2013. *The Latino Threat: Constructing Immigrants, Citizens, and the Nation.* 2nd ed. Stanford University Press.

Chinchilla, Melissa, Dahai Yue, and Ninez A. Ponce. 2022. "Housing Insecurity Among Latinxs." *Journal of Immigrant and Minority Health* 24: 656–665.

Chishti, Muzaffar, and Charles Kamasaki. 2014. *IRCA in Retrospect: Guideposts for Today's Immigration Reform*. Migration Policy Institute.

Cho, Eunice Hyunhye, Tara Tidwell Cullen, and Clara Long. 2020. *Justice-Free Zones: U.S. Immigration Detention Under the Trump Administration*. ACLU Research Report. https://www.hrw.org/sites/default/files/supporting_resources/justice_free_zones_immigrant_detention.pdf.

Cohen, Alison K., Rachel Brahinsky, Kathleen M. Coll, and Miranda P. Dotson. 2022. ""We Keep Each Other Safe": San Francisco Bay Area Community-Based Organizations Respond to Enduring Crises in the COVID-19 Era." *RSF: The Russell Sage Foundation Journal of the Social Sciences* 8 (8): 70–87.

Cohen, Amy J., and Bronwen Morgan. 2023. "Prefigurative Legality." *Law & Social Inquiry* 48 (3): 1053–1082. https://doi.org/10.1017/lsi.2023.4.

Colomé-Menéndez, Desirée, Joachim A. Koops, and Daan Weggemans. 2021. "A Country of Immigrants No More? The Securitization of Immigration in the National Security Strategies of the United States of America." *Global Affairs* 7 (1): 1–26.

Congressional Research Service. 2018. "An Overview of Discretionary Reprieves from Removal: Deferred Action, DACA, TPS, and Others." Updated April 10, 2018. https://crsreports.congress.gov/product/pdf/R/R45158.

Constable, Marianne. 2005. *Just Silences: The Limits and Possibilities of Modern Law*. Princeton University Press.

Corbett, Jim. 1986. *Borders and Crossings: Some Sanctuary Papers*. Tucson Refugee Support Group (April).

Cossman, Sarah. 2023. "Nefarious Notarios: Responding to Immigration Scams as White Collar Crime as a Matter of Public Policy." *Refugee Law & Migration Studies Brief* 1 (2): 1–8.

Coutin, Susan Bibler. 1993. *The Culture of Protest: Religious Activism and the U.S. Sanctuary Movement*. Westview Press.

———. 1995. "Smugglers or Samaritans in Tucson, Arizona: Producing and Contesting Legal Truth." *American Ethnologist* 22 (3): 549–571.

———. 2000. *Legalizing Moves: Salvadoran Immigrants' Struggle for U.S. Residency*. University of Michigan Press.

———. 2007. *Nations of Emigrants: Shifting Boundaries of Citizenship in El Salvador and the United States*. Cornell University Press.

———. 2011. "Falling Outside: Excavating the History of Central American Asylum Seekers." *Law & Social Inquiry* 36 (3): 569–596.

———. 2013. "In the Breach: Citizenship and Its Approximations." *Indiana Journal of Global Legal Studies* 20 (1): 109–140.

———. 2016. *Exiled Home: Salvadoran Transnational Youth in the Aftermath of Violence*. Duke University Press.

———. 2020. "Opportunities and Double Binds: Legal Craft in an Era of Uncertainty." In *Paper Trails: Migrants, Documents, and Legal Insecurity*, edited by Sarah B. Horton and Josiah Heyman, 130–152. Duke University Press.

Coutin, Susan Bibler, Sameer M. Ashar, Jennifer M. Chacón, and Stephen Lee. 2017. "Deferred Action and the Discretionary State: Migration, Precarity and Resistance." *Citizenship Studies* 21 (8): 951–968.

Coutin, Susan Bibler, Jennifer Chacón, Stephen Lee, Sameer Ashar, and Jason Palmer. 2021. "Shapeshifting Displacement: Notions of Membership and Deservingness Forged by Illegalized Residents." *Humanity: An International Journal of Human Rights, Humanitarianism, and Development* 12 (3): 339–353.

Coutin, Susan Bibler, and Véronique Fortin. 2015. "Legal Ethnographies and Ethnographic Law." In *Wiley Handbook of Law and Society*, edited by Austin Sarat and Patricia Ewick, 71–84. Wiley Blackwell.

———. 2021. "Exclusionary Inclusion: Applying for Legal Status in the United States." In *Precarity and Belonging: Labor, Migration, and Non-Citizenship*, edited by Catherine S. Ramírez, Sylvanna M. Falcón, Juan Poblete, Steven C. McKay, and Felicity Amaya Schaeffer, 191–208. Rutgers University Press.

———. 2023. "The Craft of Translation: Documentary Practices within Immigrant Advocacy in the United States." *PoLAR: Political and Legal Anthropology Review* 46 (1): 24–38.

Coutin, Susan Bibler, Bill Maurer, and Barbara Yngvesson. 2002. "In the Mirror: The Legitimation Work of Globalization." *Law & Social Inquiry* 27 (4): 801–843.

Coutin, Susan Bibler, Justin Richland, and Véronique Fortin. 2014. "Routine Exceptionality: The Plenary Power Doctrine, Immigrants, and the Indigenous under US Law." *UC Irvine Law Review* 4 (1): 97–120.

Coutin, Susan Bibler, and Barbara Yngvesson. 2023. *Documenting Impossible Realities: Ethnography, Memory, and the As If.* Cornell University Press.

Cox, Aimee Meredith. 2015. *Shapeshifters: Black Girls and the Choreography of Citizenship.* Duke University Press.

Cuic, Aleksandar. 2022. "Immigration After the Trump Administration: Surgical Fix or Another Band-Aid?" *Case Western Reserve Journal of International Law* 54: 259–280.

Dadhania, Pooja R. 2023. "State Responsibility for Forced Migration." *Boston College Law Review* 64 (4): 745–800.

Daniel, E. Valentine. 1996. *Charred Lullabies: Chapters in an Anthropography of Violence.* Princeton University Press.

Dauvergne, Catherine. 2020. "Revisiting *The New Politics of Immigration.*" *International Migration* 58 (6): 96–107.

De Genova, Nicholas P. 2002. "Migrant 'Illegality' and Deportability in Everyday Life." *Annual Review of Anthropology* 31 (1): 419–447.

De Graauw, Els. 2016. *Making Immigrant Rights Real: Nonprofits and the Politics of Integration in San Francisco.* Cornell University Press.

De Leon, Jason. 2015. *The Land of Open Graves: Living and Dying on the Migrant Trail.* University of California Press.

De Trinidad Young, Maria-Elena, and Steven P. Wallace. 2019. "Included, but Deportable: A New Public Health Approach to Policies that Criminalize and Integrate Immigrants." *American Journal of Public Health* 109 (9): 1171–1176.

Dery, David. 1998. "'Papereality' and Learning in Bureaucratic Organizations." *Administration & Society* 29 (6): 677–689.

Desmond, Matthew. 2014. "Relational Ethnography." *Theory and Society* 43 (5): 547–79. https://doi.org/10.1007/s11186-014-9232-5.

Diamond, Peter C. 1992. "Temporary Protected Status under the Immigration Act of 1990." *Immigration and Nationality Law Review* 14: 205–225.

Dingeman, Katie, Yekaterina Arzhayev, Cristy Ayala, Erika Bermudez, Lauren Padama, and Liliana Tena-Chávez. 2017. "Neglected, Protected, Ejected: Latin American Women Caught by Crimmigration." *Feminist Criminology* 12 (3): 293–314.

Dreby, Joanna. 2015. *Everyday Illegal: When Policies Undermine Immigrant Families.* University of California Press.

Dreisbach, Tom. 2023. "Government's Own Experts Found 'Barbaric' and 'Negligent' Conditions in ICE Detention." *National Public Radio,* August 16. https://www.npr.org/2023/08/16/1190767610/ice-detention-immigration-government-inspectors-barbaric-negligent-conditions.

Eagly, Ingrid, and Steven Shafer. 2015. "A National Study of Access to Counsel in Immigration Court." *University of Pennsylvania Law Review* 164 (1): 1–92.

Edwards, Frank, Kelley Fong, Victoria Copeland, Mical Raz, and Alan Dettlaff. 2023. "Administrative Burdens in Child Welfare Systems." *RSF: The Russell Sage Foundation Journal of the Social Sciences* 9 (5): 214–231.

Edyburn, Kelly L., and Shantel Meek. 2021. "Seeking Safety and Humanity in the Harshest Immigration Climate in a Generation: A Review of the Literature on the Effects of Separation and Detention on Migrant and Asylum-Seeking Children and Families in the United States during the Trump Administration." *Social Policy Report* 34 (1): 1–46.

Elias, Sella Burch. 2013. "The New Immigration Federalism." *Ohio State Law Journal* 74 (5): 703–752.

———. 2017. "Immigrant Covering." *William & Mary Law Review* 58 (3): 765–856.

Enchautegui, María E., and Cecilia Menjívar. 2015. "Paradoxes of Family Immigration Policy: Separation, Reorganization, and Reunification of Families under Current Immigration Laws." *Law & Policy* 37 (1–2): 32–60.

Enriquez, Laura E. 2020. *Of Love and Papers: How Immigration Policy Affects Romance and Family*. University of California Press.

Enriquez, Laura E., Daisy Vazquez Vera, and S. Karthick Ramakrishnan. 2019. "Driver's Licenses for All? Racialized Illegality and the Implementation of Progressive Immigration Policy in California." *Law & Policy* 41 (1): 34–58.

Falzarano, Francesca, Hillary Winoker, Rebecca V. Burke, Jose A. Mendoza, Francisco Munoz, Ana Tergas, Paul K. Maciejewski, and Holly G. Prigerson. 2022. "Grief and Bereavement in the Latino/a community: A Literature Synthesis and Directions for Future Research." *Health Equity* 6 (1): 696–707.

Faria, Caroline, Sarah Klosterkamp, Rebecca Maria Torres, and Jayme Walenta. 2020. "Embodied Exhibits: Toward a Feminist Geographic Courtroom Ethnography." *Annals of the American Association of Geographers* 110 (4): 1095–1113.

Faricy, Christopher G. 2011. "The Politics of Social Policy in America: The Causes and Effects of Indirect versus Direct Social Spending." *Journal of Politics* 73 (1): 74–83.

———. 2015. *Welfare for the Wealthy: Parties, Social Spending, and Inequality in the US*. Cambridge University Press.

Fassin, Didier. 2011. "Policing Borders, Producing Boundaries. The Governmentality of Immigration in Dark Times." *Annual Review of Anthropology* 40: 213–226.

Felbab-Brown, Vanda. 2017. "Hooked: Mexico's Violence and U.S. Demand for Drugs." *Brookings Institute* May 30. https://www.brookings.edu/articles/hooked-mexicos-violence-and-u-s-demand-for-drugs/.

Felstiner, William L. F., Richard L. Abel, and Austin Sarat. 1980–1981. "The Emergence and Transformation of Disputes: Naming, Blaming, Claiming . . ." *Law & Society Review* 15 (3–4): 631–654.

Flores, Andrea, Kevin Escudero, and Edelina Burciaga. 2019. "Legal–Spatial Consciousness: A Legal Geography Framework for Examining Migrant Illegality." *Law & Policy* 41 (1): 12–33.

Fox, Ashley, Wenhui Feng, and Megan Reynolds. 2023. "The Effect of Administrative Burden on State Safety-Net Participation: Evidence from Food Assistance, Cash Assistance, and Medicaid." *Public Administration Review* 83 (2): 367–384.

Galanter, Marc. 1983. "Reading the Landscape of Disputes: What We Know and Don't Know (and Think We Know) about our Allegedly Contentious and Litigious Society." *UCLA Law Review* 31 (1): 4–71.

Galli, Chaira. 2023. *Precarious Protections: Unaccompanied Minors Seeking Asylum in the United States*. University of California Press.

García, Angela S. 2014. "Hidden in Plain Sight: How Unauthorised Migrants Strategically Assimilate in Restrictive Localities in California." *Journal of Ethnic and Migration Studies* 40 (12): 1895–1914.

García Cruz, Gabriela. 2020. "Contesting 'Citizenship': The Testimonies of Undocumented Immigrant Activist Women," In *We Are Not Dreamers: Undocumented Scholars Theorize Undocumented Life in the United States*, edited by Leisy J. Abrego, and Genevieve Negrón-Gonzales, 110–126. Duke University Press.

García Hernández, César Cuauhtémoc. 2013. "Creating Crimmigration." *Brigham Young University Law Review* (6): 1457–1516.

Garrett, Terence M., and Arthur J. Sementelli. 2023. "Revisiting the Policy Implications of COVID-19, Asylum Seekers, and Migrants on the Mexico–US Border: Creating (and Maintaining) States of Exception in the Trump and Biden Administrations." *Politics & Policy* 51 (3): 458–475.

Geertz, Clifford. 1973. "Thick Description: Toward an Interpretive Theory of Culture." In *The Interpretation of Culture: Selected Essays*, 3–30. Basic Books.

Gerson, Pedro. 2023–2024. "Punitive Legal Immigration." *Kentucky Law Journal* 112: 331–372.

Gill, Lindsey J. 2013. "Secure Communities: Burdening Local Law Enforcement and Undermining the U Visa." *William and Mary Law Review* 54 (6): 2055–2087.

Gilman, Michele Estrin. 2014. "The Return of the Welfare Queen." *American University Journal of Gender, Social Policy, and the Law* 22: 247–280.

Golash-Boza, Tanya. 2015. *Deported: Immigrant Policing, Disposable Labor, and Global Capitalism*. New York University Press.

———. 2018. "President Obama's Legacy as "Deporter in Chief." In *Immigration Policy in the Age of Punishment: Detention, Deportation and Border Control*, edited by Philip Kretsedemas and David C. Brotherton, 37–56. Columbia University Press.

Gomberg-Muñoz, Ruth. 2016. "The Juárez Wives Club: Gendered Citizenship and US Immigration Law." *American Ethnologist* 43 (2): 339–352.

———. 2017. *Becoming Legal: Immigration Law and Mixed-Status Families*. Oxford University Press.

Gomberg-Muñoz, Ruth, and Reyna Wences. 2021. "Fight for the City: Policing, Sanctuary, and Resistance in Chicago." *Geographical Review* 111 (2): 252–268.

Gonzalez, Gilbert G. 1999. *Mexican Consuls and Labor Organizing: Imperial Politics in the American Southwest*. University of Texas Press.

———. 2015. *Guest Workers or Colonized Labor?: Mexican Labor Migration to the United States*. Routledge.

Gonzales, Roberto G. 2016. *Lives in Limbo: Undocumented and Coming of Age in America*. University of California Press.

Gould, Jon B., and Scott Barclay. 2012. "Mind the Gap: The Place of Gap Studies in Sociolegal Scholarship." *Annual Review of Law and Social Science* 8: 323–335.

Greenhouse, Carol J. 2011. *The Paradox of Relevance: Ethnography and Citizenship in the United States*. University of Pennsylvania Press.

Guerra, Mary Dolores. 2011. "Lost in Translation: *Notario* Fraud—Immigration Fraud." *Journal of Civil Rights and Economic Development* 26 (1): 23–40.

Guild, Elspeth, and Stoyanova, Vladislava, 2018. "The Human Right to Leave Any Country: A Right to Be Delivered." In *European Yearbook on Human Rights 2018*, edited by

Wolfgang Benedek, Philip Czech, Lisa Heschl, Karen Lukas, and Manfred Nowak, 373–394. *Cambridge University Press.* https://doi.org/10.1017/9781780688008.016.

Gustafson, Kaaryn. 2009. "The Criminalization of Poverty." *Journal of Criminal Law and Criminology* 99 (3): 643–716.

Hallett, Miranda Cady. 2014. "Temporary Protection, Enduring Contradiction: The Contested and Contradictory Meanings of Temporary Immigration Status." *Law & Social Inquiry* 39 (3): 621–642.

Hamilton, Nora, and Norma Stoltz Chinchilla. 1991. "Central American Migration: A Framework for Analysis." *Latin American Research Review* 26 (1): 75–110.

Haney-Lopez, Ian. 1996. *White by Law: The Legal Construction of Race.* New York University Press.

Hansen, Thomas Blom, and Finn Stepputat. 2005. "Introduction." In *Sovereign Bodies: Citizens, Migrants, and States in the Postcolonial World,* 1–38. Princeton University Press.

Haraway, Donna. 2003. *The Companion Species Manifesto: Dogs, People and Significant Otherness.* Prickly Paradigm.

Harwood, Edwin. 1984. "Arrests without Warrant: The Legal and Organizational Environment of Immigration Law Enforcement." *UC Davis Law Review* 17 (2): 505–548.

Hasselberg, Ines. 2016. *Enduring Uncertainty: Deportation, Punishment and Everyday Life.* Berghahn Books.

Heinrich, Carolyn J. 2018. "Presidential Address: 'A Thousand Petty Fortresses': Administrative Burden in US Immigration Policies and Its Consequences." *Journal of Policy Analysis and Management* 37 (2): 211–239.

Herd, Pamela, Hilary Hoynes, Jamila Michener, and Donald Moynihan. 2023. "Introduction: Administrative Burden as a Mechanism of Inequality in Policy Implementation." *RSF: Russell Sage Foundation Journal of the Social Sciences* 9 (4): 1–30.

Herd, Pamela, and Donald P. Moynihan. 2018. *Administrative Burden: Policymaking by Other Means* New York: Russell Sage.

Hernández, David Manuel. 2010. "'My Fellow Citizens': Barack Obama and Immigration Policy." *Journal of Race & Policy* 6 (1): 24–44.

Hiemstra, Nancy. 2017. "Periscoping as a Feminist Methodological Approach for Researching the Seemingly Hidden." *Professional Geographer* 69 (2): 329–336.

Hing, Bill Ong. 2007. "Providing a Second Chance." *Connecticut Law Review* 39 (5): 1893–1910.

Hobart, Hi'ilei Julia Kawehipuaakahaopulani, and Tamara Kneese. 2020. "Radical Care: Survival Strategies for Uncertain Times." *Social Text* 38 (1): 1–16.

Holmes, Douglas R., and George E. Marcus. 2006. "Fast Capitalism: Para-ethnography and the Rise of the Symbolic Analyst." In *Frontiers of Capital: Ethnographic Reflections on the New Capital,* edited by Melissa S. Fisher and Greg Downey, 33–57. Duke University Press.

———. 2008. "Collaboration Today and the Re-imagination of the Classic Scene of Fieldwork Encounter." *Collaborative Anthropologies* 1 (1): 81–101.

Honig, Bonnie. 1998. "Immigrant America? How Foreignness 'Solves' Democracy's Problems." *Social Text* 56 (Autumn): 1–27. https://doi.org/10.2307/466763.

Horton, Sarah. 2015. "Identity Loan: The Moral Economy of Migrant Document Exchange in California's Central Valley." *American Ethnologist* 42 (1): 55–67.

Horton, Sarah B. 2020. "Introduction: Paper Trails: Migrants, Bureaucratic Inscription, and Legal Recognition." In *Paper Trails: Migrants, Bureaucratic Inscription, and Legal Recognition*, edited by Sarah B. Horton and Josiah Heyman, 1–30. Duke University Press.

Horton, Sarah Bronwen. 2016. *They Leave Their Kidneys in the Fields: Illness, Injury, and Illegality among U.S. Farmworkers*. University of California Press.

Howard, Christopher. 1993. "The Hidden Side of the Welfare State." *Political Science Quarterly* 108 (3): 403–436.

———. 1997. *The Hidden Welfare State: Tax Expenditures and Social Policy in the United States*. Princeton University Press.

Hull, Matthew S. 2012. "Documents and Bureaucracy." *Annual Review of Anthropology* 41: 251–267.

Human Rights Watch. 2023. "U.S.: Biden 'Asylum Ban' Endangers Lives at the Border." May 11. https://www.hrw.org/news/2023/05/11/us-biden-asylum-ban-endangers-lives-border.

Hunt, Alan. 1990. "Rights and Social Movements: Counter-Hegemonic Strategies." *Journal of Law & Society* 17 (3): 309–328.

Hutzler, Alexandra. 2024. "Immigration Emerges as Key 2024 Election Wedge Issue for Trump, Vulnerability for Biden." *ABC News*, January 25. https://abcnews.go.com/Politics/immigration-emerges-key-2024-wedge-issue-trump-vulnerability/story?id=106635907.

ICE (US Immigration and Customs Enforcement). 2013. "Facilitating Parental Interests in the Course of Civil Immigration Enforcement Activities." Federal Enterprise Architecture No. 306–112–002b. August 23rd. https://www.courts.ca.gov/documents/BTB_XXII_IG_5.pdf.

ICE (US Immigration and Customs Enforcement). 2023. "ICE Enforcement and Removal Operations Statistics." Last updated 12/29/2023. https://www.ice.gov/spotlight/statistics.

ICE Out of LA! n.d. "About the Campaign." http://iceoutofla.org/en/.

International Rescue Committee. 2023. "What Is President Biden's 'Asylum Ban' and What Does It Mean for People Seeking Safety?" Last updated: July 25, 2023. https://www.rescue.org/article/what-president-bidens-asylum-ban-and-what-does-it-mean-people-seeking-safety.

Islam, Gazi. 2015. "Practitioners as Theorists: Para-ethnography and the Collaborative Study of Contemporary Organizations." *Organizational Research Methods* 18 (2): 231–251.

Jackson, Jean E. 1990. "'I Am a Fieldnote:' Fieldnotes as a Symbol of Professional Identity." In *Fieldnotes: The Makings of Anthropology*, edited by Roger Sanjek, 3–33. Cornell University Press.

Jenkins, J. Craig. 1977. "Push/Pull in Recent Mexican Migration to the US." *International Migration Review* 11 (2): 178–189.

———. 1983. "Resource Mobilization Theory and the Study of Social Movements." *Annual Review of Sociology* 9 (1): 527–553.

Jones-Correa, Michael, and James McCann. 2020. *Holding Fast: Resilience and Civic Engagement Among Latino Immigrants*. Russell Sage Foundation.

Jordan, Miriam. 2023. "Biden Administration Announces New Border Crackdown." *New York Times*, February 21. https://www.nytimes.com/2023/02/21/us/biden-asylum-rules.html.

Juarez, Jose A., Jr 2017. "Flores v. United States Citizenship and Immigration Services: Clearing the Way to Admission for Temporary Protected Status Beneficiaries." *Capital University Law Review* 45 (3): 549–577.

Kafka, F. (1999). *The Trial*. Schocken Books.

Kagan, Michael. 2015. "Plenary Power Is Dead: Long Live Plenary Power." *Michigan Law Review First Impressions* 114: 21–30.

Kairys, David, ed. 1998. *The Politics of Law: A Progressive Critique*. 3rd ed. Basic Books.

Kalhan, Anil. 2014. "Immigration Surveillance." *Maryland Law Review* 74 (1): 1–78.

Kanstroom, Daniel. 2007. *Deportation Nation: Outsiders in American History*. Harvard University Press.

Kasirer, Nicholas. 2006. "The Dance Is One." In *Mélanges Offerts au Professeur François Frenette: études portant sur le droit patrimonial*, edited by Sylvio Normand, 13–32. Le Presses de L'université Laval.

Kaufmann, David. 2019. "Comparing Urban Citizenship, Sanctuary Cities, Local Bureaucratic Membership, and Regularizations." *Public Administration Review* 79, no. 3 (May/June): 443–446.

Kawar, Leila. 2011. "Legal Mobilization on the Terrain of the State: Creating a Field of Immigrant Rights Lawyering in France and the United States." *Law & Social Inquiry* 36 (2): 354–387.

Keyes, Elizabeth. 2012. "Beyond Saints and Sinners: Discretion and the Need for New Narratives in the U.S. Immigration System," *Georgetown Immigration Law Journal* 26, no. 2 (Winter): 207–256.

———. 2014. "Race and Immigration, Then and Now: How the Shift to Worthiness Undermines the 1965 Immigration Law's Civil Rights Goals." *Howard Law Journal* 57 (3): 899–930.

Khosravi, Shahram, ed. 2009. "Sweden: Detention and Deportation of Asylum seekers." *Race and Class* 50 (4): 38–56.

———. 2018. *After Deportation: Ethnographic Perspectives*. Palgrave Macmillan.

Kinosian, Sarah. 2017. "Crisis of Honduras Democracy Has Roots in US Tacit Support for 2009 Coup." *The Guardian*, December 7. https://www.theguardian.com/world/2017/dec/07/crisis-of-honduras-democracy-has-roots-in-us-tacit-support-for-2009-coup.

Kleinman, Arthur, Veena Das, and Margaret M. Lock, eds. 1997. *Social Suffering*. University of California Press.

Koh, Jennifer Lee. 2017. "Removal in the Shadows of Immigration Court." *Southern California Law Review* 90 (2): 181–236.

Krajewska, Magdalena. 2017. *Documenting Americans: A Political History of National ID Card Proposals in the United States*. Cambridge University Press.

Kreychman, Rosanna M., and Heather H. Volik. 2005–2006. "The Immigrant Workers Project of the AFL-CIO." *New York Law School Law Review* 50 (2): 561–569.

Kritzer, Herbert M. 2011. "The Antecedents of Disputes: Complaining and Claiming." *Oñati Sociol-Legal Series* 1 (6): 1–31.

Kurtzleben, Danielle. 2023. "Why Trump's Authoritarian Language about 'Vermin' Matters." *National Public Radio*. November 17. https://www.npr.org/2023/11/17/1213746885/trump-vermin-hitler-immigration-authoritarian-republican-primary.

Lai, Annie, and Christopher N. Lasch. 2017. "Crimmigration Resistance and the Case of Sanctuary City Defunding." *Santa Clara Law Review* 57 (3): 539–610.

Lakhani, Sarah Morando. 2013. "Producing Immigrant Victims' 'Right' to Legal Status and the Management of Legal Uncertainty." *Law & Social Inquiry* 38 (2): 442–473.

———. 2014. "From Problems of Living to Problems of Law: The Legal Translation and Documentation of Immigrant Abuse and Helpfulness." *Law & Social Inquiry* 39 (3): 643–665.

Lee, Eunice. 2023. "Immigration in the Shadow of Death." *University of Pennsylvania Journal of Constitutional Law* 26 (1): 126–200.

Lee, Stephen. 2019. "Family Separation as Slow Death." *Columbia Law Review* 119, no. 8 (December): 2319–2384.

Legomsky, Stephen H. 1984. "Immigration Law and the Principle of Plenary Congressional Power." *Supreme Court Review*, 255–307.

Leiden, Warren R., and David Neal. 1990–1991. "Recent Development: Highlights of the U.S. Immigration Act of 1990." *Fordham International Law Journal* 14 (1): 328–339.

León, Lucía. 2020. "Legalization through Marriage: When Love and Papers Converge," In *We are Not Dreamers: Undocumented Scholars Theorize Undocumented Life in the United States*, edited by Leisy J. Abrego, and Genevieve Negrón-Gonzales, 190–210. Duke University Press.

LeVine, Marianne, and Meryl Kornfield. 2023. "Trump's Anti-immigrant Onslaught Sparks Fresh Alarm Heading into 2024." *Washington Post*, October 12. https://www.washington post.com/elections/2023/10/12/trump-immigrants-comments-criticism/?=undefined.

Levit, Nancy, and Robert R. M. Verchick, 2016. *Feminist Legal Theory: A Primer*. 2nd ed. Foreword by Martha Minow. New York University Press.

Ley especial transitoria para establecer el estado civil de personas indocumentadas afectadas por el conflicto. D.L. N° 205, del 12 de marzo de 1992, publicado en el D.O. N° 57, Tomo 314, del 24 de marzo de 1992. https://www.jurisprudencia.gob.sv/DocumentosBoveda/D /2/1990-1999/1992/03/88A01.pdf.

Linton, Julie M., and Andrea Green. 2019. "Providing Care for Children in Immigrant Families." Policy Statement. American Academy of Pediatrics. https://publications.aap.org /pediatrics/article/144/3/e20192077/38449/Providing-Care-for-Children-in-Immigrant -Families?autologincheck=redirected.

Longazel, Jamie. 2018. "Relieving the Tension: Lay Immigration Lawyering and the Management of Legal Violence." *Law & Society Review* 52 (4): 902–927.

López, Jane Lilly. 2022. *Unauthorized Love: Mixed-Citizenship Couples Negotiating Intimacy, Immigration, and the State*. Stanford University Press.

Lundstrom, Kristi. 2013. "The Unintended Effects of the Three-and Ten-Year Unlawful Presence Bars." *Law and Contemporary Problems* 76, no. 3–4: 389–412.

Marcus, George E. 2005. "The Anthropologist as Witness in Contemporary Regimes of Intervention." *Cultural Politics* 1 (1): 31–50.

———. 2016. "Multi-Sited Ethnography: Notes and Queries 1." In *Multi-Sited Ethnography: Theory, Praxis and Locality in Contemporary Research*, edited by Mark-Anthony Falzon, 181–196. Routledge.

Martin, Philip L. 2004. "Mexican Migration to the United States: The Effect of NAFTA." In *International Migration. Prospects and Policies in a Global Market*, edited by Douglas S. Massey and J. Edward Taylor, 120–130. Oxford University Press.

Martin, Robyn. 1994. "A Feminist View of the Reasonable Man: An Alternative Approach to Liability in Negligence for Personal Injury." *Anglo-American Law Review* 23 (3): 334–374.

Martinez, Pedro Santiago, Claudia Muñoz, Mariela Nuñez-Janes, Stephen Pavey, Fidel Castro Rodriguez, and Marco Saavedra, eds. 2020. *Eclipse of Dreams: The Undocumented-Led Struggle for Freedom*. AK Press.

Martínez Rosas, Girsea. 2020. "Critically Accommodating 'Illegality': Anticipatory Losses within Mixed-Status Immigrant Families." *Journal of Loss and Trauma* 25 (5): 488–500. https://doi.org/10.1080/15325024.2020.1716162.

Mather, Lynn. 2021. "What Is a 'Case'?" *Oñati Socio-Legal Series* 11 (2): 355–378. https://opo.iisj.net/index.php/osls/article/view/1287.

Mather, Lynn, and Barbara Yngvesson. 1980–1981. "Language, Audience, and the Transformation of Disputes." *Law & Society Review* 15 (3/4): 75–82.

McCann, Michael W. 1994. *Rights at Work: Pay Equity Reform and the Politics of Legal Mobilization*. University of Chicago Press.

McGranahan, Carole. 2020. "Ethnographic Witnessing: Or, Hope is the First Anthropological Emotion." *Journal of Legal Anthropology* 4 (1): 101–110.

Medvescek, Ron, and Rick Wiley. 2019. "Arizona Daily Star Photographer Ron Medvescek Retires after 38 Years." *Arizona Daily Star*. Last modified February 11, 2020. https://tucson.com/news/local/arizona-daily-star-photographer-ron-medvescek-retires-after-38-years/collection_0ea7a232-91e4-11e9-a1fb-c705cbf199e7.html#19.

Menjívar, Cecilia. 2006. "Liminal Legality: Salvadoran and Guatemalan Immigrants' Lives in the United States." *American Journal of Sociology* 111 (4): 999–1037.

Menjívar, Cecilia, and Leisy J. Abrego. 2012. "Legal Violence: Immigration Law and the Lives of Central American Immigrants." *American Journal of Sociology* 117 (5): 1380–1421.

Menjívar, Cecilia, and Sara M. Lakhani. 2016. "Transformative Effects of Immigration Law: Immigrants' Personal and Social Metamorphoses through Regularization." *American Journal of Sociology* 121 (6): 1818–1855.

Merry, Sally Engle. 2012. "Anthropology and Law." In *The SAGE Handbook of Social Anthropology* Edited by Richard Fardon, Olivia Harris, Trevor H. J. Marchand, Cris Shore, Veronica Strang, Richard Wilson, and Mark Nuttall, 105–120. SAGE.

Migration Policy Institute. n.d. "Profile of the Unauthorized Population: United States." https://www.migrationpolicy.org/data/unauthorized-immigrant-population/state/US.

Miller, R. E., and A. Sarat. 1980–1981. "Grievances, Claims, and Disputes: Assessing the Adversary Culture." *Law & Society Review* 15 (3/4): 525–565.

Mitchell, Julie, and Susan Bibler Coutin. 2019. "Living Documents in Transnational Spaces of Migration between El Salvador and the United States." *Law & Social Inquiry* 44 (4): 865–892.

Mize, Ronald L. 2016. *The Invisible Workers of the US–Mexico Bracero Program: Obreros Olvidados*. Lexington Books.

Monico, Gabriela. 2020. "American't: Redefining Citizenship in the U.S. Undocumented Immigrant Youth Movement." In *We are Not Dreamers: Undocumented Scholars Theorize Undocumented Life in the United States*, edited by Leisy J. Abrego and Genevieve Negrón-Gonzales, 87–109. Duke University Press.

Moore, Ellen. 2020. "Sentencing 'Crimmigrants': How Migration Law Creates a Different Criminal Law for Non-citizens." *University of New South Wales Law Journal* 43 (4): 1271–1308.

Moore, Wilbert E. 1949. "America's Migration Treaties during World War II." *Annals of the American Academy of Political and Social Science* 262: 31–38. http://www.jstor.org /stable/1026971.

Morales, Daniel I. 2024. "The U.S.-Mexico Border as a Crisis of Social Reproduction." *Law and Political Economy Project Blog*, February 19. https://lpeproject.org/blog/the-border-as -a-crisis-of-social-reproduction/.

Morawetz, Nancy. 2000. "Understanding the Impact of the 1996 Deportation Laws and the Limited Scope of Proposed Reforms." *Harvard Law Review* 113: 1936–1962.

Morrill, Calvin, and Lauren B. Edelman. 2021. "Sociology of Law and New Legal Realism." In *Research Handbook on Modern Legal Realism*, edited by Shauhin Talesh, Elizabeth Mertz, and Heinz Klug, 413–431. Edward Elgar.

Motomura, Hiroshi. 2006. *Americans in Waiting: The Lost Story of Immigration and Citizenship in the United States.* Oxford University Press.

———. 2010. "What Is Comprehensive Immigration Reform? Taking the Long View." *Arkansas Law Review* 63 (2): 225–242.

Mountz, A., R. Wright, I. Miyares, and A. J. Bailey. 2002. "Lives in Limbo: Temporary Protected Status and Immigrant Identities." *Global Networks* 2 (4): 335–356.

Moynihan, Donald, Julie Gerzina, and Pamela Herd. 2022. "Kafka's Bureaucracy: Immigration Administrative Burdens in the Trump Era." *Perspectives on Public Management and Governance* 5 (1): 22–35.

Moynihan, Donald P., Pamela Herd, and Hope Harvey. 2015. "Administrative Burden: Learning, Psychological, and Compliance Costs in Citizen-State Interactions." *Journal of Public Administration Research and Theory* 25 (1): 43–69.

Muñiz, Ana. 2022. "Gang Phantasmagoria: How Racialized Gang Allegations Haunt Immigration Legal Work." *Critical Criminology* 30 (1): 159–175.

Napolitano, Janet. 2012. "Exercising Prosecutorial Discretion with Respect to Individuals Who Came to the United States as Children." Memorandum. June 15, 2012. https://www .dhs.gov/xlibrary/assets/s1-exercising-prosecutorial-discretion-individuals-who-came -to-us-as-children.pdf.

National Immigration Law Center. "DACA." https://www.nilc.org/issues/daca/.

NDLON. 2013. "Immigrant Activists Gather with a Message: 'Not One More Deportation.'" October 14. https://ndlon.org/immigration-activists-gather-with-a-message-not-one -more-deportation/#.

Nessel, Lori A. 2022. "Enforced Invisibility: Toward New Theories of Accountability for the United States' Role in Endangering Asylum Seekers," *UC Davis Law Review* 55, no. 3 (February): 1513–1582.

Nesteruk, Oleana. 2018. "Immigrants Coping with Transnational Deaths and Bereavement: The Influence of Migratory Loss and Anticipatory Grief." *Family Process* 57 (4): 1012–1028.

Ngai, Mae M. 2004. *Impossible Subjects: Illegal Aliens and the Making of Modern America.* Princeton University Press.

Novy, Nicolas A. 2019. "The Problem of Coerced Consent: When Voluntary Departure Isn't So Voluntary." *University of Kansas Law Review* 68 (2): 315–349.

Obinna, Denise N. 2020. "Wait-Times, Visa Queues, and Uncertainty: The Barriers to American Legal Migration." *Migration and Development* 9 (3): 390–410.

Office of the Texas Governor. 2023. "Operation Lone Star Buses Over 50,000 Migrants to Sanctuary Cities." October 6. https://gov.texas.gov/news/post/operation-lone-star-buses-over-50000-migrants-to-sanctuary-cities.

———. 2024. "Operation Lone Star." https://gov.texas.gov/operationlonestar.

Ordóñez, Juan Thomas. 2016. "Documents and Shifting Labor Environments among Undocumented Migrant Workers in Northern California." *Anthropology of Work Review* 37 (1): 24–33.

Pace, Molly, Sarah Al-Obaydi, Maziar M. Nourian, and Akiko Kamimura. 2015. "Health Services for Refugees in the United States: Policies and Recommendations." *Health* 5 (8): 63–68.

Panebianco, Stefania. 2022. "The EU and Migration in the Mediterranean: EU Borders' Control by Proxy." *Journal of Ethnic and Migration Studies* 48 (6): 1398–1416.

Pavey, Steve, and Marco Saavedra. 2016. "'Make Holy the Bare Life': Theological Reflections on Migration Grounded in Collaborative Praxis with Youth Made Illegal by the United States." In *Religion, Migration, and Identity: Methodological and Theological Explorations*, edited by Martha Frederiks and Dorottya Nagy, 132–151. Brill.

PBS News Hour. 2023. "Ukraine Deal by Year-End Seems Unlikely as GOP Ties It to Border Security." PBS News Hour, December 9. https://www.pbs.org/newshour/politics/ukraine-aid-deal-by-year-end-seems-increasingly-unlikely-as-gop-ties-it-to-border-security.

Pearson, Susan J. 2021. *The Birth Certificate: An American History*. Online version. University of North Carolina Press.

Pedroza, Juan Manuel. 2018. "Underreporting Makes Notario Fraud Difficult to Fight." *ABA Journal* 104: 57–59.

Pham, Huyen, and Pham Hoang Van. 2019. "Subfederal Immigration Regulation and the Trump Effect." *New York University Law Review* 94 (1): 125–170.

Pierce, Sarah, Jessica Bolter, and Andrew Selee. 2018. "U.S. Immigration Policy under Trump: Deep Changes and Lasting Impacts." *Migration Policy Institute* 9 (July): 1–24.

Pineda, Erin R. 2021. *Seeing Like an Activist: Civil Disobedience and the Civil Rights Movement*. Oxford University Press, 2021.

Pound, Roscoe. 1910. "Law in Books and Law in Action." *American Law Review* 44 (1): 12–36.

Provine, Marie, Monica Varsanyi, Paul G. Lewis, and Scott Decker. 2012. "Growing Tensions between Civic Membership and Enforcement in the Devolution of Immigration Control." In *Punishing Immigrants: Policy, Politics, and Injustice*, edited by Charis E. Kubrin, Marjorie S. Zatz, and Ramiro Martínez Jr., 42–61. New York University Press.

Reed-Danahay, Deborah. 2016. "Participating, Observing, Witnessing." In *The Routledge Companion to Contemporary Anthropology*, edited by Simon Coleman, Susan B. Hyatt, and Ann Kingsolver, 57–71. Routledge.

Reese Sady, Stephen, and Clio Reese Sady. n.d. "Families Behind Barbed Wire." https://insidewitness.files.wordpress.com/2015/02/fbbw_english.pdf.

Reichman, Daniel. 2011. "Migration and Paraethnography in Honduras." *American Ethnologist* 38 (3): 548–558.

Reidman, Nadia. 2023. "Give Me Your Tired, Your Poor, Your Huddled Masses . . . Or Don't." *This American Life*, December 1. https://www.thisamericanlife.org/817/the-cavalry-is-not-coming/act-two-16.

Reyes, Kathryn Blackmer, and Julia E. Curry Rodríguez. 2012. "Testimonio: Origins, Terms, and Resources." *Equity and Excellence in Education* 45 (3): 525–538.

Riles, Annelise. 2011. *Collateral Knowledge: Legal Reasoning in the Global Financial Markets.* University of Chicago Press.

Robben, Antonius CGM, and Marcelo Suárez-Orozco, eds. 2000. *Cultures under Siege: Collective Violence and Trauma.* Cambridge University Press.

Robinson, Leah, Penelope Schlesinger, Alana Rosenberg, Kim M. Blankenship, and Danya Keene. 2023. "'Being Homeless Can Burn You Out': A Qualitative Study of Individuals' Experience of Administrative Burden When Accessing Homeless Services." *Journal of Social Distress and Homelessness*: 1–10. https://doi.org/10.1080/10530789.2023.2237242.

Rose, Nikolas, Pat O'Malley, and Mariana Valverde. 2006. "Governmentality." *Annual Review of Law and Social Science* 2: 83–104.

Rosen, Sarah. 2022. ""Trump Got His Wall, It Is Called Title 42": The Evolution and Illegality of Title 42's Implementation and Its Impact on Immigrants Seeking Entry into the United States." *Northeastern University Law Review* 14 (1): 229–274.

Rosenbaum, Carrie L. 2018. "Immigration Law's Due Process Deficit and the Persistence of Plenary Power." *Berkeley La Raza Law Journal* 28: 118–156.

———. 2021. "Systemic Racism and Immigration Detention." *Seattle University Law Review* 44 (4): 1125–1182.

———. 2023. "Arbitrary Arbitrariness Review." *Denver Law Review* 100 (3): 773–816.

Rosenbloom, Rachel E. 2013. "The Citizenship Line: Rethinking Immigration Exceptionalism." *Boston College Law Review* 54 (5): 1965–2024.

Rubenstein, David S., and Pratheepan Gulasekaram. 2017. "Immigration Exceptionalism." *Northwestern University Law Review* 111 (3): 583–654.

Ruth, Terrance, Jonathan Matusitz, and Demi Simi. 2017. "Ethics of Disenfranchisement and Voting Rights in the US: Convicted Felons, the Homeless, and Immigrants." *American Journal of Criminal Justice* 42: 56–68.

Saavedra, Marco. 2020. "Que?!" In *Eclipse of Dreams; The Undocumented-led Struggle for Freedom*, edited by Pedro Santiago Martinez, Claudia Muñoz, Mariela Nuñez-Janes, Stephen Pavey, Fidel Castro Rodriguez, and Marco Saavedra, 77–78. AK Press.

Sacchetti, Maria. "Deportations of Migrants Rise to More than 142,000 Under Biden" *Washington Post.* December 29, 2023. https://www.washingtonpost.com/immigration/2023/12/29/immigrants-ice-border-deportations-2023/.

Saito, Natsu Taylor. 2003. "The Enduring Effect of the Chinese Exclusion Cases: The Plenary Power Justification for On-Going Abuses of Human Rights." *Asian Law Journal* 10: 13–36.

Sanchez, Elizabeth, Sandy P. Philbin, and Cecilia Ayón. 2021. "Y el luto sigue (and the grief continues): Latinx Immigrant's Experiences of Ambiguous Loss in the Age of Restrictive Immigration Policy." *Family Relations* 70 (October): 1009–1026.

Sanchez, Linda E. 2018. "When I Got DACA, I Was Forced to Revert to a Name I had Left Behind." *The Conversation*, January 11. https://theconversation.com/when-i-got-daca-i-was-forced-to-revert-to-a-name-i-had-left-behind-89130.

———. 2023. "Exclusion by Design: The Undocumented 1.5 Generation in the U.S." *Frontiers in Sociology* 8: 1–11. https://doi.org/10.3389/fsoc.2023.1082177.

Sanchez, Sandra. 2023. "GOP Hopefuls Debate Immigration, Defending Southern Border." *abc27 News.* August 24. https://www.abc27.com/news/gop-presidential-hopefuls-debate-immigration-defending-southern-border/.

Sarat, Austin. 1985. "The Litigation Explosion, Access to Justice, and Court Reform: Examining the Critical Assumptions." *Rutgers Law Review* 37 (2): 319–336.

Sassen, Saskia. 1989. "America's Immigration 'Problem.'" *World Policy Journal* 6 (4): 811–832.

———. 2014. *Expulsions: Brutality and Complexity in the Global Economy*. Belknap Press of Harvard University Press.

Sati, Joel. 2020. "'Other' Borders: The Illegal as Normative Metaphor," In *We are Not Dreamers: Undocumented Scholars Theorize Undocumented Life in the United States*, edited by Leisy J. Abrego and Genevieve Negrón-Gonzales, 23–44. Duke University Press.

Scheper-Hughes, Nancy. 1995. "The Primacy of the Ethical: Propositions for a Militant Anthropology." *Current Anthropology* 36 (3): 409–440.

Schmidt, Paul Wickham. 2019. "An Overview and Critique of U.S. Immigration and Asylum Policies in the Trump Era." *Journal on Migration and Human Security* 7 (3): 92–102.

Schneider, Dorothee. 2001. "Naturalization and United States Citizenship in Two Periods of Mass Migration: 1894–1930, 1965–2000." *Journal of American Ethnic History* 21 (1): 50–82.

Scott, James C. 1998. *Seeing Like a State: How Certain Schemes to Improve the Human Condition Have Failed*. Yale University Press.

Seif, Hinda. 2011. "'Unapologetic and Unafraid': Immigrant Youth Come Out from the Shadows." *New Directions for Child and Adolescent Development* 2011 (134): 59–75. https://doi.org/10.1002/cd.311.

Shannon, Careen. 2009. "Regulating Immigration Legal Service Providers: Inadequate Legal Service Providers: Inadequate Representation and Notario Fraud." *Fordham Law Review* 78: 577–622.

Shibley, Mariela G., and Matthew G. Holt. 2022. "The Appraisal of Exceptional and Extremely Unusual Hardship for Cancellation of Removal." In *Conducting Immigration Evaluations: A Practical Guide for Mental Health Professionals*, edited by Mariela G. Shibley and Matthew G. Holt, 41–60. Routledge.

Simpson, James. 2020. "Navigating Immigration Law in a "Hostile Environment": Implications for Adult Migrant Language Education." *Tesol Quarterly* 54 (2): 488–511.

Siskin, Alison. 2015. "Alien Removals and Returns: Overview and Trends." *Congressional Research Service Report*. February 3. https://sgp.fas.org/crs/homesec/R43892.pdf.

Smith, Linda Tuhiwai. 2012. *Decolonizing Methodologies: Research and Indigenous Peoples*. 2nd ed. Zed Books.

Starr, June, and Mark Goodale. 2002. "Introduction: Legal Ethnography: New Dialogues, Enduring Methods." In *Practicing Ethnography in Law*, edited by June Star and Mark Goodale, 1–10. Palgrave Macmillan.

Stevens, Jacqueline. 2011. "US Government Unlawfully Detaining and Deporting U.S. Citizens as Aliens." *Virginia Journal of Social Policy and Law* 18 (3): 606–720.

Strathern, Marilyn. 1999. "The Ethnographic Effect I." In *Property, Substance, and Effect: Anthropological Essays on Persons and Things*, 1–28. Athlone Press.

Stuart, Forrest. 2016. *Down, Out, and Under Arrest: Policing and Everyday Life in Skid Row*. University of Chicago Press.

Stumpf, Juliet. 2006. "The Crimmigration Crisis: Immigrants, Crime, and Sovereign Power." *American University Law Review* 56 (2): 367–419.

Suchman, Mark C., and Elizabeth Mertz. 2010. "Toward a New Legal Empiricism: Empirical Legal Studies and New Legal Realism." *Annual Review of Law and Social Science* 6: 555–579.

Tepeli, Natalie. 2013. "Keeping Families Together: The Facade of the I-601A Provisional Unlawful Presence Waiver." *Public Interest Law Reporter* 19 (1): 43–49.

Ticktin, Miriam. 2005. "Policing and Humanitarianism in France: Immigration and the Turn to Law as State of Exception." *Interventions* 7 (3): 346–368.

———. 2014. "Transnational Humanitarianism." *Annual Review of Anthropology* 43: 273–289.

———. 2019. "From the Human to the Planetary: Speculative Futures of Care." *Medicine Anthropology Theory* 6 (3): 133–160.

Tolkein, J. R. R. 1937 (1966 ed.). *The Hobbit*. Ballentine Books.

Torpey, John. 2000. *The Invention of the Passport: Surveillance, Citizenship, and the State*. Cambridge University Press.

Tuckett, Anna. 2018. "Ethical Brokerage and Self-Fashioning in Italian Immigration Bureaucracy." *Critique of Anthropology* 38 (3): 245–264.

Urla, Jacqueline. 2019. "Governmentality and Language." *Annual Review of Anthropology* 48: 261–278.

USCIS (US Citizenship and Immigration Services; *hereafter just USCIS*). 2009. "American Baptist Churches v. Thornburgh (ABC) Settlement Agreement." Updated September 3, 2009. https://www.uscis.gov/humanitarian/refugees-and-asylum/asylum/american-baptist-churches-v-thornburgh-abc-settlement-agreement.

USCIS. 2012. History Office and Library. "Overview of INS History." https://www.uscis.gov/sites/default/files/document/fact-sheets/INSHistory.pdf.

USCIS. 2018a. Asylum Division. "NACARA Cumulative Report 6–21–99 through 8–31–18." https://www.uscis.gov/sites/default/files/document/data/PED_NACARA_Report_August2018.pdf.

USCIS. 2018b. "Provisional Unlawful Presence Waivers." Updated January 5, 2018. https://www.uscis.gov/family/family-of-us-citizens/provisional-unlawful-presence-waivers.

USCIS. 2019a. N-400, "Application for Naturalization." September 19. Available from author upon request.

USCIS. 2019b. N-400, "Application for Naturalization, Instructions." September 19. Available from author upon request.

USCIS. 2021a. I-821D, "Consideration of Deferred Action for Childhood Arrivals." August 31. Available from author upon request.

USCIS. 2021b. I-821D, "Consideration of Deferred Action for Childhood Arrivals, Instructions." August 31. Available from author upon request.

USCIS. 2021c. "USCIS Reaches Settlement Agreement in 'No Blank Space Rejection Policy' Case." Last modified August 19, 2021. https://www.uscis.gov/newsroom/news-releases/uscis-reaches-settlement-agreement-in-no-blank-space-rejection-policy-case.

USCIS. 2023a. "Citizenship Resource Center, Interagency Strategy for Promoting Naturalization." Modified September 15, 2023. https://www.uscis.gov/promotingnaturalization.

USCIS. 2024a. "Consideration of Deferred Action for Childhood Arrivals (DACA)." Modified April 8, 2024. https://www.uscis.gov/DACA.

USCIS. 2024b. "Policy Manual, Vol. 3, Humanitarian Protections and Parole, Part D: Violence Against Women Act, Chapter Two: Eligibility Requirements and Evidence." Modified July 18, 2024. https://www.uscis.gov/policy-manual/volume-3-part-d-chapter-2.

USCIS. 2024c. "Policy Manual, Vol. 7, Adjustment of Status, Part A, Adjustment of Status Rules and Procedures, Chapter Ten: Legal Analysis and Use of Discretion." Modified July 18, 2024. https://www.uscis.gov/policy-manual/volume-7-part-a-chapter-10.

USCIS. 2024d. "Policy Manual, Vol. 9, Waivers and Other Forms of Relief, Part B, Extreme Hardship, Chapter Two: Extreme Hardship Policy." Last modified July 18, 2024. https://www.uscis.gov/policy-manual/volume-9-part-b-chapter-2.

USCIS. 2024e. "Policy Manual, Vol. 9, Waivers and Other Forms of Relief, Part B, Extreme Hardship, Chapter Four: Qualifying Relative." Last modified March 15, 2024. https://www.uscis.gov/policy-manual/volume-9-part-b-chapter-4.

USCIS. 2024f. "Policy Manual, Vol. 9, Waivers and Other Forms of Relief, Part B, Extreme Hardship, Chapter Five: Extreme Hardship Considerations and Factors." Last modified March 15, 2024. https://www.uscis.gov/policy-manual/volume-9-part-b-chapter-5.

USCIS. 2024g. "Policy Manual, Vol. 12, Citizenship and Naturalization, Part D, General Naturalization Requirements, Chapter 9, Good Moral Character." Last modified July 18, 2024. https://www.uscis.gov/policy-manual/volume-12-part-d-chapter-9.

USCIS. 2024h. "Victims of Criminal Activity: U Nonimmigrant Status." Last modified April 2, 2024. https://www.uscis.gov/humanitarian/victims-of-criminal-activity-u-nonimmigrant-status.

US Department of Health and Human Services. n.d. "Aid to Families with Dependent Children (AFDC) and Temporary Assistance for Needy Families (TANF)—Overview." https://aspe.hhs.gov/aid-families-dependent-children-afdc-temporary-assistance-needy-families-tanf-overview.

Valdivia, Carolina. 2020. "Undocumented Young Adults' Heightened Vulnerability in the Trump Era." In *We are Not Dreamers: Undocumented Scholars Theorize Undocumented Life in the United States*, edited by Leisy J. Abrego and Genevieve Negrón-Gonzales, 127–145. Duke University Press.

Van der Woude, Maartje, Vanessa Barker, and Joanne Van der Leun. 2017. "Crimmigration in Europe." *European Journal of Criminology* 14 (1): 3–6.

Van der Woude, Maartje, and Joanne van der Leun. 2017. "Crimmigration Checks in the Internal Border Areas of the EU: Finding the Discretion that Matters." *European Journal of Criminology* 14 (1): 27–45. https://doi.org/10.1177/1477370816640139.

Vangala et al. v. USCIS et al., No. 4:20-cv-08143 (N.D. Cal.).

Varsanyi, Monica W. 2008. "Rescaling the 'Alien,' Rescaling Personhood: Neoliberalism, Immigration, and the State." *Annals of the Association of American Geographers* 98 (4): 877–896.

Vázquez, Yolanda. 2015. "Constructing Crimmigration: Latino Subordination in a Post-Racial World." *Immigration and Nationality Law Review* 36: 713–772.

Vega, Irene I. 2018. "Empathy, Morality, and Criminality: The Legitimation Narratives of US Border Patrol Agents." *Journal of Ethnic and Migration Studies* 44 (5): 2544–2561.

Vismann, Cornelia. 2008. *Files: Law and Media Technology*. Translated by Geoffrey Winthrop-Young. Stanford University Press.

Voces de la Frontera. n.d. "Citizenship for All." https://vdlf.org/citizenship-for-all/.

Wadhia, Shoba Sivaprasad. 2011. "The Morton Memo and Prosecutorial Discretion: An Overview." Special Report. *Immigration Policy Center, American Immigration Council*

(July). https://www.americanimmigrationcouncil.org/sites/default/files/research/Shoba
_-_Prosecutorial_Discretion_072011_0.pdf.

———. 2015. "The History of Prosecutorial Discretion in Immigration Law." *American University Law Review* 64 (5): 1285–1302.

Warren, Robert. 2018. "US Undocumented Population Drops below 11 Million in 2014, with Continued Declines in the Mexican Undocumented Population." *Journal on Migration and Human Security* 4 (1): 1–15.

Watkins, Josh. 2017. "Bordering Borderscapes: Australia's Use of Humanitarian Aid and Border Security Support to Immobilise Asylum Seekers." *Geopolitics* 22 (4): 958–983.

Welch, Michael. 2002. *Detained: Immigration Laws and the Expanding I.N.S. Jail Complex.* Temple University Press.

White House. 2021. "Preserving and Fortifying Deferred Action for Childhood Arrivals (DACA)." January 20. https://www.whitehouse.gov/briefing-room/presidential-actions/2021/01/20/preserving-and-fortifying-deferred-action-for-childhood-arrivals-daca/?ct=t(AgencyUpdate_012120).

———. 2023a. "Fact Sheet: Biden-Harris Administration Announces New Border Enforcement Actions." January 5. https://www.whitehouse.gov/briefing-room/statements-releases/2023/01/05/fact-sheet-biden-harris-administration-announces-new-border-enforcement-actions/.

———. 2023b. "Remarks by President Biden on Border Security and Enforcement." January 5. https://www.whitehouse.gov/briefing-room/speeches-remarks/2023/01/05/remarks-by-president-biden-on-border-security-and-enforcement/.

Williams, Patricia J. 1987. "Alchemical Notes: Reconstructing Ideals from Deconstructed Rights." *Harvard Civil Liberties-Civil Rights Review* 22: 401–434.

———. 1991. *The Alchemy of Race and Rights: Diary of a Law Professor.* Harvard University Press.

Willman, Nubia Batista. 2017. "Reaping Whirlwind: How U.S. Interventionist Foreign Policies Created Our Immigration Crisis." *Public Interest Law Reporter* 23, no. 1 (Fall): 36–49.

Wong, Tom K. 2017. *The Politics of Immigration: Partisanship, Demographic Change, and American National Identity.* Oxford University Press.

Ybarra, Megan. 2021. "Site Fight! Toward the Abolition of Immigrant Detention on Tacoma's Tar Pits (and Everywhere Else)." *Antipode* 53 (1): 36–55.

Yu, Lilly. 2023a. "'A Good Fit': Client Sorting among Nonprofit, Private, and Pro Bono Attorneys." *Law and Society Review* 57 (2): 141–161.

———. 2023b. "Third-Party Brokers: How Administrative Burdens on Nonprofit Attorneys Worsen Immigrant Legal Inequality." *RSF: Russel Sage Foundation Journal of the Social Sciences* 9 (4): 133–153.

Zotti, Antonio. 2021. "The Immigration Policy of the United Kingdom: British Exceptionalism and the Renewed Quest for Control." In *The EU Migration System of Governance: Justice on the Move*, edited by Michaela Ceccorulli, Enrico Fassi, and Sonia Lucarelli, 57–88. Palgrave MacMillan.

INDEX

Founded in 1893,
UNIVERSITY OF CALIFORNIA PRESS
publishes bold, progressive books and journals
on topics in the arts, humanities, social sciences,
and natural sciences—with a focus on social
justice issues—that inspire thought and action
among readers worldwide.

The UC PRESS FOUNDATION
raises funds to uphold the press's vital role
as an independent, nonprofit publisher, and
receives philanthropic support from a wide
range of individuals and institutions—and from
committed readers like you. To learn more, visit
ucpress.edu/supportus.